a conflict of principles

a conflict of principles

The Battle over Affirmative Action at the University of Michigan

Carl Cohen

 University Press of Kansas

Published by the
University Press of
Kansas (Lawrence,
Kansas 66045), which
was organized by
the Kansas Board
of Regents and is
operated and funded
by Emporia State
University, Fort Hays
State University,
Kansas State
University, Pittsburg
State University, the
University of Kansas,
and Wichita State
University

© 2014 by the University of Kansas

Library of Congress Cataloging-in-Publication Data

Cohen, Carl, 1931– author.
A conflict of principles : the battle over affirmative action at the
University of Michigan / Carl Cohen.
pages cm
Includes index.
ISBN 978-0-7006-1996-2 (hardback)
ISBN 978-0-7006-2043-2 (ebook)
1. Discrimination in higher education—Law and legislation—
Michigan. 2. Universities and colleges—Admission—Law and
legislation—Michigan. 3. Affirmative action programs in education—
Law and legislation—Michigan. 4. University of Michigan—Trials,
litigation, etc. I. Title.
KFM4592.2.C64 2014
344.774'0798—dc23
2014019706

British Library Cataloguing in Publication Data is available.

Printed in the United States of America

10 9 8 7 6 5 4 3 2 1

The paper used in this publication is recycled and contains
30 percent postconsumer waste. It is acid free and meets
the minimum requirements of the American National Standard
for Permanence of Paper for Printed Library Materials z39.48-1992.

Contents

Prologue

Most of my adult life has been devoted to the University of Michigan. Of all worldly institutions, beside my family and my country, I love this university most. I am a professor of philosophy at Michigan; democracy has been central among my philosophical concerns. I am deeply committed to the principle that in a democratic community all persons should be treated equally, without regard to their race. This commitment has brought me into sharp conflict with my university.

The conflict arose because the University of Michigan, seeking to increase the number of minority students enrolled, gave explicit preference to minority applicants for admission. How they did this I will soon explain. These preferences, although honorably motivated, were a form of racial discrimination, which every decent community should forbid. The Equal Protection Clause of the U.S. Constitution reads: "No state . . . shall deny to any person within its jurisdiction the equal protection of the laws." Discrimination by race is wrong. I have opposed it all my life. In this book I tell the story of my efforts to defend the equal treatment of the races at my university.

a conflict of principles

CHAPTER 1

How It All Began

The racial discrimination that has pervaded the University of Michigan for decades did not arise from malice, but from an ardent desire to do good. My opponents in this controversy have been decent people with honorable motives. But good motives do not make wrong actions right. Discrimination by race cannot be justified because good-hearted administrators and professors believe that worthy objectives can be achieved if only we will accept the institutional uses of racial categories.

My involvement in this dispute began far from the university, while I was serving as a member of the National Board of Directors of the American Civil Liberties Union (ACLU) in the early 1970s. As chairman of the Michigan affiliate of the ACLU I had long been active in efforts to eliminate racial discrimination. Long-entrenched racial discrimination in the United States has left minorities painfully underrepresented in our colleges. Responding to this racial imbalance, new programs were devised to increase the number of minorities in the universities. Many of these programs I supported vigorously. I testified before the U.S. House of Representatives Subcommittee on the Judiciary in support of the Equal Opportunity Act of 1995,[1] part of whose purpose was to encourage the active recruitment of minorities in colleges and in private employment.

Some efforts to increase minority enrollments gave deliberate preference to blacks and to Hispanics seeking university admission. Giving such preference was a kind of racism, although nothing like the vicious racism our country had so long endured. The larger ends of these preferential programs were admirable, but those ends cannot justify means that are morally wrong. Deliberate preference by race is most assuredly a moral wrong and also a clear violation of the U.S. Constitution and our laws. As a professor of philosophy at a leading university I thought it fitting for me to speak out strongly in opposition to the race preferences promoted at many universities, including my own.

The issues presented by "affirmative action" first reached the Supreme Court of the United States in the case *DeFunis v. Odegaard*,[2] which arose from a preferential program at the University of Washington. At the National Board of Directors meetings of the ACLU we debated this case. Marco DeFunis was a white applicant to the University of Washington Law School whose academic credentials were outstanding. A program in that law school gave substantial preference to black (and other minority) applicants for admission. DeFunis was rejected and went to court. The board of the ACLU discussed the merits of his case at length. I urged my colleagues on the board to defend DeFunis and by so doing to underscore our commitment to equal treatment for all races. I failed to convince them.

The ACLU is a highly principled organization, but our principles sometimes conflict with one another, giving rise to the knottiest of moral controversies. When issues involving racial justice arose, our debates (in those days at the Barbizon Plaza Hotel in New York City, long since demolished) were often intense and lengthy. We fought vigorously over which side the ACLU ought to take in the *DeFunis* case. The board at that time was sharply divided.

On the one hand we understood that increasing minority success in colleges and universities was a critical step in the improvement of minority circumstances generally—a goal we all earnestly shared. On the other hand we were committed to the equal treatment of the races and had long opposed any preferences given to any persons because of their skin color or national origin. In my view, this principle of equal treatment for all is paramount and must govern in such conflicts. I was joined in this effort by one of the most eloquent and learned jurisprudents of our time, William Van Alstyne, then a professor of law at Duke University and also a member of the board. Leading the forces on the other side of this argument was Frank Askin, a good and passionate man, also a professor of law (at Rutgers) who cared deeply about the oppression of blacks and who was prepared (in my view) to sacrifice full equality of treatment for what he thought to be the interests of minorities. We could come to no resolution of our conflicting principles. That fiery argument in the Barbizon Plaza began my involvement in this controversy, which continues to the present day.

The outcome of the *DeFunis* case was peculiar, and it was that peculiarity that led me to publish a controversial essay during the whirlwind of this debate. Here is the story: Marco DeFunis had applied for admission to the University of Washington Law School in 1970 and again in 1971; his academic qualifications were superb, but he was rejected both times. The law school was at that time openly giving weighty preferences to applicants of color, and DeFunis learned that many of those who had been accepted by the law school had academic credentials much inferior to his. Had his own skin been black he would certainly have been accepted. DeFunis contended that those preferences, mainly for blacks over whites, given by the University of Washington (whose president was Charles Odegaard, a former dean here at Michigan), had denied him the equal protection of the laws guaranteed by the U.S. Constitution. In my view he was dead right.

He won that suit in the lower state court, which found that the university's differential treatment, quite openly based on race, was a violation of the U.S. Constitution. The court ordered DeFunis's immediate admission to the University of Washington Law School. His legal studies began there in 1971.

As DeFunis continued his legal studies, the university appealed. Eventually the Washington Supreme Court heard the case and reversed the judgment of the trial court, holding that the preferential admissions policy did not violate the Constitution.[3] Although this opinion was reasonable in tone, well constructed, and even persuasive, I was sure that the case had not been decided correctly, that the race preference at the law school was not consistent with the Equal Protection Clause of the Fourteenth Amendment to our Constitution, adopted in 1868. I was troubled and dismayed. DeFunis was by this time in his second year at the law school.

The judgment of the Washington Supreme Court was stayed by Justice William O. Douglas of the U.S. Supreme Court, pending final disposition of the case by the High Court. DeFunis remained in law school and was in the first term of his third and final year when, in the fall of 1973, the U.S. Supreme Court agreed to hear the case. It was argued before the Court in February of 1974.

At that oral argument one of the justices raised this question: If the university were to prevail in this case, what would happen to DeFunis? The university's attorney had anticipated that question and informed the Court that DeFunis had performed well in the law school and was almost certain to graduate at the end of the current term, his last, then in progress. No effort would be made to eject him.

The opinion of the U.S. Supreme Court in *DeFunis v. Odegaard* was issued on 23 April 1974. The Court concluded that because the object of DeFunis's suit was admission to the University of Washington Law School, and because he had been admitted to that law school and was now very soon to graduate from it, there was no longer any real controversy to be decided. The justices held the case moot.

The unsigned majority opinion, however, did acknowledge that race preference in university admissions, the central issue in the case, had not been resolved and was almost sure to arise again: "If the admissions procedures of the Law School remain unchanged, there is no reason to suppose that a subsequent case attacking those procedures will not come with relative speed to this Court, now that the Supreme Court of Washington has spoken."[4]

The most liberal member of the Court, William O. Douglas, was plainly angry that the majority had held the case moot. In a sharply worded dissent he pointed out that university preference programs were widespread; their legitimacy was plainly not moot. This was the time, he held, for the Court to speak out clearly, and forcefully, against racially discriminatory admission systems. He went on to say, "The Equal Protection Clause commands the elimination of racial barriers, not their creation in order to satisfy our theory as to how society ought to be organized. The purpose of the University of Washington cannot be to produce Black lawyers for Blacks, Polish lawyers for Poles, Jewish lawyers for Jews, Irish lawyers for the Irish. It should be to produce good lawyers for Americans."[5] Later in his dissent he added, "A segregated admissions process creates suggestions of stigma and caste no less than a segregated classroom, and in the end it may produce that result despite its contrary intentions. . . . That Blacks or Browns cannot make it on their individual merit . . . is a stamp of inferiority that a state is not permitted to place on any lawyer."[6]

Justice William Brennan also dissented, observing that the constitutional issues raised by race preference, which the Court avoided, concern vast numbers of people, organizations, and colleges and universities: "Few constitutional questions in recent history have stirred as much debate, and they will not disappear. They must inevitably return . . . to this Court."[7]

I cheered at these dissents, but the case had been held moot, and I was frustrated. The little jackal barks, but the caravan marches on. I feared that many might suppose that the U.S. Supreme Court had authorized race preferences in admissions, because holding the case moot allowed the decision of the Washington Supreme Court to stand without objection. I was determined to present strong objection publicly, and I did so.

For about a decade I had been an irregular contributor to *The Nation*, a left-leaning weekly journal of opinion, then under the editorship of Carey McWilliams. I was proud to publish there. *The Nation* was (and still is) an intellectually serious periodical in which complicated argument is often presented at length. One of my predecessors in the Department of Philosophy at the University of Michigan, John Dewey, had published essays in *The Nation* many years before. Dewey, a great philosopher, had written: "Philosophy recovers itself when it ceases to be a device for dealing with the problems of philosophers, and becomes a method, cultivated by philosophers, for dealing with the problems of men."[8] I heartily agreed and sought to follow Dewey's example. *The Nation* (unlike most academic periodicals) was a place from which one's philosophical arguments might enter the public arena and might be widely read.

All my essays in *The Nation* addressed civil liberties issues: the protection of privacy, the uses of conscientious objection to military service, civil disobedience, and above all freedom of speech. In an essay in *The Nation* I later defended the right of the U.S. Nazi Party to march in the streets of Skokie, Illinois.[9] The ACLU (on my side in this matter, of course) distributed that essay widely. When the attorney for the Village of Skokie wrote a vigorous response to my defense of the march, McWilliams published that too, along with my rejoinder, in an exchange quite warmly appreciated by readers of *The Nation*.[10]

I hoped to publish my response to the Washington Supreme Court's *DeFunis* decision in *The Nation*. That did not go smoothly, however. Although an honorable man and a fine editor, Carey McWilliams was concerned about the reaction of his readership to the position I had taken. In those years that readership was largely enthusiastic in supporting programs thought to advance minority interests. An attack on university admissions preferences for minorities, therefore, was not going to be received with pleasure by many subscribers. When I told McWilliams that I was preparing a sharp rebuttal to the Washington Supreme Court, he was troubled. He thought of me as one of his regular contributors, and we were friends, but he had a readership to cultivate.

I wrote that essay, quite prepared to publish it elsewhere if McWilliams turned it down. My criticism of the university's race preferences and my rejection of the court's argument defending them were sharp. When McWilliams read the piece he told me, in plain words, that "his people" were not going to like it at all. If he were to publish it, he said, he would take a lot of heat, which he did not need. The decision, of course, was his to make.

My essay "Race and the Constitution" was published in *The Nation* on 8 February 1975. McWilliams told me he had concluded that my arguments were strong and that, even if I were mistaken, his readers would profit from having those arguments put before them. I had long admired Carey McWilliams, and from that time I admired him yet more. (A few years later *The Nation* was purchased by Victor Navasky, a sophisticated and intelligent ideologue who had no use for professors who would not support minority preferences in admissions.) My time with *The Nation* came to an end. For the many subsequent essays of mine on this subject I was obliged to find other publishers, and I did.

The invitation plainly extended by the U.S. Supreme Court in *DeFunis*, to bring the issue of race preferences in university admissions back to the Court, was sure to be accepted. Indeed, the landmark case with which it was accepted—*Regents of the University of California v. Bakke*[11]—was already brewing while DeFunis was still in law school. The major features of the race preferences at issue in the two cases were quite similar. In the *Bakke* case also I became very much involved, as I will explain, but before that I need to set forth briefly my reasons for finding the position of the Washington Supreme Court[12] in *DeFunis* seriously in error.

To put a complicated matter summarily, the court had framed its argument in the form of answers to three questions; I argued each of those answers was mistaken.

1. Are classifications on the basis of race, for purposes of school admissions and the like, per se unconstitutional? The court's answer was no, holding that there are some cases in which the Equal Protection Clause does not preclude the uses of race. I argued that this was a fundamental error, that the Fourteenth Amendment to the Constitution, which provides, "No state . . . shall deny to any person within its jurisdiction the equal protection of the laws" was formulated to prohibit precisely *all* preferential uses of racial classifications. In that sense our Constitution is and must be color-blind. The principle that a person's race or color is simply not relevant in the application of the laws ought never be sacrificed. Race preferences are not permissible even for the sake of some needed and hoped-for benefits. If I were right in this, the Washington Supreme Court must have been mistaken.

2. But if, for the sake of argument, we suppose that classification on the basis of race is under some circumstances permissible, what standards must be applied to programs like that of the University of Washington? The court said the law school must be prepared to show that its uses of race were necessary for the accomplishment of a compelling state inter-

est. That much is surely correct, but my position was that more than that is needed. If there are cases in which a state is justified in using racial classifications (say, in giving a specific remedy for a specific racial injury done earlier), it would certainly have to ensure that no one else would be injured simply by virtue of race. This is not possible in the case of race preference at a selective college, where what is given to some by race must be taken from others by race. The Supreme Court of Washington, to its credit, did explicitly recognize that race preferences of the sort in question could not be "benign." Some students are certain to be hurt by them; some persons—like Marco DeFunis in this case—do not get what they would otherwise have received because their skin was the wrong color.[13] Such an outcome, I argued, could not be acceptable under the Equal Protection Clause.

Where the basis for a classification is "suspect" (as race has long been held) the standard for review must be, as the U.S. Supreme Court had written, "exacting." My position was that the Washington Supreme Court's standard was not exacting enough.

3. Suppose the consideration of race is under some circumstances permissible, and (for the sake of argument) that the correct standard is the one the court proposed. Had the law school in this case met that standard in its uses of race? No, I argued, it had not. Even if the policy objectives of the university were worthy, they were not "compelling" in the sense required. However meritorious one might think them, they were certainly not objectives so critically important to the state as to warrant overriding the fundamental principle that all persons, of all races, are equal before the law.

With the publication of this essay my participation in the battles over race preference in university admissions had begun in earnest. I did not foresee the bearing of this outspoken position upon my personal and professional circumstances. I could not have known that the University of Michigan would become the eye of the coming storm surrounding "affirmative action."

CHAPTER 2

Bakke and the Rise of Diversity

When the Supreme Court of the United States did speak again on this matter in 1978, in *Regents of the University of California v. Bakke*, it did so in a way that did not resolve the question of the constitutional permissibility of preference by race. In fact, the reverse; it issued a set of confusing opinions that, taken as a group, invited sharply conflicting interpretations. The resulting uncertainty led to intense disputes about race preference, in courts and also in the universities (especially at the University of Michigan), that continued for a quarter of a century.

Allan Bakke's circumstances were much like those of Marco DeFunis. He had applied to the University of California at Davis Medical School, where preference by race was openly and proudly practiced. Admission there was highly competitive, but sixteen seats in each entering class were reserved for minorities only. This resulted in the admission of some minority students whose academic records were mediocre, far inferior to Bakke's. Like DeFunis, Bakke applied twice, in 1973 and 1974, and like DeFunis he was twice rejected. Like DeFunis, Bakke knew that with his credentials he would certainly have been admitted had his skin been dark. It was *DeFunis* redux.

There was, however, one great and consequential difference between the two cases: when Bakke brought his case to the lower state court he did prevail, as had DeFunis, but unlike DeFunis, he was not admitted forthwith. The California courts struck down the preferential program at U.C. Davis, but the California Supreme Court *stayed* its own judgment pending the appeal of the case.[1] It was appealed to the U.S. Supreme Court, and, because the mills of the courts grind slowly, Bakke had to wait until 1978 for his admission to the medical school.

The U.S. Supreme Court decision in the *Bakke* case was bound to be a major statement on the uses of race in university admissions. I had awaited that statement eagerly. But the tangle of opinions that emerged produced great uncertainty; I published an interpretive essay on the case in the *Wayne Law Review*, at Wayne State University.[2] Just as the ACLU National Board of Directors had been divided, and as the nation as a whole was divided, the nine members of the Supreme Court were also divided, regrettably, on the permissibility of university admissions preferences by race. The Supreme Court of California had supported Bakke vigorously, in an opinion sharply critical of the University of California. But when the case had at last to be decided by the U.S. Supreme Court in 1978, that Court split into three groups.

Four members of the Court, led by Justice John Paul Stevens, held that the preferences at the U.C. Davis Medical School were plainly impermissible. There is no need, said they, to resort to the Constitution to establish this; the California program giving preference by race plainly *broke the law.* Title VI of the Civil Rights Act of 1964 provides in no uncertain terms that "no person in the United States shall, on the ground of race, color, or national origin, be excluded from participation in, be denied the benefits of, or be subjected to discrimination under any program or activity receiving Federal financial assistance."[3] The University of California, like most state universities, receives a great deal of federal financial assistance. By its own account it was discriminating on grounds of race and national origin. The Civil Rights Act is a congressional implementation of the Equal Protection Clause of the U.S. Constitution. However one may interpret that clause, the Civil Rights Act stands independently as law by the full authority of Congress. The fact that California's preferences broke that law (said these four justices) is beyond doubt.

Four other justices, moving directly to the U.S. Constitution, held that the preferences were permissible because the Equal Protection Clause does not forbid the consideration of race in university admissions. That critical clause was part of the Fourteenth Amendment to our Constitution, adopted in 1868. Its clear intention was to protect blacks newly freed from slavery. It is not reasonable, they argued, now to invalidate a program aimed at advancing the welfare of blacks because of the wording of an amendment designed to support their advancement.

The ninth justice, Lewis Powell, was torn. A man of the highest integrity, he hated racial injustice and joined the first four in holding that the California program must be struck down. His reasoning was based not on the Civil Rights Act but on the Equal Protection Clause of the Constitution. By reserving some seats in each entering class for blacks only, the

U.C. Davis admissions system was (he concluded) plainly discriminatory and unacceptable.[4]

Powell's opinion was long, confusing, and perhaps internally inconsistent. After holding the California race preferences unconstitutional, he struggled to find a justification for such preferences that might withstand constitutional attack in some subsequent case. Perhaps the First Amendment, he suggested, protecting the freedom of speech, can serve to support efforts to increase the diversity of entering classes by enriching debate, and speech, on university campuses. This diversity, said Powell, could be the constitutional interest that might justify preferential programs if (as he thought possible) they were administered in a nondiscriminatory way.[5]

There is another way to look at this set of inharmonious Supreme Court opinions. We can say that there were two groups of five, one of which held that the U.C. Davis program was plainly unacceptable, either as a violation of the law or of the Constitution, and a second group of five that held that the consideration of race was not absolutely precluded by the Constitution. Justice Powell was the fifth member of both groups. His convoluted opinion was the source of many agonies to follow. Was his opinion the decision of the Court? Did his opinion establish diversity as a justification for race preference? That was disputed in an ocean of ink over the following twenty-five years.

The immediate upshot of the *Bakke* decision was clear. The preferential program at the University of California was struck down. Allan Bakke entered (and eventually graduated from) the U.C. Davis Medical School. How the decision would bear upon other preferential programs was not clear. The controversy grew more heated. Widely differing interpretations of the *Bakke* decision stemmed from the fact that Justice Powell's opinion, grounded in the Constitution, was the critical fifth vote on the Court in both respects; his analysis was therefore taken by many to be controlling. But if it were, what was the constitutional status of the quest for racial diversity? Powell apparently had in mind an admissions system in which each applicant was considered as an individual, not as a member of a racial group, so that all of his or her merits and characteristics might be weighed by admissions officers, including the applicant's race or national origin. Being black might then be a "plus factor" that the university could reasonably weigh. He thought it possible to defend the constitutionality of weighing some racial considerations as a legitimate effort to increase the diversity of the entering class.

It is hard to see how such racial considerations could be weighed in a nondiscriminatory way. The mere fact that they are weighed at all is discriminatory. Nevertheless, appealing to Powell's authority, that quest for diversity became the justification heavily relied upon at a good many universities, including the University of Michigan.

This was not at all the justification of preference that the University of California had put forward. Its justification had been, unapologetically, that the university was right to devise a scheme that would *compensate* minorities for the oppression of generations past. That justification— preference as redress for injury—the Supreme Court found totally unacceptable, a violation of our Constitution. Redress may be appropriately given to an individual who has suffered an injury; individuals have rights. But ethnic groups—whites, blacks, Hispanics—are not individuals and do not hold rights. For the state to provide compensation today to an individual black because of damage done earlier to other blacks, with the consequence that some entirely innocent third party must bear the burden of the compensation because he or she is of the same color as those who did the earlier injury, is not constitutional, not even common sense. Under a constitution such as ours, which certainly treats the rights of citizens as *individual* rights, not the rights of ethnic groups, the compensatory defense of preference must fail. The university preference for minority applicants as compensation for earlier societal injury was flatly rejected by the Supreme Court. This has become settled law in our country.[6]

But that compensatory approach, the view that preference is at bottom a kind of remedy for earlier damage, continues to appeal to many. For most Americans today, if minority preferences are ever to be justified, that could only be as *turnabout*, in light of the preferences that the white majority has so long enjoyed. This moral reasoning, rejected by the Court as a matter of constitutional law, is also rightly rejected by a thoughtful morality. Governments ought not seek to benefit B at the expense of A simply because A has the same skin color as W, who had done an injury to persons with the same skin color as B. Redress by skin color cannot justify race preference.

With the Supreme Court's demolition of the attempted compensatory justification of race preference by U.C. Davis, tenacious defenders of preference were obliged to seek some other justification. Justice Powell gave them what they needed, a constitutional defense of preference as a support for *diversity*.[7]

Much later, as we shall see, diversity did become the justification of racial preference upon which a Supreme Court decision relied. But at the time of the *Bakke* decision this possible argument seemed strained at best and was not taken very seriously. Eight separate opinions were issued in the *Bakke* case, the justices falling into the three groups noted above—but only one justice, Lewis Powell, even mentioned diversity as an objective; no other justice was willing to join him in his speculations. His central position in the *Bakke* case, however, gave to colleges and universities, among them the University of Michigan, an arguably plausible defense of race preference.

The ensuing enthusiasm for diversity as the justification of race preference was often sheer hypocrisy. Many, perhaps most of those who extolled the alleged centrality of diversity in higher education, and its overriding value, silently harbored the belief that the real justification is compensatory, even if that could not be defended in court. But there was no alternative. The case for race preference in admissions might withstand constitutional scrutiny only if ethnic diversity were its justification.[8]

The word *diversity* became (and remains) the universal buzzword of the universities. Across the country there arose diversity projects and programs, diversity offices, diversity deans. At the University of California at San Diego, for example, there is today a massive diversity apparatus that includes the chancellor's diversity office, the assistant vice chancellor for diversity, the graduate diversity coordinators, the staff diversity liaison, the undergraduate student diversity liaison, the chief diversity officer, the director of development for diversity initiatives, the Office of Academic Diversity and Equal Opportunity, and the Diversity Council. To all of this there has recently been added a new, full-time vice chancellor for equity, diversity, and inclusion.[9] Colleges and universities are made more diverse by enrolling minorities, chiefly blacks and Hispanics. Black and Hispanic students are diverse! The praise of diversity became effusive and ubiquitous. Claims about the absolutely essential role of diversity in higher education reached almost absurd extremes. All this was quite remarkable in view of the fact that until Justice Powell had opened this possible line of argument, the universities had pursued race preference vigorously with little or no mention of diversity as their concern.

The diversity argument had become the last argument standing. All chips were to be placed on that bet. Twenty-five years later, when the University of Michigan was obliged to defend its race preferences in federal courts, it staked everything on that defense. The compensatory argument, upon which the University of California had relied in the 1970s, was a sure loser, and Michigan repudiated it explicitly.

Lee Bollinger became president of the University of Michigan in 1996. He was a professor of law and had been dean of our law school. He affirmed repeatedly that the diversity justification offered hypothetically in Powell's *Bakke* opinion was "good law." With backing like his, the diversity defense now well formulated and at hand, and with little to fear, universities did not think themselves obliged to abandon race preference programs after *Bakke*, or even to cut back on them. On the contrary, race preferences in admissions soon became almost universal among selective colleges and universities.

Having a diverse student body became essential for good repute. The absolute number of black and Hispanic students who could win admission to Harvard or Michigan on their own academic merits, or to Stanford or Wisconsin, was not great, certainly not great enough to provide for all of these schools the racial numbers they sought. The competition for the enrollment of academically able black students became intense. If minority applicants could not win admission on their own, but were thought to have the potential to succeed, they were sought out, given special support, admitted to special programs, enrolled in the universities, and protected there by altering internal evaluative systems. After the *Bakke* decision race preference ran riot.

My own involvement in the controversy, before *Bakke* and after, grew deeper. I published essays on the topic in widely differing journals: in the *Texas Law Review*,[10] in the *Civil Liberties Review*,[11] in *The Chronicle of Higher Education*,[12] and elsewhere. I was determined to expose the immorality of race preference and what I thought to be the fraudulence of the "diversity defense" of it. In one place above all I found a solid and supportive intellectual platform for the presentation of my critical views. *Commentary* magazine, the widely esteemed monthly publication of the American Jewish Committee, took an editorial position that was thoughtfully and energetically on my side. Its editor, Norman Podhoretz, and his associate Neal Kozodoy, who eventually succeeded him, were respected public intellectuals of great influence. They became my friends and long-continuing supporters. It was in *Commentary* that I published the most extensive and most effective attacks on the race preference that had so widely infected our national community. The first of these was a long and forceful essay, "Why Racial Preference Is Illegal and Immoral," in June of 1979.

CHAPTER 3

From *The Nation* to *Commentary*

The main vehicle for the expression of my views shifted from a journal well known for its left-leaning position, *The Nation*, to a journal, equally distinguished, well known for its right-leaning position. During those years *Commentary* became, and remains, quite conservative in its political views. On many matters it is much more conservative than I was, or am. This did not trouble me. If the editors of *Commentary* enthusiastically held, as they did, that race preference was intolerable in the United States, they were on my side. Whatever their larger political views may have been, they and I were in this respect in fullest harmony. I did not shift from left to right. The position I had defended as the truly liberal position, the position that respects equality before the law above all transitory social goals, I defended in *Commentary* in the very same spirit that I had defended it in *The Nation*. In what were called "liberal" quarters, race preference was finding favor. If now the expression of an authentic liberalism, a liberalism that rejects racism in every form, was to be found in other quarters, so be it. I did not hesitate to go there.

In the movie *Annie Hall*,[1] a clever remark is made by Woody Allen's character: *Commentary*, he thought, had merged with the periodical *Dissent* (a socialist journal much to the left of *The Nation*), and it was to be called *Dysentery*. But of course those sharply opposed periodicals did not merge in me. Perhaps, in me, those sharply opposed periodicals did find some common ground.

Commentary is one of those periodicals in which an author is expected by its editors and readers to present an argument in full. If the argument is complicated or multifaceted, well, the presentation of it must reflect that and may need to be lengthy and detailed. The editors expected contributors to maintain the highest standards in intellectual substance and in rhetorical form. In *Commentary*, letters critical of an earlier essay might be pages in length; rejoinders would be lengthy as well. Getting the argument right was (and is) what counts in that journal. They may have failed on occasion, but its editors try hard.

I became a regular contributor to one of the leading conservative journals of the day. My essays did not address political campaigns, or environmental legislation, or the country's foreign policy—these being spheres in which *Commentary* was far to my right. In two arenas I was much at home there. I shared *Commentary*'s sympathetic support of Israel, which I had expressed vigorously in *The Nation* years before ("Democracy in Israel," 20 July 1974). And I found all race preference, as my *Commentary* editors did, illegal and immoral.

The essay in which I refined and formulated those convictions was provoked by race preference given not in universities but in industrial employment. The case in which such preference came to a head, *United Steelworkers of America v. Weber*,[2] was infamous, its ultimate outcome shocking, the argument in defense of that outcome intellectually disreputable. Even today professors of constitutional law hold it up as a model of what a Supreme Court opinion ought not be like. Although the particulars of this case are not directly relevant to the universities, its central theme—whether the Civil Rights Act of 1964 forbids race preference—certainly is. Here follows the layout, in brief.

Brian Weber, a white, unskilled steelworker, was Bakke's analogue. He sought admission to a job-training program for skilled workers at the Grammercy, Louisiana, plant of the Kaiser Aluminum and Chemical Corporation. He was denied that opportunity because he was white. A quota of black trainees had to be filled first.

Consider the context: not one of the more junior black employees who were admitted to the program had faced discrimination there in any way. There had been a no-discrimination clause in the labor contract at that plant from the day it had opened. Weber himself had discriminated against no one. The United Steelworkers Union, colluding with Kaiser, simply wanted more minorities in the skilled trades and had devised a scheme to achieve this objective by giving a marked preference to black applicants for skilled job-training programs. In the world of private industry seniority is invariably the way priorities in such competitions are decided. Weber had absolute seniority in that plant—but the preferential program there overrode his seniority.

The possibility of such racial discrimination had been foreseen by the authors of the Civil Rights Act. The pertinent passage of that act (in Title

VII) reads: "It shall be an unlawful employment practice for any employer, labor organization, or joint labor-management committee controlling . . . on-the-job training programs, to discriminate against any individual because of his race, color, religion, sex, or national origin in admission to . . . any program established to provide apprenticeship or other training."[3] The racial discrimination that Weber suffered, costing him a treasured place in that job-training program, a place that would certainly have been his had he been black, was an egregious violation of the law.

My first essay in *Commentary*, published before this case was decided, explored and explained the factual setting of this dispute in great detail.[4] Every possible defense of the discriminatory preference was set forth, examined closely, and found wanting. The United Steelworkers Union and Kaiser's management together had simply found it convenient to advance their objective by giving preference to blacks, and they did so in defiance of the law.

When race preference had deprived Allan Bakke of his rightful place in a medical school two years earlier there had been a flood of protest on his behalf; scores of amicus briefs were submitted to the Court, many of them rightly excoriating the racial discrimination practiced then by the University of California. (Happily, that is today no longer possible in California; a statewide initiative in 1996 amended the California Constitution to forbid all preference by race or national origin in that state.)[5] But that widespread concern for Bakke, for the fair treatment of upper-middle-class college students, was not duplicated when the victim was an unskilled worker in a steel plant. This was cruelly unfair, and I was doubly offended—by the discrimination itself and by the victimization of a vulnerable nobody in the workaday world. My argument attacking the Kaiser/United Steelworkers Union's scheme was meticulous and solid. The facts were not in dispute; the language of the Civil Rights Act was unambiguous. I was confident that the U.S. Supreme Court would affirm the decision of the 5th Circuit Court of Appeals[6] and put discriminatory job-training programs finally to rest.

I was mistaken. Only seven justices participated in deciding this case. Justice Lewis Powell was ill. Justice John Paul Stevens, the author of the opinion in *Bakke* in which four justices held the medical school preferences in violation of the Civil Rights Act, was obliged to recuse himself because he had once served as an attorney for Kaiser. The majority opinion that emerged, approving the Kaiser race preferences in on-the-job training placement, was nothing short of outrageous. It was written by

Justice William Brennan. Neither he nor the four others who joined him are any longer on the Court.

My distress was shared by my editors at *Commentary*. How were we to respond to this dreadful miscarriage of justice? Of course I would write the essay, and I did. We discussed at length the title that essay was to carry. Podhoretz wanted fierce words—Justice Betrayed. I shared his anger but wanted not to be guilty of an accusation that might be thought excessive in its vitriol. I was to be the author; I had my way. *Weber* was decided on 27 June 1979; my essay considering its every detail, "Justice Debased: The *Weber* Decision," appeared in *Commentary* that September, three months later. It was, I will say frankly, a scathing attack on a decision not worthy of our Supreme Court.

How could the plain words of the statute have been ignored? Well, said Brennan and his associates, it was not the intent of Congress to forbid racial preference having the wholesome purpose this Kaiser program did. It is not the "literal" meaning of the statute, but its "spirit" (said they) that must govern here. By studying the history of the Civil Rights Act one can, they said, discover the purposes of Congress in its adoption. The Kaiser plan, if not "within the letter of the statute" is yet "within its spirit, . . . within the intentions of its makers."[7] Said they in effect, the purpose of Congress and the purpose of this quota plan are consonant. Therefore Congress could not have intended to forbid this plan. If the literal language of Congress says otherwise, we must interpret that language to mean what it did not say, while saying what it did not mean.

This was an abuse of judicial authority; it was justice debased. There was no need for the Court majority to examine the history of the legislation to determine what was really intended by Congress through its passage. The language of the statute was straightforward and lucid; it has been held up as a model of legislative clarity. Sometimes the exploration of congressional intent is needed; in this case it was no more than a device employed to reach a result that the plain words of the law would not permit. That, however, was not the worst of it.

The worst of it was this: when the legislative history of the act is closely examined, when one studies what was actually said by senators and representatives in the course of the long debate leading up to the passage of the Civil Rights Act in the summer of 1964, one finds that its authors did indeed mean to forbid all preferences of the kind employed by Kaiser and the United Steelworkers Union. I went to our university library here in Ann Arbor; I pored over the *Congressional Record* of 1964. The congressional debates of that summer, which I cited at length in my essay, extend intermittently over exactly 13,000 pages (from page 1,511 to page 14,511) of ten massive tomes. In the Senate that controversial bill was not submitted to committee but taken up directly on the floor. Many representatives and almost every senator rose to put his or her judgment on record. Many were eloquent. All were forceful. There was an acute consciousness, throughout the Congress, of the need for a clear legislative history to guide the courts in interpreting and applying the Civil Rights Act. The language used by Congress in those debates was utterly unambiguous.

Careful inspection of the legislative history of the Civil Rights Act leaves no doubt that it was intended to protect *all* citizens, and *all* workers, of *all* races, against racial preference of every kind. Whites as well as blacks were to be protected. Preference by race in employment, addressed in Title VII of the act (as also preference by institutions receiving federal financial assistance, addressed in Title VI) was to be eliminated. Writing this essay for *Commentary* had obliged me to immerse myself in the Civil Rights Act as never before. I had become deeply engaged in the struggle to put an end to preference by race.

CHAPTER 4

From Washington to Berlin and Beyond

My essays on the *Weber* case were widely noted. I was invited to testify before the U.S. Senate Committee on the Judiciary, which I did in September of 1979. The issue on that occasion was how, with legislation, we might avoid the sorts of preference that the Supreme Court had found acceptable in *Weber*, in the face of its apparent violation of the Civil Rights Act of 1964. In that 96th Congress, the Senate was considering amendments to the Fair Housing Act of 1968, and I was asked to comment on proposed amendments. It seemed to me evident that Congress in 1979, as in 1964, had *intended* with its legislation to preclude all preferences by race. Yet the language of the Civil Rights Act had not succeeded in achieving that. I presented the case for a set of words in the amendments then being considered that would make the intentions of Congress so very clear that no court could evade them.[1]

If the need for fairness were expressed only in general terms to facilitate passage of the legislation, subsequent judicial interpretation of the statute might once again conclude that if race preferences had been honorably motivated (as in fact they almost always are), they could withstand constitutional objections. A number of amendment formulations were entertained by the committee. I repeated my response: the language of the amended statute must be precise, specific, unambiguously prohibiting deliberate preference for any persons, in any ethnic group. One might think, as I did (and do), that the language of the Civil Rights Act was clear enough. Yet it had been evaded in *Weber*. The task of the Committee on the Judiciary was to frame the statute so as to make such evasion no longer possible.

On the international scene also preferences had become controversial. Which ethnic groups were to be the beneficiaries of preferences varied, of course, with the circumstances of the country in which the preferences had been enacted. I addressed these matters in Berlin in 1983, where I had been invited by the *Dahlem Konferenzen*, devoted that year to this sensitive topic. It was sensitive in Germany because of the unhappy condition of the Turkish minority there, many of whom had come to Germany originally as guest workers. Having made their homes in Germany, members of the younger generation of Turks had not assimilated well. To advance their assimilation (some thought), the Turks in Germany were in need of special consideration in education and employment. In France that same attitude was expressed by those who believed that only through preferences might the conditions of the growing Muslim minority be brought up to the national standard. Our experience in the United States, introducing preferences for the black and Hispanic minorities, was painful, but not very long. A global view, I argued, provides a substantial body of evidence of the negative consequences of preferences instituted by national legislatures on behalf of what are called "group rights."[2]

In India, ethnic preferences have been established longer than in any other nation. "Positive discrimination" goes back to British rule and was built into the Indian Constitution in 1947. In the United States we often hear it said that race preferences will be temporary, lasting only a few years. When the U.S. Supreme Court found preferences in some contexts permissible, its majority opinion (in 2003) expressed the "expectation" that it would be needed for not more than twenty-five years. That was the original view in India, where the preferences (for the Dalits, or "untouchables") were adopted at first with the understanding that they would last for only twenty years. But these "reservations," or quotas, have been extended repeatedly in India and are no longer regarded as transitory there. Moreover, the categories of beneficiaries (the "backward classes") steadily increase in number. They now constitute more than three-quarters of the Indian population. At universities not more than 50 percent of the available places may be reserved. Reservations for the most backward groups often go unfilled there, but quotas for "other backward classes" rarely go unfilled—with the result that the majority of reserved places go to those who deserve them least.

The system doesn't change; politicians buy support by confirming preferences and extending them to more and more ethnic groups. As I write this in 2014 there is strong pressure on the national legislature to extend these "reservations" to the sizable Muslim minority in India. The lesson of the Indian experience is plain: race preference does not wind down; it winds up. Proliferation is the rule.

In Malaysia there is a well-established system of ethnic preferences that are the consequence of a labor policy not unlike that of Germany—bring guest workers from abroad to do the work that locals won't do. In this case the guest workers were Chinese, brought in long ago to work the rubber plantations. But the Chinese, generally adopting a frugal lifestyle and investing heavily in the education of their children, pulled themselves from the plantations and built businesses across the country. They now dominate retail establishments in Malaysia, of which they owned about 85 percent at the time I presented my arguments against preferences in Berlin in 1983.

The economic domination by the Chinese minority was reduced somewhat by the expulsion of Singapore, a largely Chinese island that became an independent country in 1965. Shortly before my visit to Berlin, I had taught for two months as a visiting professor at the National University of Singapore. It was (and remains) an ethnically Chinese city, densely populated and prosperous. Its independence could not stop the intellectual advance of the ethnic Chinese who remained in Malaysia. When university admissions there were determined by examination results, only 20 percent of the places went to Malays, most of the rest to ethnic Chinese.

To protect the Malay majority the government of Malaysia set out to achieve racial balance in employment. It did this by giving formal preference to Malays in hiring. Group membership trumped individual performance. To further increase the number of Malays in higher education, the Malay language became the only medium of instruction in schools as well as in universities. Preferences have become pervasive in Malaysia, where their purpose is not to advance an oppressed minority but to protect the majority, performing relatively less well, from the intellectual and economic advances of the ethnic Chinese. The ethnic problems in Malaysia were quite different from those faced in Europe, but the Malaysian experience does teach a lesson wisely borne in mind: the relatively inferior performance of some ethnic groups is not always a consequence of discrimination against them.

Then there is Nigeria, a nation encompassing a vast array of ethnic groups and regions—largely Islamic in the north, largely Christian in the south. Tension between the two halves of the country often becomes violent. Nigeria had never been a country until colonial rulers made it one. With the abolition of colonial rule, the changing governments of Nigeria have regularly indulged in favoritism toward one or another of the many scores of tribes and ethnic groups.

Preferences are demanded in Nigeria, and justified by its Constitution of 1979, which requires that national activities "reflect the federal character of the country." This principle has been applied to school admissions, to promotions in school, and even to membership on the national soccer team. Every activity must "look like Nigeria." Almost every policy issue becomes a matter of ethnic dispute, intensified by charges of ethnic favoritism.

The violence that often accompanies disputes in Nigeria has been in part the product of the politicization of ethnic differences—and that politicization takes the form of preferential treatment for various ethnic groups. To reduce discord, separate ethnic enclaves have been carved out and given formal status. Heterogeneity has produced a spoils system in which ethnic conflicts are mitigated by gerrymandered homogeneity within states. Even for nations not threatened by internal violence there is a lesson to learn: when racial balance is advanced by granting preferences, diversity often produces conflict rather than harmony.

It is often supposed that ethnic groups all exhibit similar dispositions and talents and that if given equal chances, all will perform with equal competence. Marked disparities by group, in employment or education, are therefore taken to be a sure sign of oppression. When ethnic proportionality becomes the unquestioned standard of fair play, ethnic preferences will be sought for the sake of fairness.

The reality is this: for a host of reasons, some of which we know and many of which we do not know, some of which spring from malign oppression and some of which do not, ethnic groups behave differently, perform differently, learn differently, and exhibit different talents and temperaments. This is not crude stereotyping; it is plain fact. Devising preferences to overcome that fact by engineering proportionality is futile and a recipe for disaster. Ethnic preferences, I told my international audience in 1983, are dynamite.

CHAPTER 5

Naked Racial Preference

The quest for racial proportionality spread from the universities, where it was common by the late 1970s, to the public schools. In Jackson, Michigan—not far from my home in Ann Arbor—a school board's efforts to achieve racial proportionality in its workforce gave rise to a dispute eventually resolved by the U.S. Supreme Court. In that conflict I came to learn how the *mechanics* of preference could have cruel consequences.

"Naked Racial Preference" was the title of the essay in which I recounted the facts and the arguments in this extraordinary case; it appeared in *Commentary* in March of 1986. I used the title again for a small book that I published nine years later.[1] The case, *Wygant v. Jackson Board of Education*, was decided by the Supreme Court later that same year.[2] The opinion of the deciding plurality was forceful, and I was heartened by the way in which one concurring justice, Sandra Day O'Connor, rejected the supposition that racial justice always entails racial proportionality.

In the Jackson schools, white teachers with high seniority were laid off to protect the jobs of other teachers, with less seniority, who were "Black, American Indian, Oriental, or of Spanish descendancy."[3] Those teachers whose jobs were protected had not been discriminated against, and the teachers whose jobs were sacrificed to protect them had not themselves discriminated against anyone. With layoffs unavoidable in the school district, which teachers were to keep their jobs, and which would not, depended largely on race.

As in the universities it became a racial numbers game, but the rules of this particular game were astounding. In 1981, when Wendy Wygant was laid off *for the seventh time* to protect minority teacher ratios, blacks constituted 9.7 percent of the population of Michigan, had been awarded

10 percent of the degrees in education in Michigan, but constituted 13.5 percent of the teachers in the public schools. Minorities *exceeded* their number in the relevant labor pool by about 30 percent. Why then the scheme to protect them? Because the percentage of minority teachers in the district was substantially below the percentage of minority *students* in the district! The premise was that every ethnic subset, every minority group, is entitled to a proportion among its public school *teachers* equal to the proportion that subset constitutes among public school *students*. The steadily increasing departure of white families from the cities and white students from the urban public schools resulted in a steadily increasing proportion of minority students—reaching 70 and even 80 percent in some districts. The flow of available teachers, white and black, is largely determined by altogether different factors. The proportionality principle applied in that school district was absurd. It was also completely unrealistic, because if it were achieved in a few districts using race preferences, that could happen only at the cost of resegregating other districts. This principle would undermine honest efforts to integrate all the public schools. Here was an example of the way in which race preference is not only unfair (in the repeated layoffs of senior teachers by race) but also counterproductive and injurious to the entire community.

The district's defense of its racial layoff scheme was faulty for a deeper reason: it relied upon the assumption that, absent discrimination, all ethnic groups would be randomly distributed among all categories of employment. After that is supposed, any showing of statistical "underrepresentation" becomes the warrant for racially preferential instruments to get the proportions right. The convictions underlying that argument are not only unrealistic, they are unwholesome. Even where discrimination is wholly absent, patterns of employment (or recreation, or education, etc.) are rarely random across ethnic groups. Human beings commonly work, play, live, and associate with members of the ethnic groups—religious, racial, and national—with which they identify themselves. The numerical proportionality of ethnic groups in employment or education never can be realized and never should be thought ideal.

The mistake is dangerous. When the reports of the numerical representation, say of blacks or of Jews, in some profession, is framed in such a way as to suppose that racial proportionality is the proper moral standard, deviations from it come to be viewed as "societal discrimination." Much discrimination there has been, we know; but it is foolish to suppose that discrimination alone is the paramount cause of every nonrandom ethnic distribution. The drive to achieve racial "balance" has consequences the very reverse of those desired. Wanting racial justice, the advocates of preference to achieve balance end up producing racial injustice. Seeking to eliminate discrimination by race, they encourage and employ it. For decades we have struggled to reduce interracial tension and distrust; now we engender distrust and exacerbate tension with deliberate racial favoritism.

The unfairness of race preference, I argued in that essay of March of 1986, is underscored by the impossibility of determining justly who really is a member of any given minority. How are we to decide, in a rational and consistent way, *who* is a *what*? This problem has no solution. I believed then and have become ever more fully convinced that every scheme that relies upon racial classifications, whether its intention be malicious or honorable, must founder on this rock.

In the notorious case of *Plessy v. Ferguson*, decided in 1896,[4] the "separate but equal" doctrine was established in our country, resulting in a half century of racial segregation and oppression. But Homer Plessy, the central figure in that case, according to the Court record, was seven-eighths white, and the "mixture of colored blood was not discernible in him."[5] He was a black man under Louisiana law. The "one-drop" rule was absurd, but nonetheless often applied.

In these days, when preferences are designed to benefit minorities, one's classification as black, Native American, or Hispanic may offer significant advantages. In New York City, in the autumn of 1985, racial quotas were instituted in making police department promotions. In response, petitions were received from individual officers seeking to change the racial designation on their employment records to that of some minority. Recently, membership in some Native American tribes has been claimed by persons hoping to receive some of the benefits of a profitable casino newly permitted on those tribal lands. But how is the tribal court to determine the legitimacy of such claims? Where Wygant had been laid off in Jackson, Michigan, being of "Spanish descendancy" could save one's job. But how determine that? The attorney for the school board, when arguing his case before the Supreme Court, was pressed on this matter. He responded, "I guess we just didn't think about it, Justice Powell, at that point. I think we were looking at Hispanic people."[6] But looking how? If a teacher's name were Gonzalez, as was her grandfather's, she was likely to have received special protection—unless that forebear happened to be her maternal grandfather, in which case the categorization is not clear. But wherever racial preference is given there must be some rules, some standards with which to determine whether the required mixture of blood, or required skin color, is really there. Then there must be public officials with the authority to apply those rules—not unlike the boards that sought with great scrupulosity in Hitler's Germany to determine who was truly Aryan.[7] Such tasks confront us inevitably when we begin to think with our blood. In Michigan, in Germany, in New York it was, as it always must be, a nasty business.

The decision of the Supreme Court in the *Wygant* case, three months later, was especially heartening in four respects. First, reinforcing and emphasizing the outcome in *Bakke*, the Court firmly rejected the argument that "societal discrimination," discrimination experienced in the society at large, might justify preferences for minorities now. For the Court Justice Powell wrote, "This Court has never held that societal discrimination alone is sufficient to justify a racial classification. Rather, the Court has insisted upon some showing of prior discrimination *by the governmental unit involved* before allowing limited use of racial classifications in order to remedy such discrimination."[8]

Second, the Court flatly rejected the argument that the need for "role models" might justify minority preferences. Powell again: "The role model theory . . . has no logical stopping point. [It] allows the [School] Board to engage in discriminatory hiring and layoff practices long past the point required by any legitimate remedial purpose."[9]

Third, the Court reaffirmed the principle that whenever any law or regulation uses a suspect category, such as race, to classify persons, that classification will be subject to the most scrupulous examination to determine if it is warranted; *strict scrutiny* has been and must remain the standard for the evaluation of racial classifications.

And fourth, strict scrutiny requires that when a governmental unit has relied upon race, it must be shown that the remedial plan implemented is *narrowly tailored* to address the problem at hand. Justice Sandra Day O'Connor echoed the argument I had presented in *Commentary*: because the hiring goal for minority teachers (that the layoff provision was designed to protect) was tied to the number of minority *students* in the school district, it was indefensible. "It cannot be adjudged 'narrowly tailored' to effectuate its asserted remedial purpose."[10] My confidence in Justice O'Connor grew.

Justice Byron White condemned the naked preference crisply: "The discharge of white teachers to make room for blacks, none of whom has been shown to be a victim of any racial discrimination, . . . is violative of the Equal Protection Clause [and hence] unconstitutional."[11]

CHAPTER 6

The University of Michigan Comes into Focus

A critical turning point for me was reached in 1995. It was triggered by an extraordinary article in the *Journal of Blacks in Higher Education* (*JBHE*), to which I was a subscriber. In its August issue the *JBHE*, by making penetrating requests of the admissions offices of many fine colleges and universities, assembled a substantial body of data about the acceptance rates of white applicants and black applicants in those institutions.[1]

Universities had not been forthright about their admissions policies. Their efforts to enroll larger numbers of minority students had been commonly described in language that was agreeable, but vague and deliberately obscure. Here at the University of Michigan, for example, we had announced the Michigan Mandate (about which I will say more shortly), which was to revolutionize our minority enrollments. But how? What policies were really being applied, behind closed doors, to increase the number of minority students? Few of us knew. We learned eventually that some universities, including my own, did not always tell the truth. In a sidebar at the end of every formal publication of the university, this statement appears: "The University of Michigan is committed to a policy of non-discrimination and equal opportunity for all persons regardless of race, sex, color, religion, creed, national origin, or ancestry . . . in employment, educational activities, and admissions." The practice of my university, as I soon came to learn, was not at all consistent with that often-repeated profession. But I do not believe that the authors of this passage were deliberately lying. In large institutions it is often the case that the right hand knoweth not what the left hand doeth.

The editors of the *JBHE* had requested admission figures from twenty-five highly esteemed universities and from another twenty-five highly esteemed liberal arts colleges. Each was asked, What percentage of all students applying to your institution is accepted? And then, what percentage of black applicants is accepted?

Among the universities, ten of the twenty-five—including Harvard, Princeton, Yale, Stanford, Duke, and Columbia—refused to supply the data requested. Of the fifteen that did respond, twelve revealed acceptance rates for blacks were (in the words of the *JBHE*) "significantly higher than acceptance rates for whites." At the University of Virginia, for example, 54.2 percent of black applicants were accepted in 1995, as opposed to an overall acceptance rate of 36.6 percent. At Rice, the acceptance rate for blacks in that year was 51.7 percent and that for whites was less than half of that. This pattern was nearly universal.

Among the liberal arts colleges approached by the *JBHE*, the figures showed even greater partiality. Amherst, for example, reported an overall acceptance rate of 19.2 percent in 1995, but its acceptance rate for black applicants was 51.1 percent. For Bowdoin the figures were 30.4 percent and 70.2 percent. And so on. The director of admissions at Williams, declining to respond, said gingerly, "We think these figures should remain in-house because of the current anger over affirmative action."

One might expect the acceptance rate for a given group to be higher if its earlier academic performance had been stronger. But that could not explain the admissions disparities revealed in this report by the *JBHE*, because the earlier performance of minority groups accepted at greatly higher rates was significantly weaker, not stronger, than that of other groups. In many cases it was even weaker than the performance of many applicants rejected.

Reading and thinking about this report, I was obliged to ask myself what was happening at the University of Michigan. Until this time I had addressed the issues without focusing on my own university. I am unable to say now, in retrospect, how I had managed to keep my attention on the general problem while somehow avoiding its bearing, now obvious, on our circumstances in Ann Arbor.

That acrobatic position couldn't be maintained. I decided that I had to learn whether, in fact, my university was giving outright admissions preference to minority applicants. How was I to do that? Some years before I had served on the Undergraduate Admission Steering Committee, which, its members being appointed faculty members and administrators, recommended admissions policies to the central administration. Chiefly (in those much earlier days) this committee sought to determine what the size of the entering class ought to be, that is, how many new undergraduates we thought could be happily accommodated. It was only an advisory body; I don't recall how the actual admissions target was decided upon. The matters we discussed, although important, were not terribly controversial. I cannot recollect any discussion of race or minority enrollments during my service on the Undergraduate Admission Steering Committee more than twenty years earlier.

In more recent years I had served on the Admissions Committee of the Medical School. In 1985 I had been recruited by our Medical School, and during the decade 1985–1995 my appointment had been divided between the College of Literature, Science, and the Arts (our Michigan name for the liberal arts college, commonly referred to as LSA) and the Medical School, where I was also a professor of philosophy and director of the Program in Human Values in Medicine. But at the Medical School, a much more hierarchical institution than LSA, we who served on the Admissions Committee were never given, by the dean, an opportunity to address questions of policy. We were asked to review application dossiers and then to interview candidates for admission, which we did, usually in groups of two or three interviewers, with great energy and care. We would make a report to the director of admissions with our recommendations regarding each of the applicants who had come before us. There were many small groups of faculty interviewers on our committee. To my knowledge none of us were ever invited to comment in any way on the larger policies of the Medical School regarding minority applicants. The director of admissions at the Medical School during the latter years of my tenure there was Prof. Paul Gikas, a distinguished member of the Department of Pathology now retired, a good friend. He was a straightforward person, of great good sense; I liked and admired him. To the best of my recollection Gikas and I never discussed minority enrollment. I do recall that I later had occasion to send him some data suggesting race preference in the Medical School that I had subsequently gathered, but I do not know what he did with it. Nor do I know whether admissions policy decisions were in his hands. Probably such decisions were made, in the Medical School, by the dean and his cabinet, whose authority in that school was quite complete.

So, having resolved in the late summer of 1995 that I needed to learn what admissions policies were in force at my own university, I had to decide first how to pursue that inquiry. I had come to believe, without direct evidence, but in the light of reports like that of the *JBHE*, that we were giving substantial admissions preference to minority applicants to LSA.

Were we giving race preference at the Medical School? That seemed highly probable to me. I had been teaching large lecture classes in medical ethics for the Medical School, required classes for all second-year medical school students. Initially I was asked to prepare multiple-choice questions in ethics for the second-year final exams. I declined to do that; multiple-choice questions simply cannot examine successfully in ethics. My medical colleagues, anxious to retain formal instruction in medical ethics, insisted that the final exams *had* to include some attention to ethical issues, for if they did not, medical students would come quickly to the conclusion that such "soft" material was not taken seriously by the school. Medical students are, indeed, a goal-oriented lot; understandably they would ask, What role does this material play in my education? If medical ethics were to be important for them the subject would have to be shown to be important to the school itself. To that end we had to examine them on the subject. But if that could not be done with multiple-choice questions, some essay-type exams for the sophomores would have to be devised. It was not difficult for me to set the essay topics, in the light of my earlier lectures and the readings I had assigned. The practical problem then confronted was the evaluation of the essays submitted. The only person at the Medical School who could do that was me. During my ten years at that school this proved an arduous and time-consuming task. My classes had more than 200 students, sometimes 250 or more. The benefit to the students and to the profession justified my labors. But I admit that the days I spent reading and evaluating those exam essays were among the least agreeable in my university year.

In reading and commenting on those essays I learned a good deal about the quality of thinking of our medical students. Standards at the University of Michigan Medical School are high. Many of our students wrote superb short essays; most of them wrote essays that demonstrated at least a reasonable understanding of, and some ability to resolve, the moral complexities presented to them in those exams.

A few of those student essays, however, were shocking: confused, disorganized, in some cases almost illiterate. I knew the names, but not the race of those who had written those dreadful responses, but in the few cases in which my comments on the exams brought their authors to my office, I learned that these authors were, without exception, minority students. I came to believe, although I had no direct evidence for it at that time, that these were students enrolled by the Medical School even though their academic credentials would not normally have justified their admission. I was pretty sure that we were accepting students whom we knew to be subpar.

The Medical School appeared desperate to retain the minority students already enrolled. Increasing the number of minority doctors graduated was a demand the central administration of the university had made. Medical Board exams, given to all students at the end of their sophomore year, were supposedly designed to screen out students unsuited to the practice of medicine. But some students who failed the board exams were given a second opportunity to take them. When the exams were failed by a minority student a second time, a *third* opportunity was offered. Then sometimes a *fourth*! My colleagues told me that it was almost impossible for a minority medical student to flunk out.

This had the unfortunate consequence of associating inferior performance with skin color. Surely many minority students not given preference in admissions did superbly on their exams, but whether preference had been given to them or not, who knew? Students themselves could not have known with certainty (although some surely must have suspected) that they were among the preferred. The knowledge that some of the students we were graduating were not likely to be good physicians caused some of my medical colleagues to refrain from recommending minority doctors in their consultations with patients. One colleague told me flat out that, knowing what he knew about what we were doing to increase the number of minority physicians we graduated, and what that meant for the quality of the resultant graduates, he thought such risky recommendations should be avoided. It was racism—an unhappy racism that our own system had engendered. Some of the second-year medical students who submitted awful essays may not have been minority students. Mostly I did not know the race of the authors. But I did know that whoever had written those chaotic, sometimes horrific, exam responses, they were not persons to whom I would want to entrust my health or the health of anyone else.

My strong suspicions about the way in which admissions criteria at my Medical School had been distorted by the consideration of race could have been confirmed (or disconfirmed) by a dean willing to report candidly what the policies of the school really were. But I knew enough about the Medical School to know that I would never encounter such candor in the deanery. All delicate matters there were treated confidentially, and even not-so-delicate matters were kept within tightly closed circles. From the Medical School I would not learn the truth.

At the University of Michigan Law School—one of the finest in the country—I was pretty sure that preference had been regularly given to minority students. Because my essays and books often concerned political and legal philosophy, I had occasion now and then to discuss controversial issues with members of the law faculty. In one of those comfortable Law School meeting rooms we had held such a theoretical discussion, long before, on the *DeFunis* case—about which I had written in 1976. Some professors in the Law School were my friends, whom I greatly admired. With some I was quite close. They told me nothing explicit about admissions policies there, but from voice tone and facial expression it was not difficult to infer what some of them thought about their admissions policies. But the faculty of the Law School (vastly smaller than that of the Medical School, of course) was a tight fraternity whose policies, if they might be in some quarters suspect, would certainly not be reported to inquiring outsiders.

One experience of mine involving a student at our Law School will show why I had little doubt that race preference was given there. My professorship was in the Residential College of the university, which was (and remains) a unit within LSA; we offered undergraduate instruction in a more informal, but not less demanding, environment. My office was in East Quadrangle, where our students lived and our classes were taught. As an educational experiment, and one of the first of its kind, our college was highly successful. I had helped to plan the Residential College and had been a member of its faculty from the time of its founding. One of the courses I regularly taught there (I called it "Logic and Language") was an introduction to both formal and informal logic, supported by extensive philosophical readings. I was coauthor of the logic textbook on which we relied.[2] This was, and remains, a demanding course, but students thrive in it, and I love teaching it.

One of my students in that course, some few years before the events of 1995, had become my good friend. His grasp of complicated arguments was penetrating; his skills in technical logic were quite remarkable for one so young. I would like to name him here, but (in view of what came to pass) I think that would not be kind. I will call him Ali, although that was not his name. His father was a distinguished professor in our university, originally from Kenya, a graduate of Oxford, a splendid scholar who was drawn away from our university in 1989 by a very attractive offer from the State University of New York at Binghamton. Ali graduated from the University of Michigan with honors, of course, and soon after applied for admission to its Law School. I supported that application vigorously, but my support was hardly necessary; his superb record won him admission. We remained in touch after his graduation, but only occasionally.

Early in his law school studies Ali was appointed an editor of the *Mich-*

igan Law Review. This was a distinct honor. The *Michigan Law Review,* run entirely by students at the Law School, had long chosen its editors on intellectual grounds alone. In that high-powered realm, nothing counted but sheer intelligence and writing skills; Ali was a standout.

I received a telephone call from Ali in 1992, after the lapse of some time; email had not yet become the standard mode of communication. He wanted to talk to me about an important matter. Might we meet in my office? Of course. We had a long conversation there. It was revelatory.

The problem he reported was this: the *Michigan Law Review* had many participating editors, but he was the only black editor. Appointment was based upon writing samples evaluated blindly, with the applicant's grade-point average in completed law classes then factored in. This system, long in force, did not yield minority editors (Ali being the sole exception), although the number of minority students in the Law School was by this time about 12 percent of its student body. The editors were determined to correct this imbalance.

Ali showed me a memorandum—I have it in my files—from the *Michigan Law Review* Association, dated 3 April 1992. In it a new system for the selection of editors was proposed, designed to ensure the "same percentage of minorities on its staff as there are minorities in the Law School." If the existing procedures "fail to identify a sufficient number of minority candidates for positions on the *Law Review,* we will supplement these procedures by considering an applicant's *affirmative action eligibility . . .* that is, on the basis of whether an applicant is a Black American, Mexican American, Native American, or Puerto Rican raised on the American mainland." The memorandum went on to explain that under this new system minority students would be identified by the Law School office as having "affirmative action eligibility" (i.e., they were indeed African American, Native American, etc.), and this would be noted on their sample writing entries. In the end a "sufficient number of positions will be offered to those applicants from minority groups with the highest writing scores or augmented grades." What number is "sufficient" was not specified, but one must infer from the introduction that it would be the number that would cause the *Michigan Law Review* staff to exhibit the same proportion of minority students as that in the Law School at large.

The essence of this policy is clear enough: when minority students are not good enough to make it on their own, the best minority applicants available will be appointed to ensure the racial numbers sought. To avoid the risk of dreadful embarrassment by the appointment of persons utterly incompetent, the *Michigan Law Review* policy concludes with the following proviso: "Positions will not be offered to applicants who score a zero in the writing competition and whose grades fall below a threshold to be determined by the Editor-in-Chief and Managing Editor."

Learning of this newly proposed preferential system, Ali was greatly distressed. He sought my advice. "Carl," he said, "that policy will ruin me, will *undermine* me. Everyone to whom I later apply for positions will 'know' how I got on *Law Review*—although it wasn't like that at all!" In my office that afternoon, telling me about this proposed change, Ali was near tears. Probably he was not as threatened as he feared; his great merit had already been established. But he was certainly right in general: after this policy had been adopted, the reputation of all black students on the *Michigan Law Review*, whether appointed by preference or by merit, would be undermined, within and outside the school. "If I put *Law Review* on my resume," Ali later wrote, "that only means that I didn't both write a competition piece worthy of a zero and fall below some unknown minimum grade-point average. And here in the school I have to face the resentment of white students who applied for *Law Review* but didn't make it."

I had little advice to give him. I found his distress painful and his arguments against the proposed policy strong. There was nothing I could do to help him, of course. I urged him to write his fellow editors of the *Law Review*, putting his arguments before them as persuasively as he could; it was conceivable that he could change their minds. He did write that letter, long and eloquent, a copy of which I retain. After considering the many hurts that would be done to students black and white, along with damage to the *Law Review* itself, he concluded his letter thus: "Personally, I'm tired of having my achievements doubted. When my wife told her workmates that I had been accepted by the U of M Law School, one person muttered, 'It's no wonder. He's black and he's blind.' On the *Law Review* I thought I could attain recognition for my merit rather than my color. . . . Unfortunately my membership is tainted. . . . Isn't it ironic to have blind grading tickets for everyone and colored grading tickets for minorities?"

Ali has gone on to a successful career in academic law. The preferential system for the selection of *Michigan Law Review* editors was adopted and (to the best of my knowledge) remains in effect.

That the Law School was giving preference in admissions was a pretty sure bet, but I did not have evidence that could establish that fact. A student at another law school, quoted in the *New York Times*, described the same distress that the assumption of racial inferiority creates: "I'll never forget my first week of law school. The message was clear: we were the 'slow' kids. A meeting between the Dean and a group from my section confirmed this. That experience left no one with the illusion that we were anything but charity cases. We wanted to compete but apparently the law school had some doubt that we could. We were only there for diversity's sake."[3]

And in our own university newspaper, a minority student in mechanical engineering wrote poignantly, "Nobody expects you to know what you're doing. . . . You're always the last lab partner picked."[4]

By late 1995 I was utterly convinced that the University of Michigan was giving admission preference by race. If that were so, I believed that we would have been breaking the law, the Civil Rights Act of 1964, and also violating the Equal Protection Clause of the U.S. Constitution. But I could not prove it.

CHAPTER 7

Confrontation

It became clear to me that if I were to learn what our University of Michigan admission policies really were, I would have to do so in my own college, the College of Literature, Science, and the Arts (LSA). In this college I had served for three years, during the 1970s, as a member of the Executive Committee. In the university at large I had been chair of the Faculty Senate, representing the entire faculty at meetings with our president and with our Board of Regents. My friends in the college were numerous, some close and many casual, in various departments. I was widely known and well respected. The dean of our college at this time was Edie Goldenberg, with whom I was not close. But having been active in the governance of the college in years past, I knew how it worked. I had served the college loyally, and I loved it. One of the associate deans at the time was a distinguished professor of history, Terrence McDonald, who became dean in 2003 and who remained our successful and much-admired dean for more than a decade.

What I did not know with certainty was whether, in 1995, we in LSA were giving preference by race to applicants for admission, and if we were, what principles were guiding us. I was determined to find out.

In our college there was an Admissions Committee on which sat several colleagues, not to be named here, from whom I thought I might learn, informally, about the minority admissions policies that had been troubling me. I went to one of them and asked him if he could tell me, roughly, what was going on. Were we treating admissions applications differently according to race? He was silent for a while, and then said,

"Carl, this is a matter I simply cannot talk to you about."
"Why not?"

"It's Committee business, and we've agreed to keep it that way."

"But admission policies are the business of the entire College."

"Sorry, I can't talk to you about this."

I urged him to confide in me. I was not an outsider; I was not hostile to the college or seeking to damage it. I just wanted to know whether in fact we were giving special consideration to minority applicants. If we were I would of course seek to have that policy changed, but in-house, without injury to the reputation of the college. I learned nothing from him, although, of course, my suspicions were heightened by his insistence on committee confidentiality. When I approached another member of the committee whom I knew less well, the conversation was even shorter. I was making no progress. I was troubled by all of this, of course, but I also realized that each of these colleagues had acted honorably. The members of the Admissions Committee had apparently agreed to keep all discussion of race-related policies strictly within the committee. The fact that I was a longtime member of the college faculty—that I had myself served on that committee (or its predecessor) years ago—was not relevant in their view. Keeping agreed-upon confidence was a serious obligation, and they would not be moved. My reputation as a critic of race-based policies they knew; they probably supposed that if they confided in me (or indeed anyone), the issues might become public in ways that could be treated sensationally and that could seriously damage the university.

If committee members were of that mind, it was a certainty the director of undergraduate admissions, a member of the administration and not a faculty member, would have the same fears. Policies that bear on race are always problematic, delicate. There was no hope that I might get what I sought from him or his office.

But if, as now seemed to me virtually certain, there were formal policies giving preference by race, there ought to be some way to learn what they were. Michigan, like all states, has a Freedom of Information Act (FOIA), which makes it possible for ordinary folks to obtain documents prepared by public bodies if those documents concern public matters. There are important exceptions built into the law: documents that would invade the privacy of persons, certainly of students, would not be available under the FOIA. If some matter was in litigation in which the institution from which the documents were requested was a party, public access might be denied. These exceptions did not apply in the case of the policies I sought to learn about. As far as I was concerned, no individuals need be named or be in any way identifiable, and what I wanted to learn about had no bearing upon any litigation involving the University of Michigan at that time. I believed that I was entitled to the information I sought, but I wanted to confirm this belief.

While I had served on the Executive Committee of LSA, years before, I had become acquainted with a staff member of the college, an attorney, who had given the committee advice on various matters. I thought I recalled that she had served for a while in the Freedom of Information Office in our central administration. Her name was Virginia Nordby; I respected her intelligence and balance of mind. She could advise me concerning the legitimacy of my quest. When I sought to locate her I learned that she had retired some years earlier. I called her at her home, on the north side of Ann Arbor, and asked if I might talk with her about a matter I preferred not to get into on the phone, one that was proving to be awkward for me. She was interested and invited me to her home.

Virginia Nordby had been a loyal servant of the university; she liked me and was anxious to be of help to me. What was my problem? I put it before her, in confidence, explaining that I sought information about university admissions policies that I was unable to get from Admissions Committee members. In short, Did our university have admissions policies that gave preference by race? If so, What are they? I told her that I was nearly certain that we did give such preference, but that I was unable to learn the facts. There must be documents—memoranda, instructions to personnel in the Office of Undergraduate Admissions, correspondence among administrators—that would reveal these policies. I asked her, Was I entitled to obtain such documents, if they existed, under the Michigan FOIA?

She put a number of questions to me about the object of my inquiry. The point of these questions was plainly to determine, in her own mind, whether, under the Michigan statute, the documents I was seeking might be protected from public request. Relevant litigation was simply nonexistent. I assured her repeatedly that I wanted no information about any individuals in any category; as a civil libertarian I fully shared the belief that the privacy of student records must be protected assiduously. What I sought was information about university policy. Was I not entitled to that?

Thinking like an attorney, she avoided categorical judgments. Moreover, she may have feared that the information I was seeking, if made public, would damage the university she also loved. But mine was a reasonable question. Ultimately she said, in effect:

"Yes, Carl, very probably you are entitled to the policy documents you seek. I cannot see any grounds on which they could be withheld. I would urge you, as a friend, not to request those documents under the Freedom of Information Act."

"Why do you say that?"

"Because once you submit an FOIA request, the university will begin to treat you as an adversary. University administrators will comply with the law, of course, but they will view your request as an effort to devise weapons against them, and they will see you, and think of you, as their opponent, even though you are not. I know you and I know of your work. It would be a pity to create tension between the university and yourself, after the many years you have taught here."

"I see that, Virginia. Submitting an FOIA request is not something I had planned to do. But how then am I to proceed? What can I do short of that to learn the truth in this matter?"

"You must get the information you seek through informal channels, through people you know, who trust you."

"I'm not sure they do trust me anymore. And anyway, Virginia, I have tried that." I recounted to her my experiences in finding the subject not even discussable in informal conversations.

"Yes, Carl, but you must do it that way. You don't want to submit an FOIA request. That's not you, and it won't be good for you. Don't do it."

I promised her that I would try informal channels once again, although I was not sanguine about the outcome.

As I said I would, I returned to colleagues with a plea for an informal report on the role of race in our admissions policies. I virtually begged. I said to them, as I recall, something like this: "Look, you know me. I could be sitting in your place. Having served as chair of the University Senate, I am practically 'Mr. Inside'! It just doesn't make sense that you should keep me from learning what I have a right to know about our university." It was to no avail. They had given their word that they would keep confidence about the matter. I was greatly irritated, of course, but I honored their position.

I now wonder what I would have done had they broken their word and told me all they knew. If I were to do anything with the information thus obtained, I certainly could not then have identified them as my source— so it is perhaps for the best that I learned nothing from them. That left me with the decision I had been warned about. Should I submit an FOIA request?

FOIA requests come to the University of Michigan (and most universities) in substantial number, commonly from newspaper reporters and other representatives of the press. Michigan law requires the university to respond fully and to do so within a limited number of days—ten days, as I recall. In the central administration building of the university there is a Freedom of Information Office, the person in charge there being a well-paid attorney. He or she and the small staff see that the university complies with its duty while also protecting the university from unreasonable requests and from the careless provision of internal materials. The chief freedom of information officer is an important figure in the university; the office, in the same building as that of the president, is a sensitive place at which the university comes into contact with the general population of the state it serves.

I decided, after long deliberation, to reject Virginia Nordby's advice and request what I was after under the Michigan FOIA. I had never before made an FOIA request. If such requests are to be effective, I learned from colleagues in California, they must be framed very carefully. If the holes in the net one casts are too large the fish will escape; if the holes are too small, one may catch tons of fish one does not want and with which one cannot cope. The university will respond precisely to the request it confronts. It will comply with the law. But it has no obligation to go beyond that. Its responders will not seek to be helpful; they will not suggest how one's request should or might be framed. You get exactly what you request. If you ask for the wrong things, you get those; if you ask for everything, the university may bring it to you in a large truck—and under the law has the right to charge you for the labor of finding, duplicating, and delivering the documents requested. New documents will not be prepared for you. If the material sought does not sit somewhere in the files of that institution you are out of luck. One must be careful, precise.

Ultimately I did receive a good deal of material in response to my request, although it came forth slowly, as I will explain. But because the documents I received later came to play a prominent role in the controversy over race preference at the University of Michigan, and even to play an important part in later court cases, I have reported the exact text of my FOIA requests in Appendix A of this book. There were two such letters, and the reason for this is that, as the reader will discover, after sending the first I realized that to understand what was really going on I needed yet more information. The FOIA officer of the university at that time (and for some years thereafter) was Lewis A. Morrissey, whom I had never met, but whom I came to know and respect.

My attention had turned expressly to the University of Michigan after I read the article, earlier described, in the *Journal of Blacks in Higher Education*, in August of 1995. Many weeks had gone by since then, during which I had been deliberating about the course I ought to follow. I was also very much involved during these months with a federal case, *Hopwood v. the University of Texas*, going forward at that time, which concerned race preference at the University of Texas.[1] This was a significant case; I was to publish a long essay about it in *Commentary* the next year, in 1996. (I will write more about that case shortly.) Also during that autumn of 1995 I was busy preparing testimony I presented on 7 December before the U.S. House Committee on the Judiciary, Subcommittee on the Constitution, on the Equal Opportunity Act of 1995 (which never did become law).[2]

In any event, I sent my first letter of request under the FOIA to the freedom of information officer after my classes ended in mid-December of 1995. It was replete with needed legalisms and off-putting repetition, but it came essentially to this: I sought memoranda, correspondence, meeting minutes, directives, guidelines, or any like documents from or to the director of admissions for LSA, the Medical School, and the Law School pertaining to policies regarding minority admissions. What goals and timetables had been adopted by those three colleges, I asked, concerning ethnic admissions—the admission of applicants who were black or white or Hispanic or in any other identified ethnic category? I emphasized the fact that I did not seek any information about the consideration or admission of any named individuals. It was the admissions *policies* of these colleges that I sought to learn; I requested all the documents that might bear upon these policies. An exact copy of this letter is in Appendix A.

Almost immediately after putting this letter into the mail on 18 December 1995, I realized that my request was seriously deficient. Rereading it, I found it quite alright as far as it went, but I also saw that it did not cover an important set of documents that my full understanding of the situation would surely require. That first letter asked for documents containing or referring to ethnic guidelines and directives that would reveal university policies. I expected such documents to be framed in guarded and mushy language. But whatever their formulation, those documents would not tell me what the university actually does. To learn that, I needed hard numerical data about applications and actual admissions by ethnicity. In addition to the *policies* of the three colleges (LSA, Medicine, and Law), which I certainly did want, I needed information about the *actual past conduct* of those admissions offices. How many offers of admission had been made, over recent years, to applicants in identifiable ethnic groups? How many students in those minority groups actually had been enrolled?

I wrote a second letter the next day, with the same formal structure, in which I requested all available *data* regarding the admissions of students by ethnic group in those three colleges for the immediately preceding years, 1995 and 1994. From colleagues in California I had earlier received copies of documents they had obtained in which minority admissions data of this kind was clearly reported for the University of California at Los Angeles (UCLA) Medical School and the University of California at Berkeley Law School. I sent copies of these California reports to Lewis Morrissey with my FOIA letter, to illustrate the kinds of data I was seeking, whether reported in that form or some other. Again I made it clear that I wanted no information pertaining to any named students, or any other information that might constitute an invasion of the privacy of any applicant. It was *the actual numbers and grade-point averages (and LSAT scores and MCAT scores) of admitted applicants, by race and ethnicity,* that I sought. I volunteered to come to his office to discuss more thoroughly the nature of the information I was seeking. An exact copy of this letter is in Appendix A. This second letter, as it turned out, produced results that proved, much later, to be of great consequence.

Virginia Nordby had warned me that by submitting an FOIA request I would be taking an adversarial position, or at least be seen as an adversary by the university administration. I supposed that was true, although at that time I felt no antagonism toward my university; I was mainly trying to find out what we had been doing. I had no idea what response would actually be forthcoming. Would I receive records of the kind received by my friends in California? No telling.

The University of Michigan was (and is) my employer. Readers may wonder about my wisdom in making an inquiry that might well cause me to be viewed as an adversary by my employer. In fact, that never was a great concern for me. The classes I taught and the academic writing I did all continued with satisfaction on the part of my students and my colleagues. I was a small part of a great university; I knew that any formal judgments made about me would be based upon the quality of the teaching and scholarly work I had done and was doing. The peculiarity of my circumstances, however, did lead to some troubling twists, as I will soon explain.

When people later commented about the position I had put myself in vis-à-vis the university, I would call attention to the fact that I was, and am, a professor of philosophy with tenure. Tenure is granted to university professors just because it is generally understood that they may, in the course of their work, feel compelled to say things or publish writings that are highly controversial. Then I would add: "After all, this is the University of Michigan!"

CHAPTER 8

Pulling Teeth

The first response I received (sometime in early 1996) to my Freedom of Information Act (FOIA) requests was stunning. It was a short, polite letter from Lewis Morrissey in which he first summarized what I had requested (probably a standard pattern in replying to FOIA requests) and then concluded, "There are no documents responsive to your request." That line has stuck in my mind from that day to this.

This was a false report, but it would not be at all fair to say that Lewis Morrissey lied to me. One has to appreciate the circumstances of the freedom of information officer. He cannot himself, or even with the help of his staff, dig through the enormous files of the several schools and departments of the university. His job is to get the materials requested, but to do that he must rely on the cooperation of administrators and faculty members who have that information.

He must have taken my letters to the officers of the three schools I had identified, the College of Literature, Science, and the Arts (LSA), the Law School, and the Medical School, and asked them to provide whatever documents and records in their files would be responsive to my requests. The upshot was extraordinary, however. The school officers apparently produced nothing. It was not his job to upbraid them; those administrators had their jobs, and he had his. In all likelihood nothing was given to him that would fit the descriptions of records requested in my letters of 18 and 19 December. Hence his response to me.

I began to feel antagonistic. I knew that the report I received from Morrissey could not be correct. Documents were being hidden, but I did not know who was doing the hiding. There was no doubt in my mind that documents of the sort I had described must exist. Universities at that time were exceedingly sensitive about the percentage of minority students they were enrolling, always eager to report increases in the numbers of minority students. Such reports couldn't be made—either to the press, or to the regents—if the numbers of applicants and enrolled students in the various ethnic categories had not been carefully recorded. Of course they had those documents! The officers in the several schools may have believed that had they produced those records they would be opening the proverbial can of worms. To view the matter more generously, it may be that these administrators simply failed to take my requests seriously, giving a routine negative response to the Freedom of Information Office.

In any case, I had been given a formal response that was certainly false. I knew, as Lewis Morrissey knew well, that truthful responses were expected under the law, and that if the university could be shown to have deceived or lied in its FOIA responses, he and his office would be subject to serious complaint. His reputation and the good name of the university were at stake in these matters.

Morrissey's office was located near the president's in the building named after Robben Fleming, president of our university from 1968 to 1978. President Fleming had led the university adroitly during the rockiest days of U.S. higher education, in the turbulent late 1960s and early 1970s. I knew him well; as chairman of the Senate Advisory Committee on University Affairs (SACUA), the executive arm of the University Senate, I had been the principal representative of the faculty to him and to the regents of the university during some of those difficult times. Students were then in high dudgeon, outraged by the Vietnam War and indignant about archaic regulations governing their personal conduct. President Fleming managed to keep almost all parties in the university at peace with one another. He had a way of treating personal attacks, verbal abuse, and unfair accusations with generosity and calm rationality. While universities in much of the country were exploding—at the University of Wisconsin quite literally—here at the University of Michigan rational discourse and decent order were largely maintained. That was due in great measure to the wisdom and good humor of our central administrators. Robben Fleming was a labor-management arbitrator, as I was also, practiced in settling disputes judiciously. A genuine civil libertarian, he received recognition of that in a formal award from the American Civil Liberties Union (ACLU) of Michigan. I had been proud of his presidency and grew a bit sentimental whenever I visited the building named after him.[1]

From the Fleming Administration Building, Morrissey had written a fairly routine response—probably one of many—telling requesters there were no documents responsive to their requests. Of course he couldn't send me what he didn't receive from the several colleges of the university. But I would not allow the matter to end there. Sometime in mid-January of 1996 I called his office and asked to sit down with him to discuss my requests and his response. He was courteous and welcoming. We set a date, and I went to the Fleming Administration Building to talk with him, carrying with me a batch of papers that I had received from colleagues at the University of California—copies of what they had received in response to their FOIA request.

We sat together at a table in a small conference room adjoining his office. He asked an assistant to join us, and she—her name I cannot recall—was with us for the following hour or so. I aimed to convince Lewis Morrissey that it could not be the case that there were no documents responsive to my requests. I reviewed the kinds of reports universities were frequently making. I think I brought a copy of the *Michigan Daily* that carried a report, derived from official university sources, of the growth in our minority enrollments over recent years. I pointed out that we could not collect such records, or adjust our policies in that realm, unless someone—the director of undergraduate admissions or his agent—had sent memoranda or instructions in some form to the workers in the admissions offices. Those directives *had* to be there; Morrissey's letter to me, however honestly reporting his beliefs, was surely mistaken about the facts and had to be corrected. He listened patiently, and our subsequent conversation was friendly, even though I may have become a bit heated in conveying my convictions. I wanted the truth, but so did he. Sending false reports was precisely what he was there to prevent.

We looked together at the copies of records coming from the University of California. He finally nodded in agreement; perhaps there were some relevant documents that had not been retrieved. Would I mind, he asked, if he "took another crack at it?" Of course not, I replied. We briefly discussed the time limits set by the statute. He asked if I would grant him an extension of time to look into the matter. Without hesitation I said that I would. I was not angry or impatient; I just wanted his full cooperation.

He promised to call me when he had something further to report. Years later he and I encountered one another at some afternoon reception and talked, drinks in hand, about that first meeting, and we chuckled.

I cannot recall exactly how long it was before he called. It must have been at least two weeks—and his message then was not substantive. He courteously asked for some additional time; the matter was proving more complicated than he had thought. I was quite happy to give him all the time he needed. I hadn't even thought about what I would do with the information when I did finally receive it. He may have called me a second time for an additional extension; my memory is not clear about that. I have pretty good files holding documents of substantive importance, but I was not keeping a day-to-day journal of these events, and I didn't imagine then that I would be recounting those events as I am now, nearly twenty years later.

CHAPTER 9

Revelation

Documents from the University of Michigan Freedom of Information Office began to arrive in February of 1996 and continued to arrive until early March. My recollection of these dates is not exact, but this is essentially correct. There were several packets; I don't recall how many. When all had arrived there was a pile of papers about two inches high. They reported policies and included records at all three colleges: Law, Medicine, and the College of Literature, Science, and the Arts (LSA). (I presume that the earlier delinquency in withholding them received some reproof from the central administration.)

The content of these documents was remarkable. To make good sense of all that follows I must now report the substance of much of it. But first I must say that I was shocked. What had been sent me made incontrovertible the fact that the University of Michigan had long been engaging in deliberate, blatant racial discrimination in its admissions systems. I had expected some indication of race preference, but I had not imagined that such grossly discriminatory devices had been employed or such grossly discriminatory results achieved. I read and reread them and was dumbfounded.

My first task was to sort through what I had received in order to understand its practical import. A complete recounting here is impossible, but a review of the kinds of documents I received, and the kinds of things they revealed, will make what follows more fully understandable.

The College of Literature, Science, and the Arts (LSA) is the central undergraduate college to which most high-school graduates seeking admission to the University of Michigan must apply. From LSA I received documents of three kinds: (1) *guidelines* prepared for lower-level officers, called "counselors" in admissions, explaining the ways in which responses are to be made, by ethnic group, to admission applications when they are first received; (2) *reports* detailing actual past admissions by grade-point average (GPA) and SAT (originally the Scholastic Aptitude Test, later the Scholastic Assessment Test, and now just the SAT, an empty acronym) score for all students—and then separately for students in the category called "underrepresented minorities"; and (3) *criteria* to determine the cutoff levels by scores and grades when considering applications for special programs in the college, for minority applicants separately, and for all other applicants. The impact of these documents will be more readily grasped if I explain some of the discriminatory techniques that they reveal.

Regarding guidelines. The University of Michigan is rightly called a "selective" university. We receive, every year, a huge number of applications for admission. (In 2014 the number was more than forty-nine thousand.) We can accept for admission only a fraction of these applicants. Each application for admission, with its dossier of high-school records, SAT scores, recommendations, and so on, must receive a response. A final decision may be postponed for some; for others a decision can be made upon first examination. Some of the documents I received were designed to guide the admissions counselors in making those first responses. For many applicants that immediate response—rejection or admission—made by a junior admissions officer concludes the matter.

One document I received (in March of 1996) was titled "COLLEGE OF LITERATURE, SCIENCE, AND THE ARTS: GUIDELINES FOR ALL TERMS OF 1996." Its authors, and other persons to whom admissions counselors might send queries, were listed at the top of the first page: the associate director of admissions, the director of academic services, and the associate dean for administration. This was a document of more than twenty pages, covered by a table of contents, probably prepared during the fall of 1995. At the top of the first page is the authority from which it comes: the Office of Undergraduate Admissions. Next to that, in large bold capitals, is the warning "CONFIDENTIAL INTERNAL USE ONLY."

How could the Office of Undergraduate Admissions cope with thousands upon thousands of applications? As a first step, applicants must be put into different categories, sorted by the kinds of information about the applicant that each file contained. At this time, 1996, every application was first put into one of ninety groups. It was done in this way: a large grid was prepared, ten rows from top to bottom, nine columns from left to right, yielding ninety cells (see pages 54–55). The horizontal rows of the grid displayed the applicants' high-school GPAs. A four-point scale was used: every grade of A yielded four, B yielded three, C yielded two, and D yielded one. The points produced by an applicant's entire set of grades were averaged, producing his or her grade-point average.

The top row of the grid was for students applying with an all-A record in high school, a 4.0 GPA. The second row was for students whose high-school GPA was 3.8 or 3.9, third row 3.6 or 3.7, and so on down to the bottom row, in which the GPA was 2.2 or 2.3. Applicants falling into the top row were plainly outstanding; those in the bottom row were not likely to be admitted.

The vertical columns of the grid identified performance on the SAT, on which the maximum possible score was then 1,600, which all applicants were expected to take. The right-most column was for those with scores between 1,500 and 1,600 (outstanding). The next column to the left was for scores of 1,360–1,500; then moving leftward, 1,280–1,360, 1,200–1,280, 1,090–1,200; and so forth. The worst scores, 400–840, were in the left-most column.

One could determine immediately the general character of a student's academic performance in secondary school by noting his or her location on this grid. Students whose grades and test reports put them in a cell near the upper right-hand corner were plainly superior and likely to be admitted to the university; students whose credentials put them into one of the cells near the bottom-left corner had performed poorly, and their chances of admission were slight. The great majority of applicants, of course, fell into the cells in the approximate center and upper center of the grid.

Admissions counselors were instructed by this document to send one of a number of alternative form letters to each applicant. Which form letter an applicant received depended entirely on the cell into which his credentials had placed him or her. There were several letters, identified by code on one of the sheets of the document: A = admit, R = reject, and D = delay (i.e., postpone). On the code sheet some of these were qualified in various ways: delay for scores (DFS), delay for grades (DFG), and so forth. Those in the top-right cells were sent an A letter—an outright admit. All those in the bottom row and most of those in the cells near the lower-left corner were sent an R letter—an outright reject. But most applicants fell somewhere in the middle, and it was therefore necessary to indicate, in each cell, which letter of response was to be sent to applicants with that combination of grades and test scores. Letters from the code sheet (A, R, etc.) were inserted in each cell on the grid to guide the counselors in selecting the called-for first response (accept, reject, etc.) to the applicant. All this was quite mechanical and perhaps unavoidable and reasonable in view of the large number of applicants awaiting response.

What was extraordinary about the grid was the fact that each cell contained not one code letter, but two, one above the other, and in some cases three! How then was the counselor to know which of the two code letters to use in responding to an applicant falling into a given cell? That was the key to the system: at the top of the grid appears the following instruction in bold letters: **"In general, use the top row in each cell for majority applicants and the middle and bottom rows for underrepresented minorities and other disadvantaged students."** The same cell could yield different outcomes for the applicant depending simply upon his or her race.

That is the thrust of this LSA rating system: in cell after cell in the center and upper center of the grid, eighteen cells in all, the letter on the top row for whites and Asians was R (reject), and the letter on the middle or bottom row for blacks and Hispanics was A (admit). It was a crude system in which, by careful design, blacks and Hispanics in the middle categories were given a marked preference in admission.

Admissions preferences by race are sometimes defended as a reasonable way to tip the scales just a wee bit, giving the nod to a minority applicant over his or her white competitor when the records of the two were essentially the same, or close—a sort of "plus factor," some called it, a light thumb on the scale. But what was done at the University of Michigan was nothing like that. The preferences given, as this document proved beyond doubt, were substantial and were given automatically simply on the basis of race. When all these matters later came before the federal courts, one attorney called these LSA guidelines a "smoking gun." This system of grids with code letters was later held by a federal court plainly inconsistent with the Equal Protection Clause of the Constitution of the United States.

What I have just reported concerns the guidelines, the intention of LSA, its *policy*. Did this preferential policy have, in fact, a genuinely discriminatory *result*? You bet. A second set of documents I received from LSA reported in detail the actual outcome of that policy in the preceding year, 1994. One such document was headed "Profile of the University of Michigan, Fall, 1994." Here again a large grid appears, with GPAs identifying eleven rows: 4.0, 3.80–3.99, 3.60–3.79, 3.40–3.59, and so on down to "less than 2.20" for the bottom row. Across the top were the same nine categories of SAT scores identifying the nine columns: 1,500–1,600 at the right, then 1,400–1,490, 1,300–1,390, and so on, with the left-most column for the scores 400–790. On this chart additional provision is made for those who have taken the American College Test (ACT), which for some schools replaced the SAT, with a maximum possible score of 36, so at the top of each column is the appropriate analogous score on the ACT: 35–36 in the right-most column (equivalent to SATs of 1,500–1,600), then 33–34, 31–32, and so on, with the left-most column 1–19, equivalent to SATs of 400–790 (see pages 56–57).

This chart is one of actual performance; it tells us how many applicants were in fact admitted in the fall of 1994 in each of the cells thus identified. This information is given in revealing form. Three numbers appear in each cell; the explanation at the top of the sheet reads: "Each cell contains: Applications, as the top number, Admits, as the second number, Paids as the third number." ("Paids" refers to those who had actually enrolled after being admitted, important for university administrators, of course, but not relevant to the question of whether the college policy had resulted in discriminatory admissions, because for that we need know only how many letters of admission [admits] were sent in each cell. Therefore I will ignore the third number.)

To illustrate: in the fall of 1994 consider the cell for applicants with SAT scores between 1,300 and 1,390 (ACT 31–32) whose high-school GPA was 4.0, or perfect. The cell shows 654 such applicants. It also shows how many of those were actually sent letters admitting them: 643. That's 98 percent. For the cell with the same SAT scores but a high-school GPA between 2.80 and 2.99, the number of applicants (in 1994) was 88, and it shows the number admitted was 17, less than 2 percent. The document exhibits the academic profile of the entire entering class in this fashion.

But there is a second document, a sheet exactly identical in form that gives an exactly parallel report about the percentage of admissions in each performance cell, prepared for "UNDERREPRESENTED MINORITIES" only (caps in the original). It is thus easy to determine whether, in fact, race preference had been given. We need only compare, with respect to any given cell, the percentage of *all* applicants in fact admitted and the percentage of *minority* applicants admitted. Here are some illustrations: in the cell described just above, SAT score 1,300–1,390 and GPA 2.80–2.99, an undistinguished performance in which the percentage of all students admitted was 2 percent, we find on the second sheet in that same cell only six applications from minority students. The number admitted was six: 100 percent.

Take another cell, one in which the GPA was just above a B, 3.0–3.19, and SAT scores were good but not splendid, 1,200–1,290 (ACT 29–30).

Considering all students who applied in 1994 there were 372 such applicants, but only 128 were admitted, or about one-third. That was not at all what it was like for minority students, of whom 27 were in that cell. For them the number admitted was 27, again 100 percent. So it went in cell after cell after cell. Admission rates in most cells, for all students, were not high; Michigan is indeed a selective university—but admission rates in most cells for "underrepresented minorities" (elsewhere in these documents defined as Native Americans, Black/African Americans, and Hispanic/Latino Americans) were startling: 32 out of 33, 42 out of 43, 58 out of 58. In actual admission rates the University of Michigan had been discriminating by race with a heavy hand.

It was in fact worse than those numbers disclose for three reasons: first, the numbers on the chart for "all students" include minority students. If one were to subtract the number of minorities from the numbers both of applications and admissions in each cell of the overall chart, the contrast between majority and minority applicants would be even greater.

Second, counselors are instructed in the document to admit minority students "as soon as a high probability of success can be predicted." It is certainly not the case for the vast majority of applicants that admission is granted as soon as a high probability of success can be predicted. Counselors are advised that minority students with poor records who may receive special form letters (DFG, DFS, etc.) but who do not qualify for "ON THE SPOT REVIEW might be admitted under CSP or Bridge Program guidelines after fall semester grades and/or tests are submitted" (caps are in the original). The number of such later admissions is not given; the principles to be applied in on-the-spot review are also not given. The Bridge Program was one in which minority students were, in effect, enrolled in a probationary term not included in these numbers. What the CSP program is I never learned.

Third, there is a separate heading on page 13 of the guidelines, "Special Considerations," under which it is noted that there are some applicants with "severe earlier life experiences" after which is added the following: "Only underrepresented minority students are considered under Affirmative Action Objectives." I later sought to find out what our "Affirmative Action Objectives" had been, or then were, but no one was either willing or able to tell me. The phrase "only underrepresented minority students are considered" indicates that that ethnic category was in many contexts a threshold consideration, quite unlike other student characteristics.

It's apparent that the discriminatory performance of the college was much in line with its discriminatory intentions. But a third, particularly

LSA Freshman Guidelines —All 1996 Terms—Table I

CONFIDENTIAL

Instate and Legacy: First Review Decisions

In General, use the top row in each cell for majority applicants and the middle and bottom rows for underrepresented minorities and other disadvantaged students.

R and r = reject
A = admit
D = delay

GPA	0-17 / 400-840	18-19 / 850-920	20-21 / 930-1000	22-23 / 1010-1080	24-26 / 1090-1190	27-28 / 1200-1270	29-30 / 1280-1350	31-33 / 1360-1490	34-36 / 1500-1600
> 4.00	rtst	rtst	rtst..PDTE	PDTE..a	a	A	A	A	A
		A..ACSP..	A..ACSP..	A..ACSP	A	A	A	A	A
	*	ABP..DSF	DSF						
3.8 - 3.9	rtst	rtst	rtst	PDTE	a	A	A	A	A
		A..ACSP..	A..ACSP..	A..ACSP	A..ACSP	A	A	A	A
	*	ABP..DSF	DSF						
3.6 - 3.7	rtst	rtst	rtst	PDTE	PDTE	PDTE	a	a	a
		A..ACSP..	A..ACSP..	A..ACSP	A..ACSP	A	A	A	A
	*	ABP..DSF	DSF						
3.4 - 3.5	rtst	rtst	rtst	PDTE..rtst	PDTE	PDTE	PDTE	a	a
		A..ACSP..	A..ACSP..	A..ACSP	A..ACSP	A	A	A	A
	*	ABP..DSF	DSF						
3.2 - 3.3	RTST	RTST	RTST	rtst	PDTE..DSSR	PDTE..DSSR	PDTE..DSSR	PDTE..DSSR	PDTE..DSSR
		A..ACSP..	A..ACSP..	A..ACSP	A..ACSP	A..ACSP	A..ACSP	A	A
	*	ABP..DSF	DSF						
3.0 - 3.1	RTST	RTST	RTST	rr&t	rssr	rssr	rssr	rssr	PDTE..DSSR
		A..ACSP..	ACSP	ACSP	A..ACSP	A..ACSP	A..ACSP	A..ACSP	A.. ACSP
	*	ABP..DSF	DSF						
2.8 - 2.9	RR&T	RR&T	RR&T	rr&t	rssr	rssr	rssr	rssr	PDTE..DSSR
		DGSF	DGSF	DGF	DGF	DGF	DGF	DGF	DGF
	*	(BP)	(ACSP)	(ACSP)	(ACSP)	(ACSP)	(ACSP)	(ACSP)	(ACSP)
2.6 - 2.7	RR&T	RR&T	RR&T	RR&T	RSSR	RSSR	RSSR	RSSR	rssr
		DGSF	DGSF	DGSF	DGF (BP)	DGF (BP)	DGF (BP)	DGF (BP)	DGF (BP)
	*	(BP)	(ACSP..R/MIN)	(BP)					

READING THE CELLS

A. TOP ROW

1. Majority decisions are made based on the acronym in top row of each cell. All admit or reject BOLD CAP markups are done automatically by clerks. Lower case admit and reject decisions are made by counselors. All decisions determined through SCUGA adjustments are made by counselors.

2. Due to the variety of Letters that can be ordered with a single Action code, the acronym in the top row of each cell is an Action code rather than a Letter code. Counselors need to refer to the accompanying Guide for Action/Letter combinations to determine the appropriate letter to order.

3. In the past few years, for expediency, we eliminated sending Delay for Grades (DGF/Delay for Scores (DSF/ Delay for Grades and Scores (DGSF) letters to majority students in LSA and Engineering units. If the student's credentials fell in a postponed cell, we always entered a postponed (PDTE Action code) markup, and sent the Delay Decision (DD) letter. This year, counselors have the option to mark up either a PDTE Action Code and send the DD letter, or if they have concerns about the trend in a student's grades and need more information before determining what the Action should be a DGF letter can be ordered requesting fall semester grades. The Action code for this delay is DSSR. Either PDTE or DSSR can be appropriate depending on the specific circumstances.

B. MIDDLE AND BOTTOM ROWS

1. Counselors use middle and bottom rows of a cell to make decisions on all underrepresented minority or other disadvantaged students.

2. The underrepresented minority and other disadvan-

2.4 - 2.5	RR&T RR&T R/MIN	RR&T RR&T R/MIN	RR&T DGSF (BP) R/MIN	RR&T DGSF (BP) R/MIN	RSSR DGF (BP) R/MIN	RSSR DGF (BP) R/MIN	RSSR DGF (BP) R/MIN	RSSR DGF (BP) R/MIN	rssr DGF (BP) R/MIN
≤ 2.3	RR&T RR&T R/MIN	RR&T RR&T R/MIN	RR&T RSSR R/MIN	RR&T RSSR R/MIN	RSSR RSSR R/MIN	RSSR RSSR R/MIN	RSSR RSSR R/MIN	RSSR RSSR R/MIN	rssr RSSR R/MIN

Generally, admit students at the 98% or 99% if there are no serious deficiencies. Generally admit top 5% from counties other than Livingston, Macomb, Oakland, Washtenaw or Wayne if there are no serious deficiencies. Discuss all exceptions for majority applicants that fall outside the guidelines with MM.
* Asterisk means usually not to be admitted. Discuss all exceptions for minority applications that fall outside the guidelines with IV.
NOTE: All admits to Summer Bridge must be approved by either GT, IV, or MM before going to letter production.

taged student pool has several specific letters to send depending on each unique circumstance, and therefore,
3. The admit and delay acronyms on the middle and bottom rows of the cell are Letter codes, not Action codes. Counselors need to refer to the Guide for Action/Letter combinations to enter the correct Action code acronym.
4. The reject acronyms are Action codes with the R/MIN letter as the personalized reject letter to be sent.
5. The acronym in parenthesis is the letter to be sent if requested information is acceptable. Questions are to be referred to IV.

This grid was used by admissions counselors to determine the response to be given to each applicant for undergraduate admission to the University of Michigan. From left to right, nine columns indicate performance on SAT (or ACT) exams. From top to bottom, ten rows indicate high-school GPA.

Within each cell appears the coded instruction for response to applicants falling into that cell. "A" or "a" is short for "accept"; "R" or "r" is short for reject. Other letters qualify the response.

This grid reports the intention of the university to discriminate by race. For majority applicants (whites and Asians) the top row in each cell is to be applied; for minority applicants (blacks and Hispanics) the middle and bottom rows in each cell are to be applied.

All the grids displayed in this book were received in February of 1996 from the University of Michigan, in response to a Freedom of Information Act Request submitted by Carl Cohen in December of 1995.

Office of Undergraduate Admissions

Key to chart:
Group: For All Units (as of 6-20-94) **Applied-Admitted**
Group: Underrepresented Minorities (as of 9-19-94) **Applied-Admitted**

Best Test Score ▶ SAT: ACT:	0400-0790 01-19	0800-0890 20-21	0900-0990 22-23	1000-1090 24-26	1100-1190 27-28	1200-1290 29-30	1300-1390 31-32	1400-1490 33-34	1500-1600 35-36	Number	% Adms-Appl Paids-Adms
Former School GPA ▼											
Missing	38-1	28-1	72-26	146-69	146-106	106-88	56-43	23-21	0-0	615-355	57.7%
	12-1	5-0	3-0	6-0	0-0	4-0	1-1	0-0	0-0	31-2	6.5%
4.00	2-2	10-8	37-33	178-173	303-294	516-507	654-643	442-433	98-94	2240-2187	97.6%
	1-1	4-4	7-7	10-10	15-15	25-25	15-15	10-10	1-1	88-88	100.0%
3.80 - 3.99	16-6	47-27	148-95	537-483	804-772	1023-988	918-903	393-385	38-37	3924-3696	94.2%
	7-4	18-16	30-28	58-56	39-39	43-40	19-18	7-7	0-0	221-208	94.1%
3.60 - 3.79	32-17	74-38	194-62	580-374	803-719	815-793	591-580	208-205	12-12	3309-2800	84.6%
	25-15	33-33	30-28	58-54	59-57	48-47	22-21	3-3	0-0	278-258	92.8%
3.40 - 3.59	45-17	90-43	194-61	530-225	696-602	652-602	407-392	114-112	13-13	2741-1991	72.6%
	25-12	36-33	43-42	58-58	57-57	33-31	12-12	3-3	0-0	267-248	92.9%
3.20 - 3.39	57-16	93-44	216-67	514-134	552-222	526-346	321-281	77-73	6-6	2362-1189	50.3%
	36-14	41-37	55-49	64-63	42-42	18-18	15-15	5-5	0-0	276-243	88.0%
3.00 - 3.19	72-22	117-54	186-57	373-112	405-80	372-128	201-108	50-40	3-2	1779-603	33.9%
	50-20	52-45	36-32	68-67	33-32	27-27	9-9	2-2	0-0	277-234	84.5%
2.80 - 2.99	59-14	85-31	139-53	221-69	247-55	191-32	88-17	15-8	0-0	1045-279	26.7%
	45-13	34-22	39-36	44-38	31-31	11-11	6-6	0-0	0-0	210-157	74.8%

GPA										Total	%
3.00 - 3.19	72-22	117-54	186-57	373-112	405-80	372-128	201-108	50-40	3-2	1779-603	33.9%
	50-20	52-45	36-32	68-67	33-32	27-27	9-9	2-2	0-0	277-234	84.5%
2.80 - 2.99	59-14	85-31	139-53	221-69	247-55	191-32	88-17	15-8	0-0	1045-279	26.7%
	45-13	34-22	39-36	44-38	31-31	11-11	6-6	0-0	0-0	210-157	74.8%
2.60 - 2.79	49-6	57-18	86-27	150-37	135-29	90-19	41-8	8-2	0-0	616-146	23.7%
	32-4	22-13	24-17	30-25	17-15	9-8	2-2	0-0	0-0	136-84	61.8%
2.40 - 2.59	32-3	35-7	56-9	68-19	43-11	45-6	21-5	1-0	0-0	301-60	19.9%
	18-2	16-5	17-9	18-12	8-7	1-1	2-2	0-0	0-0	80-38	47.5%
2.20 - 2.39	24-2	29-4	36-3	42-11	27-2	10-1	8-1	4-0	0-0	180-24	13.3%
	12-1	11-2	10-1	16-8	3-1	4-1	1-1	0-0	0-0	57-15	26.3%
Less than 2.20	40-4	20-1	27-2	33-2	16-0	13-0	2-1	1-0	0-0	152-10	6.6%
	28-3	10-0	13-0	14-0	2-0	4-0	0-0	1-0	0-0	72-3	4.2%

This grid shows from left to right in nine columns the performance on the SAT (or ACT). From top to bottom appear eleven rows indicating high-school GPA. The upper row in each cell shows the actual total number of applications in that cell in the fall of 1994 and the actual total number of those accepted that term. The lower row in each cell shows the actual number of minority applicants in that cell in the fall of 1994 and the actual number of minorities in that cell accepted in that term. The two columns on the far right show the total numbers, and percentages, of applicants admitted at that GPA level: the upper row for all applicants, the lower row for minority applicants. Paid admissions (the number actually enrolled) are ignored on this table.

interesting, category of information was provided that flatly contradicted one claim the university made frequently when describing its admissions principles in general terms. After being admitted, the university proclaimed, all students were treated alike without regard to race. This was false, as the documents I received that March made clear.

At that time it was possible for students with proven ability and great determination to enroll as first-year students in a combined LSA and Medical School program that made it possible for them to graduate, six years after enrolling, with both a bachelor's degree and an M.D. After having been admitted to the university one might apply for the Integrated Premedical-Medical Program (called Inteflex); acceptance was highly prized but open only to applicants with exceptional academic records.

Pages 9 and 10 of the guidelines identified the responses to be given to applicants for this program. Those responses differ markedly for "minority" and "nonminority" applicants after their admission.

For nonminorities (whites and Asians): "Highest category is granted to non-minorities having ACT score of 30+ or SAT score of 1,320+ and GPA of 3.8 (if out-of-state) and 3.6 (if in-state)."

For minorities (blacks and Hispanics): "Highest category is granted to minorities having ACT score of 26+ or SAT score of 1,171+ and GPA of 3.4, in-state and out-of-state."

There we have it: the documents provided to me by the University of Michigan in February and March of 1996 made it impossible to claim honestly that the University of Michigan treated applicants of all races alike.

CHAPTER 10

Further Revelations

The account of admissions policies and actual past admissions in the preceding chapter reports only what was revealed by documents received from the College of Literature, Science, and the Arts (LSA). Race preferences in the professional schools, especially the Law School and the Medical School, were also extraordinary. Because what was going on in the Law School at that time became of great importance in later litigation, as I will explain subsequently, it's important for me to report also some of what I learned, as a result of my Freedom of Information Act (FOIA) request, about admissions to our professional schools.

First the Medical School: although I had become convinced, from my experience teaching there, that marked preferences were being given to some Medical School applicants, the voluminous documents I received from that school in response to my FOIA request did not enable me to determine the policy details there. Many of the figures on the documents I received were organized in ways I could not reliably decipher.

The practice of the Association of American Medical Colleges at that time was to classify minorities into four groups: "Mexican Americans, Mainland Puerto Ricans, African Americans, and Native American Indians." Our Medical School clumped the four groups under the heading "Minority." Some detailed report regarding minority applicants to the Medical School for the previous year had probably been prepared, but no such report appeared in any of my packets. What did appear was enough to confirm marked preference by race. One document, "Annual Report of Admission, 1995," shows the number of *applicants* to the Medical School and the number of *offers of admission*, in total and for minorities.

Total applications to the Medical School in 1995 numbered 5,873. Of these, 791 were applications by minorities, and 5,082 were applications by nonminorities. Total *offers of admission* to the Medical School number 245. Of these 46 were offers to minority applicants and 199 were offers to nonminority applicants. It can thus be readily determined that the *rate of admission* to the Medical School for *nonminority* applicants (in 1995) was 3.9 percent. The rate for *minority* applicants was 5.8 percent.

Other documents I received revealed that this substantial difference was consistent with the practice of preceding years. During the years 1992, 1993, and 1994, the average rate of admission for all minority applicants was 7.4 percent. The average rate of admission for nonminority applicants was 4.2 percent.

The table reporting applications and offers to minorities and to nonminorities, which appeared in the annual report, does not disclose all Medical School applications and offers. A footnote qualifying the figures for the academic year 1995–1996 and the three preceding years reads as follows: "Figures include only the standard admission pool (not including students entering from special programs such as the postbaccalaureate program.)" The special programs referred to are designed specifically to enlarge the number of minorities admitted. One may reasonably infer that, with the inclusion of admissions granted through these special programs, the contrast between minority and nonminority admission rates in the Medical School would be yet greater.

Admission into the University of Michigan Medical School is not and was not easily achieved, but (in those years) it was nearly twice as hard for a white student as it was for a black student.

It was in the Law School, however, that preferential admissions, as determined from the documents the university delivered to me, were most marked. Ethnic preference there was astounding.

The formally adopted minority admissions policy, which would exhibit the intentions of the Law School, was not sent to me. There was such a policy (adopted by the Law School faculty in 1992, as I later learned), and its provisions became highly controversial. But in its response to my FOIA request the Law School neglected—or simply declined—to include its policy statement regarding minority admissions.

Actual performance, however, could not be hidden. At that time (but no longer) the Law School Admissions Office prepared a document (the latest version I received was dated 7 December 1995), "Admission Grid of LSAT [the Law School Admissions Test] and GPA for All Applicants." This is a table of what had actually been done, a full report of the profile of all completed admissions for the year 1995 (see pages 62–63). It was very similar to the performance grid for LSA described in the preceding chapter, save that here the standardized exam scores across the top were not those of the SATs but of the LSATs, and the GPAs on the vertical axis of the Law School grid report the grades received in undergraduate university study, not high school. All law school applicants for that year (1995) appear on the grid in one of 120 groups, or cells.

In each cell both the number of applicants and the number of offers of admission ("admits") are given. The percentage rate of admissions within each category can thus be easily calculated. The different rates of admission for different ethnic groups cannot be at all hidden because of the way in which the various grids were prepared. The Law School constructed a *separate* grid of this kind, on a separate sheet, for each of the several ethnic groups distinguished: "Native Americans," "African Americans," "Caucasian Americans," "Mexican Americans," "Other Hispanic Americans," "Asian/Pacific Island Americans," and "Puerto Ricans." No grid was prepared (or at least was not sent to me) for minorities as a whole.

The contrasts between the admissions rates for "Caucasian Americans" and the admissions rates for other ethnic groups is stunning. Here are four illustrations:

1. For applicants with GPA of 3.00–3.24 (B) and LSAT scores of 161 and up (top range):
   Caucasian Americans: applications 115, admits 17, rate 14.8 percent
   Mexican Americans: applications 7, admits 7, rate 100 percent
2. For applicants with GPA of 3.25–3.49 (B+) and LSAT scores of 161 and up (top range):
   Caucasian Americans: applications 217, admits 16, rate 7.4 percent
   Native Americans: applications 3, admits 3, rate 100 percent
3. For applicants with GPA of 3.00–3.24 (B+) and LSAT scores of 148–163 (six cells in midrange):
   Caucasian Americans: applications 319, admits 7, rate 2.2 percent
   African Americans: applications 35, admits 26, rate 74.3 percent
4. For applicants with GPA of 3.00–3.24 (B) and LSAT scores of 156–166 (four cells in midrange):
   Caucasian Americans: applications 124, admits 6, rate 4.8 percent
   African Americans: applications 20, admissions 17, rate 85 percent

On the chart for Caucasian American applicants with very good LSAT scores, 156–158, and GPA above 3.25, there had been 51 applicants but only 1 admit. In that same cell on the African American chart there had been 10 applicants and 10 admits! Where LSAT scores for Caucasian Ameri-

The University of Michigan Law School Admissions Office

Key to Chart:
Caucasian Americans: **Applied-Admitted**
African Americans: **Applied-Admitted**

Admissions Grid of LSAT and GPA
As of 12/07/95

GPA ▼ LSAT ▶	No LSAT	120-145	146-147	148-150	151-153	154-155	156-158	159-160	161-163	164-166	167-169	170-Above	Total
3.75 - 4.00	5-0	2-0	4-0	8-0	11-0	12-0	47-4	45-0	93-8	108-46	96-86	120-114	551-258
	0-0	1-0	1-0	1-0	1-0	0-0	1-1	2-2	3-3	3-3	0-0	1-1	14-10
3.50 - 3.74	6-0	7-0	6-0	19-0	23-0	32-3	57-2	65-2	161-14	163-62	130-96	94-89	763-268
	0-0	9-0	3-0	2-0	10-5	5-4	2-2	3-3	6-5	2-1	0-0	1-1	43-21
3.25 - 3.49	9-3	10-0	1-0	16-0	24-0	21-0	51-1	61-1	126-5	91-11	78-38	74-55	562-114
	0-0	15-0	4-0	6-2	7-3	5-4	10-10	3-3	4-4	1-1	2-2	0-0	57-29
3.00 - 3.24	6-0	8-0	4-0	16-0	13-0	15-0	26-0	19-1	42-2	37-3	19-4	17-8	222-18
	0-0	21-0	5-0	25-2	13-2	6-2	7-4	5-5	7-7	1-1	0-0	0-0	90-23
2.75 - 2.99	4-0	8-0	2-0	7-0	7-0	8-0	11-0	7-1	14-0	19-0	11-1	10-3	108-5
	1-0	29-0	7-0	12-1	9-0	9-3	5-2	5-1	4-4	2-2	0-0	0-0	83-13
2.50 - 2.74	0-0	10-0	0-0	4-0	2-0	3-0	4-0	2-0	7-0	7-1	6-3	5-0	50-4
	1-0	18-0	6-0	9-0	7-1	3-1	2-1	2-1	3-2	1-1	2-2	1-0	55-9
2.25 - 2.49	3-0	8-0	1-0	3-0	1-0	0-0	1-0	0-0	5-0	2-0	0-0	1-0	25-0
	0-0	11-0	3-0	6-0	1-0	0-0	2-0	3-0	1-0	0-0	1-1	0-0	28-1
2.00 - 2.24	0-0	1-0	1-0	1-0	1-0	0-0	3-0	1-0	0-0	0-0	1-0	1-0	10-0
	0-0	8-0	2-0	2-0	0-0	0-0	0-0	0-0	0-0	0-0	0-0	0-0	12-0

GPA													Total
2.00 - 2.24	0-0 / 0-0	1-0 / 8-0	1-0 / 2-0	1-0 / 2-0	1-0 / 0-0	0-0 / 0-0	3-0 / 0-0	1-0 / 0-0	0-0 / 0-0	0-0 / 0-0	1-0 / 0-0	1-0 / 0-0	10-0 / 12-0
Below 2.00	0-0 / 0-0	0-0 / 2-0	0-0 / 2-0	0-0 / 0-0	0-0 / 0-0	0-0 / 0-0	0-0 / 0-0	1-0 / 1-0	1-0 / 0-0	0-0 / 0-0	0-0 / 0-0	0-0 / 0-0	1-0 / 5-0
No GPA	10-0 / 12-0	1-0 / 1-0	1-0 / 0-0	0-0 / 0-0	1-0 / 0-0	1-0 / 0-0	1-0 / 0-0	0-0 / 0-0	1-0 / 0-0	0-0 / 0-0	1-0 / 0-0	2-1 / 0-0	19-1 / 13-0
Total	43-3 / 14-0	55-0 / 115-0	20-0 / 33-0	74-0 / 63-5	83-0 / 48-11	92-3 / 28-14	201-7 / 29-20	200-5 / 24-15	450-29 / 28-25	427-123 / 10-9	342-228 / 5-5	324-270 / 3-2	2311-668 / 400-106

This grid on the next page shows the actual number of applicants and admissions to the University of Michigan Law School for the coming academic year. It is the Law School analogue of the "Undergraduate Profile of the University of Michigan" grid that appeared in Chapter 9. The Law School prepared separate grids for Caucasian Americans and African Americans; to ease comparisons those separate grids have been combined in this one grid with the *total* numbers of actual applications appearing on the upper row of each cell and the actual numbers of *African American* applicants and admissions on the lower row of that cell. Paid admissions (those actually enrolled) are ignored in this grid, as are the separate grids the Law School prepared for other ethnic groups.

cans were 159–160, with a GPA above 3.25, there had been 61 applicants but only 1 admit. In that same cell on the African American chart there were 3 applicants and 3 admits! Where Caucasian Americans had scores of 161–163 on the LSATs, with a GPA of 3.25 and above, there were 126 applicants, but only 5 admits. The same cell on the African American chart showed 4 applicants and 4 admits! The indubitable preference is outrageous.

The University of Michigan Law School is always ranked in the top tier of law schools in our country; admission to it is difficult to win—that is, unless one is a minority. One should bear in mind also that Law School applicants at that time were obliged to pay a $70 nonrefundable fee with their application. Midrange applicants (B or B+ students with decent LSAT scores) who remitted that sum were for the most part wasting their time and their money—*if they were white.* But if those midrange students were Native American, Mexican American, or African American their chances of admission were excellent.

The University of Michigan publicly assures applicants that there is no discrimination by race in admissions and that applicants of all races are treated equally. Those who apply recognizing that their chances of admission are not excellent nevertheless believe (because they have been told) that they will be treated like all others with similar credentials. Here again is the exact language of the disclaimer appearing in official university catalogues (and elsewhere) in the fall of 1995: "The University of Michigan is committed to a policy of non-discrimination and equal opportunity for all persons regardless of race, sex, color, religion, creed, national origin, or ancestry . . . in employment, educational programs and activities, and admissions." Demonstrably, applicants were being lied to by those who knew what was really going on. It is fair to say that some were being defrauded.

On the basis of the documents sent to me by the University of Michigan in February and March of 1996 it is undeniable that racial discrimination in admissions was at that time pervasive and deliberate, certainly in LSA, Medicine, and Law and probably in other colleges of the university as well. When the force of this came home to me, as I read those documents here in my study, my emotions were mixed. On the one hand I felt vindicated, confident that my suspicions were warranted and my concerns entirely appropriate. But on the other hand this was the institution to which I had devoted most of my adult life. I was far from happy to learn the ugly details of what my university had been doing.

CHAPTER 11

What Was I to Do?

Having received all this data I was struck by the fact that, to the best of my knowledge, no one else had thought to ask for it. In any event here it all was in front of me, on my desk. Now what? How might I get the university to cleanse itself of this dreadful discriminatory admissions pattern? It was not going to be easy.

Confronting the admissions officers in the several schools would be fruitless, I was sure. They might be discomfited by the knowledge that their admissions mechanics had been uncovered, but I was quite certain that they weren't going to change course in response to the complaints of a lone faculty member. What was being done, in the Law School as in the other colleges, was surely the product of a decision-making process that must have originated at an administrative level higher than that of the admissions office. But how much higher?

The president of the university at that time was James Duderstadt—a strong leader with a clear vision of what he wanted the University of Michigan to do and to become. Previously, he had been a successful professor of nuclear engineering and dean of the College of Engineering. The University of Michigan had, and still has, the wholesome tradition of elevating its outstanding professors to deanships and its deans to higher administrative posts. This has a salutary effect on the spirit of our colleges because the persons thus charged with administrative duties are well known and usually trusted by their colleagues, who become their subordinates. Moreover, newly appointed deans, or central administrators, will have had direct experience with the practices and spirit of the units they are to lead. They will have taught classes in those units and done research in them. It is a system that works exceedingly well if (as has been usually true here at Michigan) the choice of these professor-administrators is carefully made with the support of the faculty they are to lead.

I had known Jim Duderstadt—not closely but as an admired colleague—for some time. I decided that I would write him, in confidence, asking him if there were some way this rather painful set of preferential admissions practices might be turned around.

But he was the president. Could it be that the president did not know what was going on in the admissions offices below him? Yes, that could be, although it was not likely. Jim Duderstadt had instituted a large set of initiatives to increase the number of minorities on campus—among the faculty as well as among students—called the Michigan Mandate. Some were preferential, but not crudely. For example, a Target of Opportunity program was begun under which academic units were given the funds to hire any minority candidate for appointment who would add useful scholarship to the department, even if there were not at that time an open slot in that scholar's specialty. In this way funding support was used to increase minority numbers. But did the Michigan Mandate involve deliberate race preference in admissions? That was not generally known. The term *Michigan Mandate* was satirized, not unfairly, as diversity-speak and gobbledygook. It was partly that—nice words of which the practical import could not be openly evaluated. Some of what had been done under that "mandate" I deemed fully appropriate and felt long overdue. The university, under Jim Duderstadt's direction, began to recruit more vigorously in the secondary schools of Detroit, where black students were in the great majority. He also provided financial incentives for the deans to increase the number of minority students in the several colleges. Many measures were taken, most of which were not publicly known, but, as far as I was able to determine, none involved outright racial discrimination, as the admission systems did. Jim Duderstadt has a clear head and a lawful spirit. I did not think he would approve of the preferential devices I had uncovered.

I carefully considered how to frame my letter to President Duderstadt. It was essential that I put before him the data, or at least of some of the data, in those admission documents I had received. But I didn't think it courteous, or wise, to write a letter burdened with all those numbers. This is what I did.

I wrote a report, a matter-of-fact summary of what I had found, and sent it to the president with a brief cover letter. A copy of that report (dated 20 March 1996) is in front of me now. It is headed "Racial Discrimination in Admissions at the University of Michigan," with my name and address at the top. Using figures such as those reported in the preceding chapters of this book, I explained what I believed would surely trouble anyone who finds racial discrimination wrongful. The university professed equal treatment but did in fact discriminate. I did not want to be argumentative or sensational. One had only to understand the numbers, which came from the university's own documents, to see the problem. I described the systems used in the College of Literature, Science, and the Arts (LSA), the Law School, and the Medical School, reporting numbers in enough detail that the reality could not be doubted. It was impossible to be brief, but it totaled only ten single-spaced pages. It highlighted the pertinent facts from the documents I had received. I concluded it by saying simply that admission practices at the University of Michigan show marked preferences by race and ethnic category. Then I asked, "Do the university officers who make the public commitment to equal treatment know that in fact our practice does not accord with that profession?" If they do, I said, troubling issues of honesty arise. If they do not, if they have been unaware of the preferences actually given, then changes ought promptly to be made. My concluding sentence reads: "Either we must change our practices to bring them into accord with the public declaration of the university, or we must change our public declaration so that it reports honestly the racial preferences that we give."

I aimed to give President Duderstadt and his cabinet the intellectual space needed to dissociate themselves from racial discrimination. Not knowing who in the administration knew what, I did not think it appropriate or wise for me to accuse anyone of wrongdoing.

A verbatim copy of that report (I'll refer to it as the "Cohen Report") appears, without any editing or alteration whatever, as Appendix B of this book, so that those interested in knowing precisely what was communicated to our administrative officers at that time can examine the complete record.

A week, then two weeks, passed; I received no response from the president. This perplexed me. Jim Duderstadt was a responsible administrator; there ought to have been at least an acknowledgment of my letter and report, even if without any comment on its content. Much later, sometime in 2010 I believe, I asked Jim Duderstadt why he refrained from all response to the report I sent him in 1996. He and I remain friends, and my query was merely one of curiosity, not at all hostile, as he understood. He said that he had absolutely no recollection of my letter or of the report, and therefore (if in fact he had received it) he couldn't answer my question. It is hard for me to believe that there could have been such a lapse in a matter anyone would have recognized as critical, yet it is conceivable that my letter did not reach him personally. But at the time I grew irritated and became more determined to push the university administration to deliver some rational response. What I hoped for above all, of course, was a cessation of race preference, but if that were going to be somehow sidestepped, I wanted to know why. When the silence persisted, I decided, somewhat reluctantly, that I would send the report to the regents of the university.

Governance of the University of Michigan is not like that of most state universities. Our regents (there are eight of them) are not appointed by the governor as in most states but are elected for eight-year terms by the citizens of Michigan, in hard-fought partisan campaigns by nominees of the political parties. Even though voters may know little about the educational philosophies of the candidates, this system has worked well, in our case, for more than 150 years. The University of Michigan is an autonomous body, recognized as such in the Constitution of the State of Michigan. We are not the instrument of the state legislature (which provides only a small fraction of our financial support) but are owned and controlled by the regents, in whom our constitution vests complete authority in all matters pertaining to the university and who feel themselves directly responsible to the electorate. We've had many splendid regents in my time at the university. In my view one of the keys to this success is tradition. The political parties take pride in their nominees, those partisan nominees are invariably graduates of this university, and they love it and devote themselves to it without pay. The position of regent is viewed by all as a great honor, and as regents they have almost invariably acted, to the best of their abilities, in the interests of the university. Few universities, anywhere, have been governed as well, with so much wisdom or loyalty.

I have had the privilege of knowing a number of our regents over the years; four of them (Tom Roach, Deane Baker, Phil Power, and Paul Brown) have been my good friends. Over my decades at the university I had had opportunities, as a representative of the faculty, to meet and talk with the regents. At the time of the "Cohen Report," 1996, I knew several of the regents personally; I had been in their homes and they in mine. I believed that they respected me. Whatever their political views, I knew that they cared deeply about the well-being of the University of Michigan.

Although I could certainly write them about these delicate matters concerning race, I felt that I could not do so addressing them as friends.

It would not have been appropriate to impose upon our friendships. My informal association with them assured me only that they would read the letter I was preparing and that they would think seriously about the issues it raised.

My brief letter was sent to them as regents, addressing each respectfully as Regent Brown, Regent Baker, and so on. With each letter I enclosed a copy of the "Cohen Report," unchanged, and I sent that packet to each regent at his or her home or business address. I doubted that the regents at that time knew any of the details of our admissions procedures. Did they know that we were giving outright preference by race? I really could not say. I thought it likely that, at least for some of them, what I reported about our admission preferences would come as an unhappy revelation. I waited for their responses.

Again no response. I was frustrated and puzzled. The regents were attorneys and businesspeople; surely they would not allow serious communications to go unacknowledged. But they did. I received not one word of response from any one of the eight regents of the university.

Unlike the instance involving President Duderstadt, I never subsequently confronted any regent about the matter. Sometime later, however, when the controversy over race preference was in the courts, I came to realize that what had probably caused their silence was the advice of the university general counsel. I do not know this for sure, but the unanimity of silence is unlikely to have been a coincidence. And if one considers the position of the regents, from the perspective of an attorney whose job is to protect the university, silence makes good sense. If they already knew what I had told them, or if they learned, upon inquiry, that what I had reported to them was indeed the truth, what were they to say to me in response?

They could not deny the facts of the report, and any admission of the truth of those facts might later prove to be seriously embarrassing. If denial was impossible and admission was unwise, what would be the point of answering Cohen, when even an acknowledgment of my letter and report might later prove awkward? No, nothing could be gained by any response. This explanation of the silence of the regents is only speculation on my part. But the silence itself was a fact.

Those in authority, whatever their knowledge or opinions may have been, were not then willing even to recognize the problem or to acknowledge my complaint. I was getting nowhere. I could only stew with the stuff in my hands.

CHAPTER 12

Point of No Return

Early in my teaching career I had been an active member of the American Association of University Professors (AAUP). The University of Michigan is not unionized, but the AAUP serves on our campus some of the functions of a union, giving faculty members an instrument with which to address some of their concerns as employees. This is a complicated matter because Michigan also has, as many good universities do, a system in which the faculty of each college is self-governing. The by-laws of the university, established by the regents, give to the faculties of the several colleges, through their elected executive committees, almost complete authority to formulate and enforce the rules and procedures of their colleges. This works rather well for us. I write from the perspective of the College of Literature, Science, and the Arts (LSA), which has been my principal home. The several colleges—Law, Medicine, Engineering, and so forth—are also quite independent and self-governing. Channels for participation and complaint, therefore, (for the faculty) do not here depend on any union-like organization.

But the AAUP actually *is* a union on some other college and university campuses, even though it is not that here. Because this is so, it became important for me that I not be a member of it, for a reason arising from my personal circumstances. For many years I have served as a labor-management arbitrator, a member of the Labor Panel of the American Arbitration Association. In that role my reputation for complete impartiality is vital and precious to me. Because I want to be free to accept appointments as an arbitrator in labor disputes in which one of the parties is the AAUP serving as a union and could not do so if I were an AAUP member, I long ago formally resigned from that organization and have no official relationship with it, here or anywhere.

I explain this because I was approached, later in the spring of 1996, by a colleague in the mathematics department, Wilfred Kaplan, at that time an officer of the Michigan Chapter of the AAUP. Now deceased, Wilfred Kaplan was a good friend and anxious always to advance the interests of the university faculty in ways that were harmonious and constructive. Under the auspices of the AAUP, he told me, he was organizing open sessions for faculty, students, and the public on admissions policies at the University of Michigan. Many controversial matters that concern admissions arise here at the university, especially the ratio of in-state to out-of-state admissions and the number from out of state to be admitted. My continuing concern about considerations of race in admission, of which he and others knew, was also a subject of interest to the AAUP. He told me that he and others would be pleased if, even though I was not a member of the AAUP, I would participate in an open session by presenting my views on race preference in admissions.

I agreed to do that. I was pleased by the invitation because it would give me an opportunity to present, in the most thoughtful and civil circumstances, the patterns I had uncovered and the concerns with which I had been troubled. Some in the university may have thought me an adversary (as Virginia Nordby had put it) because I had submitted a Freedom of Information Act (FOIA) request. But I did not think of myself that way. I had long been part of the self-governing committees of the faculty, both in LSA and in the university at large. I thought I was, as others thought of me, part of the establishment, an insider. I took great pride in our faculty self-governance, and my long-term goal was to cause the university to amend its policies in a constructive and deliberative fashion. I had not viewed the documents I had received as weapons with which to attack the university. Attacking the University of Michigan, damaging its reputation, was very far from my intention, then or ever. This was my place, and I wanted honor for it, not dishonor.

Addressing a large meeting of the faculty on the topic of race preference was therefore something I was more than ready to do. If I could persuade my colleagues that changes were in order by putting before them unhappy facts about our institutional conduct of which they probably had not been aware, we might seek to effect those changes in the best way, relying upon the self-governing practices long established at Michigan. If faculty members of LSA, for example, were to express in a formal resolution their displeasure with any system of race preference, it would be difficult, indeed nearly impossible, for administrators to resist.

So I prepared carefully for that large meeting called by the AAUP. It was to be held in the Michigan League. The League, a facility originally designed for the benefit of women, is one of two fine old buildings on our central campus (the other is the Michigan Union, which long served only men) beautifully maintained for purposes allied to the instruction and research that are our principal activities—meeting rooms, dining facilities, some light recreational facilities, and some large halls for major gatherings. In recent years both buildings serve both sexes equally, of course. The Union (on whose steps President John Kennedy first proposed the Peace Corps on October 14, 1960, in the course of his presidential campaign) has had a more historic role, but the League, only a few blocks away, is more attractive, more appealing architecturally—and one of my favorite buildings. It was in the League ballroom, a large hall, that the AAUP meeting was to be held.

I decided that I would provide copies of the "Cohen Report," which I had originally prepared for the president. Because that report could be taken to be critical of the university, I made copies of it without using any university equipment or facilities, wanting to avoid any possible complaint that I had behaved unfairly. I didn't know how many copies to prepare. I had one of the local copy shops make fifty copies at my expense, and I brought them with me to the ballroom early that evening, putting one copy on each of the chairs in the first few rows. Many more people came than I had copies.

When I was called upon to speak, I introduced my large concern briefly and asked those with copies of my report to examine it with me. I went summarily through it, explaining how I happened to write it and what documents the university had already sent me, from which the facts in the report were amassed. I summarized its findings for the benefit of those who did not have a copy. I also showed some of the actual documents I had received and had brought along that evening to illustrate the products of my FOIA request.

I had expected a lively discussion, but I was disappointed. The audience (perhaps eighty to a hundred as I recall) consisted mainly of faculty members, many students, and some townspeople. Those who did not have a copy of the report may have felt that they could not enter the conversation comfortably. But those who did have a copy in their hands were also unexpectedly silent. A few questions of fact were asked—one about my reason for submitting an FOIA request, which I explained, and several seeking clarifications of some of the numbers in the report. There was only one controversial response, a rather sharp complaint from a member of the university administration whom I knew slightly. He read the report as a criticism of the university, which I had to admit it was, although attacking the university was not my aim. He argued because I had written that the university ought, if it intended to maintain its practice of giving minority preferences, at least alter its widely repeated assurance that we treat the races with full equality, I was calling our officials hypocrites. As I have said, I did not know how much of the policy was intentionally fraudulent—but the *institutional* hypocrisy was undeniable. My critic, whose name is Lester Monts and who remains a member of our central administration, did not like the accusation. He and I had a brief, slightly heated exchange, but no one else sought to participate in what could have become an interesting debate. I have a vivid recollection of some faculty colleagues, sitting in the first rows of that hall, silently thumbing through the pages of the report. One of them, whom I did not know, was slumped in his chair, the report in front of his face, his body language pretty clearly revealing that he was not happy about what he was reading. I infer that was indeed the case for many in attendance. The meeting came to an end without much more discussion of my concerns.

As people were leaving, several came up to me with comments and questions, all reasonably friendly. One young lady introduced herself as there on behalf of a Lansing newspaper, the *Lansing State Journal.* Lansing is our state capital, about sixty miles northwest of Ann Arbor. (East Lansing is another college town, the home of Michigan State University.) The reporter asked if she could have a copy of the report I had distributed. I said that of course she could, that nothing in it was confidential as far as I was concerned. After all, I observed, the public had been invited to this discussion. She didn't have a copy, so I gave her the copy I had been using in my talk.

As I look back upon that evening I believe that I did want—more than I was willing to admit at the time—to reach the public with the data I had collected. I had not hesitated in making them public; that was in part because at the time I did not think that much would come of it. I was wrong. That evening I reached the point of no return.

Some days later I received a call from an aide in the office of one of the members of the Michigan House of Representatives. He introduced himself, explaining that some of the remarkable disclosures in my report had reached his office. He told me that his boss, the chair of the Constitution Committee of the Michigan House, would like to invite me to testify before that committee on the matters dealt with in my report. How the report had come into his hands I did not learn. Whether Michigan universities were treating the races equally, or giving preference to some, was a matter of continuing concern for the Constitution Committee. Would I come up to Lansing to give testimony on a date he specified? Yes, of course I would, I said.

I do not recall the exact date of that hearing; at the time I doubted this would be a very consequential event. I did hope that the painful facts of the preferences might cause some legislators to express their dissatisfaction to our university administrators, who had seemingly ignored me. The University of Michigan is one of three flagship state universities in Michigan, along with Wayne State University in Detroit and Michigan State University. Only a fraction of our budget comes from the state treasury, but it is an absolutely vital fraction; our administrative officers are always anxious to retain the support and goodwill of Michigan state legislators. Our university is constitutionally autonomous; they cannot tell us what we must do. But they can and do decide how much or how little state money we can do it with. We listen to them with great respect.

My testimony was to be given in one of the regular committee rooms in the Capitol Building in Lansing. The presentation of testimony before legislative committees is often seen on television; the setting of my testimony was not unusual. The committee members were arrayed in a horseshoe, with the committee chair in the center. He called me to sit at the table facing the committee members at the opening of the horseshoe, and from there I addressed them, respectfully, my papers spread before me. The public sat in many rows of chairs behind me, and the room was full. I was the first person to testify that afternoon. I had placed copies of the "Cohen Report," not one word changed, on the committee table, one copy for each member behind his or her name card. I was quite calm and comfortable since I was not the object of the committee's concern or criticism. I was only a messenger with a message that my inquiries had given me the capacity to deliver. It was my intention to explain and in some degree elaborate upon the report I had put before them.

Speaking to groups, large and small, is a central part of my work as a university professor; it is what I take satisfaction in doing. Experience and feedback indicate that I do it well. My testimony went smoothly, lasting about an hour. I took them through the report, showing them actual copies of the documents referenced in the report. I did not know it at the time, but I learned before leaving that among those in the audience was a representative of the University of Michigan Office of the General Counsel.

The committee listened intently. When I finished, a number of questions were asked by the members respecting the inferences drawn in the report, inferences that were only a restatement in prose of what the numbers had shown conclusively. I was asked why I had undertaken the inquiry; I explained that my long involvement with the ACLU of Michigan had led me to develop an acute concern for the equal treatment of the races in our state, but that, in addition, I had written extensively on the fundamental role of equality in the philosophy of democracy. I mentioned my book, *Democracy*, which at that time was readily available through the Free Press, a branch of the Macmillan Publishing Company. I was asked if I had brought the data in the report to the attention of the University of Michigan central administration. Yes, I said; I told them that I had sent a copy of the report to the president and to each of the regents, but that I had received no acknowledgment or response.

One representative on the committee, a gentleman whose name I do not remember, tried to discount the significance of the report by saying that it was merely a bunch of pages with a bunch of numbers and that anybody could put together such a collection. It had no force or value because it could all be made up, concocted. I responded courteously by observing that all the numbers in the report were taken directly from documents prepared by the University of Michigan and sent to me as a consequence of my FOIA request. "The same documents would be sent to you, sir," I observed, "if you requested them. No data in this report are a result of assumptions or suppositions of mine." He did not appear to be even slightly persuaded. I think he, and perhaps others, believed that my report had a hidden agenda or was an effort to hinder the admission of minorities to the University of Michigan. Nothing could be further from the truth. I believe that our university must be an inclusive and welcoming environment. My concern was the racially discriminatory means that the university had adopted to advance that objective.

There was a different, much less hostile response from other committee members. They seemed puzzled; some found the numbers in the report difficult to accept, although they did not question their veracity. This response was well represented by a question, in the form of a comment, that I remember vividly. I recall the words this legislator used because they were so troubling. Holding the report in her hands and looking at one of the interior pages, she said, plainly irritated, "What I can't understand, Professor Cohen, is that this [pointing at the report] is not what they tell *us*!" I assumed the remark was not so much directed at me as at her colleagues on the committee, but replied, "What the university has conveyed to you, ma'am, I have no way of knowing. But the data in the report before you come only from the university, from nowhere else."

Several other committee members were plainly disturbed, saying they now felt obliged to conclude that the university had not been telling them the truth, or at least, not the whole truth. I replied that I did not believe that university officers had made false reports to the state, or that they would ever do that. They would certainly know that false reports in this context would eventually be exposed and that the consequences for the university would be grave.

Yet here were some elected representatives who appeared to feel that they were getting two stories about admissions, one from the university directly and one indirectly through me, and that these two accounts were not consistent. How could that be? I don't know, but I will offer here a speculative answer. What I am about to say is no more than my inference, and I cannot be sure that it is correct.

The university had been under continuing political pressure to increase the number of minority students enrolled, possibly from some of the members of this committee. Administrative officers were anxious to respond concretely to that pressure, to assure everyone, elected representatives as well as the public, that they had been doing everything lawfully possible to effect this increase. As earlier noted, President Jim Duderstadt had instituted and publicized the Michigan Mandate to advance this objective. Descriptions of this "mandate" were formulated in promising and constructive language, looking forward to substantial increases of minorities at the university. There was not much in the way of concrete detail. Those cheery descriptions had almost certainly been received earlier by these Constitution Committee members, but probably there would have been nothing in the language of those program descriptions that suggested the introduction of race *preferences* in admissions. Even if it could be argued that race preferences were, after the *Bakke* decision, not unconstitutional, racially sensitive matters of this sort would not have been announced without the ground for that announcement having been well prepared. So, I speculate, the inconsistency, or apparent inconsistency, to which committee members were responding with irritation (and in some cases, I later learned, with anger) was caused by innocuous and sweetly worded accounts of effort and achievements on the one hand and the hard numbers I had brought to them on the other. Of course I could not know that for certain, then or now.

What was important was the actual response of some of the members of the Michigan House of Representatives. On that Constitution Committee there were two members whose names I do recall: one was Deborah Whyman, who later played an active role in this controversy; the other was David Jaye, an odd fellow who later had substantial difficulties because of repeated convictions for driving while intoxicated. Jaye, I recall, spoke forcefully at the committee hearing; he was sharply troubled by what he concluded was wrongful racial preference given by the university. I cannot remember whether Representative Whyman spoke at that hearing, although it is likely that she did. I recall being later asked by an aide of Representative Whyman, by telephone, for some piece of additional detail from the documents I had received, but I do not recall what it was. I would surely have responded as helpfully as I could.

That committee hearing was a turning point in the struggle over racial equality in admissions at the University of Michigan. From that time other people, far more influential than I, were in possession of what they needed to challenge the university effectively, as I could not. I was very glad to be relieved of at least some of the burden.

A few weeks later (I don't remember the exact date) I was asked to testify on the subject of admissions and race preference before the Constitution Committee of the Michigan Senate, and I did so. But in that case I was only one of several persons, each of whom made a relatively brief statement to the committee. I recall that on that occasion I did not emphasize constitutional issues those senators would already have explored, but two other points: first, the *fact* of preference by race at the University of Michigan, and second, the *damage* race preference does *to the minority preferred* and to race relations generally.

What was critical about those committee hearings at the state capitol in Lansing was their publicity. What the university had been doing covertly, its policies formulated in documents it treated as confidential, could now for the first time be examined openly. Much, much later, after the U.S. Supreme Court had decided the University of Michigan cases, I again played an active public role in this continuing controversy. But from the time of those 1996 hearings until the Michigan cases were resolved in 2003, my role was that of a private person, actively concerned but with no formal part to play. Within the university itself, however, I remained outspoken, and that produced some fascinating exchanges and reactions. The formal steps that brought the race preferences at the University of Michigan to national attention were taken by others.

CHAPTER 13

On to the Federal Courts

In retrospect it seems inevitable that this controversy would wind up in court. At the time, however, that was not at all evident. The University of Michigan was discriminating by race; I thought that was plainly not lawful, and I had hoped that our officers, realizing the gravity of the matter, would change course. But whether the university's conduct was indeed unlawful was a question about which there was genuine disagreement. Lee Bollinger, a distinguished constitutional lawyer who had been the dean of our Law School, became president of the University of Michigan in 1997. Bollinger sincerely believed that the *Bakke* decision, interpreted as he believed it ought to have been interpreted, authorized the preferences we had been giving. From that time the university, under his leadership, dug in its heels, defending its admissions preferences vigorously.

I am not a lawyer, but on these matters I had become well familiar with the governing Supreme Court cases. I had studied them and written about them at some length, in law reviews and elsewhere, as Bollinger had not. I believed that if our practices were to come eventually to the federal courts the University of Michigan would lose and would be greatly embarrassed. Head-on conflict between Bollinger and myself became difficult to avoid.

A few words about President Bollinger. He was my friend, not close but a colleague with whom I had a cordial relationship. He had first come to the University of Michigan Law School as an assistant professor in 1973. Because his central interests were in First Amendment law, especially the extent and limits of the freedom of speech, I was asked by colleagues recruiting him to the Law School to join them when they entertained him during his exploratory visit. I was a professor of philosophy, he a young lawyer who had recently been a clerk for Warren Burger at the U.S. Supreme Court. We had similar interests and, I thought, a similar spirit. We had a splendid evening together. I liked him a lot and was delighted when I learned soon after that he had accepted a position at the Law School. Subsequently he was a great success as a teacher and scholar. His big book, *The Tolerant Society*, was well received by scholars around the country.[1] In 1987, fourteen years after our recruitment dinner together, he was appointed dean of the University of Michigan Law School.

Lee was also a great success as dean. His colleagues admired and trusted him. He remained dean until 1994, when he accepted the position of provost (second in command, so to speak) at Dartmouth University, where he had a short but felicitous stay. Meanwhile, here at Michigan, Jim Duderstadt, finding it difficult to realize his goals for the university, resigned from the presidency in 1996. Late that year Bollinger came back to Michigan as our president, an appointment he accepted with delight.

As dean of the Law School, Bollinger had played a major role in devising the admissions policies that later came to be hotly contested. He had early become convinced that only by giving preference to minorities in admissions could the Law School succeed in its enrollment goals. On the justifiability of race preference he and I were sharply opposed. But we remained cordial colleagues, and even in later days, when the Michigan cases were under way, we engaged in some brief private correspondence.

However much we disagreed about admissions preferences, I continued to believe, and quite frequently contended in discussions with colleagues, that Lee Bollinger was an outstanding president of our university. He was a serious scholar. He understood what it meant to be a university professor, and he could and did promote his vision of the university as a great center for intellectual and artistic creativity. He was not, as many college presidents are, merely an agreeable manager. He is a thinker; he writes his own speeches. As a spokesperson for the university on the national stage, he excelled. I was proud of him, and in spite of our differences I was sorry, in 2001, to see him leave. He had been one of the two finalists for the presidency of Harvard but lost out to Laurence Summers. Later that year he accepted the presidency of Columbia University, his present position, where he had graduated from law school. In New York City his artistic interests and those of his wife could be more fully satisfied, and there he would be extremely well paid. As I look back upon the admissions controversy at our university I regret that he and I were so sharply in conflict.

Well, after a torturous process the University of Michigan admissions practices did come before the federal courts, and as it turned out much later, both Lee Bollinger and I were eventually found to have been correct in our legal judgments, a paradox I will later explain. I became closely associated with some of the central participants in the ensuing litigation.

As already noted, the fact that an arm of the State of Michigan, our university, gave preference by race in admissions was troubling not only to me but also to some members of the Michigan State Legislature. Representative Deborah Whyman was perhaps the most outspoken of these angry legislators, who believed, as I did, that the preferential policies of the University of Michigan were in violation of federal law as well as the Equal Protection Clause of the U.S. Constitution. Let me explain our grounds for this conviction.

Readers will recall that universities, mine among them, had continued to use preferences because they were confident that the 1978 Supreme Court decision in *Bakke* had ensured them safe harbor. They believed that they were on solid ground as long as those preferences were designed to increase diversity in entering classes, in accord with the view expressed by Justice Lewis Powell in that case. No justice but Powell had mentioned diversity in that decision, but Powell's central role in *Bakke* gave his opinion great weight, and universities relied upon it. The Court decided in that case that the preferences then given by the University of California at Davis Medical School were plainly unconstitutional. Whether some preferences for the sake of diversity might nevertheless pass the test of exacting judicial scrutiny remained to be decided.

Precisely that matter had come before the federal courts earlier in the 1990s, in a case arising from admissions preferences given by the University of Texas Law School. Cheryl Hopwood was the rejected plaintiff; she claimed, as Alan Bakke and Marco DeFunis had claimed before her, that discrimination based on skin color had corrupted the admissions process in which she had competed. In my view she was right. But would my view prevail in court? It did. Her case went eventually to the 5th Circuit Court of Appeals in New Orleans, where in March of 1996 she won hands down. The decision was powerful and forcefully written. I was elated.

In *Commentary* I published a long and vigorously argued essay[2] defending that decision and reporting some of the Michigan findings resulting from my Freedom of Information Act (FOIA) request of some months before. The preferences given at the University of Texas Law School (and struck down by the court) were almost as shocking as those I had uncovered at the University of Michigan. At the University of Texas it was done like this: all law school applicants were given a Texas Index (TI) score, a composite of their undergraduate grade-point average (GPA) and Law School Admissions Test (LSAT) scores. TI scores of 189 and above resulted in *automatic admission* for minorities. TI scores of 192 and below were held to justify *presumptive denial of admission* for whites. What was ground for automatic acceptance for those of one racial category was ground for automatic rejection for those of another racial category. The words of the appellate decision showed the court to be nearly incredulous; it concluded that such blatant race preference violated the Equal Protection Clause of the U.S. Constitution and that all efforts by the University of Texas to defend that preference were entirely unsatisfactory. The court reaffirmed the long-held principle that race-based classifications were always suspect, always invidious, and that any use of race was therefore rightly subject to "strict scrutiny"—which meant that to be justifiable any racially preferential system must be shown to serve a *compelling government interest* and then must be shown to have been *narrowly tailored* to serve that interest. Race-based admissions preferences (it was held) failed on both counts.

Are there *any* interests so compelling as to justify our government using racial classifications? Yes, there are. Persons found to have been unlawfully discriminated against because of race are surely entitled to remedy; if race had been an element in the wrong suffered, race might be an unavoidable element in the appropriate remedy. The burden upon those who would use race in this way is heavy, as it surely ought to be, but it is a burden that may in rare circumstances be sustained. It could not be sustained by the University of Texas Law School. Although the *Hopwood* decision was controlling only in three states (Texas, Louisiana, and Mississippi), it firmly proclaimed, at the judicial level just below that of the Supreme Court, one principle that bore directly upon our Michigan circumstances: diversity (they said) is not a compelling state interest that can justify race preference in admissions. The diversity defense was examined closely and skeptically by that court of appeals. Recall that diversity had become the widely relied upon justification of preference only after Justice Powell, in *Bakke*, had suggested that it might be a constitutional interest that could justify some uses of race. The *Hopwood* court, attending to carefully formulated judgments of the Supreme Court in earlier cases, found this diversity defense to be without merit.

For one thing, the court noted that the word "diversity" appears nowhere in the *Bakke* case except in Justice Powell's discourse on the topic at the end of his long, and what many found to be confusing, opinion. Not one other justice, at that time or in all the time between that decision and the *Hopwood* case that was before them, had concurred with Powell's view of diversity as a weighty constitutional interest. Even the justices who supported the U.C. Davis admissions preferences in *Bakke* suggested in their dissent that the quest for an "integrated student body" could not by itself serve as a justification for preference. Powell's opinion alone, it was held, therefore cannot bind any lower courts and may not be supposed to lay down constitutional rules governing the way race can be used. This was powerful ammunition for those of us in Michigan who were critics of our university's policy.

Indeed, decisions of the U.S. Supreme Court, which are binding, were taken by the *Hopwood* court to explicitly exclude the quest for diversity as a justification for the use of race preferences in admissions. In a 1995 case race preferences given by the Federal Communications Commission (FCC) were struck down; Justices Sandra Day O'Connor, William Rehnquist, Antonin Scalia, and Anthony Kennedy had, in that same FCC matter (in which broadcast media, not admissions, were the focus) explicitly addressed, in their dissent, the critical question even earlier in 1990: "Modern equal protection has recognized only one [compelling state] interest: remedying the effects of racial discrimination. The interest in increasing the diversity of broadcast viewpoints is clearly not a compelling interest. It is simply too amorphous, too insubstantial, and too unrelated to any legitimate basis for employing racial classification."[3]

Finally, the 5th Circuit Court observed that the use of diversity to justify race-based programs does not promote but actually undermines the goals of the Fourteenth Amendment. It enhances racial stereotypes, fuels racial hostilities, and fosters racial divisions. To strive for an entering class displaying different skin colors, said the court, "is no more rational on its own terms than would be choices based upon the physical size or blood type of applicants." In fact, using race in this manner, the court concluded, "exemplifies, encourages, and legitimizes the mode of thought and behavior that underlies most prejudice and bigotry in modern America."[4]

Although its governing force was limited to the 5th Circuit, this was an important decision. Representative Whyman in Michigan and others across the country were well aware of it. She believed that a case arising out of the preferences given at the University of Michigan would have the same result and even greater impact. Along with three other Michigan legislators, she sought, thoughtfully and persistently, to initiate such litigation in Michigan. How might that be accomplished?

The *Hopwood* case provided the intellectual model and also suggested the procedural instrument. At the 5th Circuit, Cheryl Hopwood was represented by Theodore Olson, a distinguished litigator who had been head of the U.S. Office of Legal Counsel under President Ronald Reagan. He had argued Hopwood's case on behalf of a public interest law firm in Washington, D.C., the Center for Individual Rights (CIR). The Michigan legislators, impressed by the *Hopwood* outcome, turned to the CIR with the proposal that they now do in Michigan and the 6th Circuit what they had done successfully in Texas and the 5th Circuit.

Because the Center for Individual Rights plays a central role in much of what follows, a few words about it, and my relations with it, are now in order. It is a conservative institution, much more conservative in its overall views than am I. But it consistently lives up to its name; it is a small, nonprofit firm, passionate about the rights of individuals, even when they may be unpopular individuals. In recent years the American Civil Liberties Union (ACLU) has become quite politically correct, even to the point of tolerating race preferences for what its members perceive as minority advantage. But the CIR exhibits the spirit of the old ACLU in its willingness to stand up for little folks, whether heroes or rascals, whose rights have been unfairly infringed. I had been very active in the ACLU, and the CIR was fighting, in this controversy, for what the ACLU ought to have been fighting for. A more principled organization I have not known. Founded in the late 1980s by two men, Michael Greve and Michael McDonald, the CIR was still led by them when I first encountered the group.

Greve, born in Germany, studied at the University of Hamburg and came to the United States on a Fulbright Scholarship to study at Cornell in 1981. Unhappy with the ways of big government in Germany and elsewhere, happy in the United States and proud of his new country, he received his Ph.D. in political science from Cornell and became a program officer for the Smith Richardson Foundation and later at the conservative Washington Legal Foundation. There he became the colleague and close friend of McDonald, a graduate of the George Washington University Law School. Both were strong-willed, conservative, with powerful minds; they decided to start their own public-interest law firm, through which they could advance the libertarian values that motivated them.

Funded mainly by conservative foundations and private donations, the CIR did not then, and still does not, have a lot of money. But on a shoestring the CIR was able to achieve a number of remarkable successes by carefully choosing the litigants to be represented. Because the CIR staff was quite small, Greve and McDonald adopted the policy of enlisting the support of large and powerful law firms that shared their views and were prepared to donate expensive legal time for the public good—*pro bono publico*. They defended people whose views were unpopular and who were penalized, passed over, or silenced. In one of their most interesting cases they defended a legitimate student organization at the University of Virginia that had been denied financial support for their publications that was given to other student publications. Many student organizations at that university were the ardent advocates of assorted causes; the burden of the CIR's client was that its advocacy was explicitly religious. The case went ultimately to the U.S. Supreme Court, where two great principles, the separation of church and state, and the freedom of speech and the press are of perennial concern. I had used the decision of the Supreme Court in that case, *Rosenberger v. the University of Virginia*,[5] in which these principles are in conflict, as a text in one of my courses in political philosophy. I have no sympathy whatever for the religious zealotry of that student group, but its members had been unfairly denied what other advocates had received, only because of the *content* of their views. My concern for open and robust debate of all matters on a university campus was fully matched by that of the CIR. In defending that student group its attorneys were right, and in the end they won.

Discrimination by race—against blacks, against whites, against any racial group—had been one of the targets of the CIR from its first days. In 1996 it won, in the 5th Circuit, that big *Hopwood* case against the University of Texas, described above. That was how it happened that Representative Whyman turned to them in her quest for legal action to end race preference at Michigan.

When Greve received the call from the Michigan legislators Whyman and David Jaye, he was noncommittal. I was not privy to their conversations, but I learned subsequently that she had at that time offered him some shocking admissions data given to her and her committee, data that struck a chord with the CIR. It is probable that the data she discussed with him were the data she had received from me in the "Cohen Report." The CIR became seriously interested. Not long after that both Greve and McDonald visited me in my office in East Quadrangle on the University of Michigan campus. I assumed that they had come from Washington, not only to speak with me but also to meet with Whyman. I did not know them personally, but apparently both of them had read some of the essays I had written in *Commentary*, which were sharply critical of race preference. We were in harmony. Greve, with his charming remnant of a German accent, had called well in advance, asking if they might come to examine the documents I had received as a result of my FOIA request. Yes, of course; I was quite willing to share the material with them.

When they arrived we almost immediately turned to the documents they had come to examine. The three of us sat on a sofa in my office, the two of them on either side of me, as I went over the documents with them. Some features of those documents were not obvious, and since I had scrutinized them many times I was able to explain the data in ways that expedited their grasp of what was before them. They were impressed. One document in particular struck them as extraordinary, the grid (described earlier in Chapter 9) instructing admissions counselors to give different responses to identical applications for admission, depending only upon the race of the applicant. McDonald, an experienced litigator, shook his head in amazement.

After this meeting with Greve and McDonald it was no longer possible for me to hide from myself the advocacy role I had begun to play. I was supporting the Center for Individual Rights, arming its leaders, for a legal battle with the University of Michigan. I had not spent much time with the two principal officers of the CIR before I was fully convinced of their acuity and convinced also that their opposition to race preference was as honest and intense as my own. I became then, and I remain to this day, a loyal friend and sincere admirer of the CIR.

There could be no litigation, of course, without a plaintiff, and the CIR had always been exceedingly cautious about the plaintiffs it would represent. Representative Whyman proposed to its leaders a plan, according to which she, with cooperating colleagues from the Michigan legislature, would find appropriate plaintiffs, persons who had been rejected by the university although they were highly qualified, persons clearly discriminated against because they were white. With the commitment of such persons to proceed, the CIR would (if those persons were found to be appropriate and satisfactory clients) then file suit in the federal district court in Michigan on behalf of those rejected students. Greve agreed to consider the people they produced but still did not commit the CIR.

From the documents I had provided one could conclude without doubt that minority applicants were being preferred. But conceptual injustices were not sufficient. Real plaintiffs, living persons who were injured by the preference, were needed. Many rejected applicants fit this description and were prepared to serve as litigants, but it was essential that the plaintiffs chosen have the needed outstanding academic credentials and be of such character that the cause would be well represented by them.

In May of 1997 Whyman, with three other legislators, took the critical step that led to the litigation that soon followed. Seeking appropriate plaintiffs, they issued a press release in which they attacked "discriminatory racial preference policies" at the University of Michigan in undergraduate admissions and in Law School admissions. In this press release rejected applicants were urged to contact these legislators if they believed that they had been denied admission or scholarship aid because of the university's preferential policies. The press release could not announce that litigation would eventually proceed under the auspices of the CIR, because that had not yet been agreed, but the involvement of the CIR was suggested by including a quote from Greve noting that the CIR had received a large number of requests for assistance, although it could handle only a limited number of cases. The attention of the general public to the admissions practices at the University of Michigan really began with this press release. Reports appeared in the *Detroit News* and in the *Detroit Free Press.* What happens at the University of Michigan is usually of great interest in Detroit, especially if there is any suggestion of misbehavior. Representative Whyman took it upon herself to find suitable plaintiffs, even seeking them through radio talk shows.

Potential plaintiffs came forward in substantial numbers. Told the University of Michigan was giving preference to minority applicants over white applicants, many rejected whites who believed themselves fully qualified for admission were quick to suppose that it was *they* who had been the victims of those discriminatory policies. If all of those minority applicants accepted to the university partly because of their race had been replaced by rejected white applicants, there would still have been many outstanding whites denied admission; Michigan is a highly selective institution. But no one could possibly know *which* of the rejected whites would in that case have been accepted, so it was understandable that the number of persons who believed themselves to have been discriminated against was larger than in fact could have been the case. It could never possibly be known exactly who would have been admitted had minority preferences not been given. Therefore the legislators sought rejected applicants who might very well have been among that group and who had convincing credentials.

Whyman's office in Lansing received dozens of calls from rejected students (and some from the parents of rejected students). Contact information was recorded for all callers; they were asked to send Whyman a copy of their university application, along with their grades and their test scores. Her office then forwarded all this information to the CIR, where the material was reviewed to identify promising candidates for the litigation envisaged.

Some two hundred rejected applicants, persons who saw themselves as potential plaintiffs against the university, came forward. Many of these were not suitable plaintiffs because their grades or test scores were too low, their applications too long past, or their motivation inappropriate. The task of selecting appropriate litigants was made easier by the grids that the admissions office had used in determining admissibility. One could readily determine which of the potential plaintiffs were most suitable.

The CIR made the decision to proceed with federal litigation. Particular plaintiffs would need to be chosen, but that could be done only with the involvement of the lead attorney who would be arguing the cases, so the next step was lining up an appropriate plaintiff's attorney. This would be a big case; the reputation of the CIR would be at stake. They would need an attorney experienced in complicated litigation and one who was prepared for a long and arduous proceeding. A substantial burden would have to be carried by that attorney and his firm. Selecting the attorney for the University of Michigan cases was a most critical step. As it turned out the attorney who accepted that role—Kirk Kolbo—proved marvelously well suited for the job. He and I became close friends over the next six years.

Kolbo and McDonald had been students together at the George Washington University Law School years before. Kolbo was not nearly as conservative in spirit as McDonald. He had been active in the Democratic Party in Minneapolis, as I had been active in the Democratic Party in Ann Arbor. Also like me, he had strong feelings about racial discrimination. McDonald was a conservative Republican and would be to our political right on many issues, but he and Kolbo were in full accord on the central issue of the cases envisioned.

Kolbo was practicing successfully at this time (and continues to do so) as a member of a large firm in Minneapolis, Maslon Edelman Borman and Brand—a firm founded by Jewish lawyers who had confronted antisemitism in Minnesota in the 1950s and had a history of opposing discrimination. In the 1970s Maslon lawyers had led the fight to desegregate the public schools in Minneapolis. Kolbo discussed the University of Michigan situation with his colleagues. His friend McDonald, more conservative but equally principled, had offered him the lead role in a battle that he was eager to undertake. The burden on the firm would be long-continuing and substantial. To Kolbo's great pleasure, his partners agreed that he should take the case pro bono. Corporate litigation can be tedious; this case, in which he would be defending fundamental constitutional rights against a great university, promised to be lively and satisfying. Kolbo proved to be a penetrating and valiant force in the litigation that was to ensue. He had the penetrating intelligence, extraordinary patience, and enormous energy required.

Kolbo made an important visit to Michigan in September of 1997, the first of many. For a second time Michael McDonald, now with Kolbo, came to my office. It was my practice to have lunch in my office, always just a beer and a bagel; I offered them each a beer. We became comrades, comfortable with one another, sharing the same objectives, enthused about the chances of success. We reviewed again the documents I had uncovered, documents with which Kolbo would soon become exceedingly familiar.

Their next step was to decide who, among those who had applied, would become the plaintiffs. There would have to be two cases; that was plain from the outset because there were two admissions systems against which complaints would be registered: the system of preferences used in the Law School—as the data obtained from my FOIA request made evident—was quite different from that used in LSA, the undergraduate college. By now, the large batch of rejected applicants had been whittled to a short list of six. Kolbo and McDonald set up a small conference room at the hotel in the Detroit Metropolitan Airport where they could comfortably meet and interview the candidate plaintiffs.

Kolbo and I later talked about this process. When he came to Ann Arbor we would dine together and discuss the progress of the cases: the timetable ahead of us, the depositions he was taking, the probable outcomes of the various motions and hearings, and the many personalities involved. These conversations are the basis of much of what is reported in this account. I had no formal role in the cases. Kolbo did not need me as a witness, but he did want me to testify if I were willing to do so. I told him that although there could be no secret about my partisanship in this litigation, I would not be comfortable testifying in court against my own university. He understood, and I was never called to testify. But my frequent meetings with Kolbo, and my subsequent close friendship with the plaintiffs, kept me well informed about the proceedings for years to come.

There was another, related association that brought me great satisfaction and much stimulation as we thought about the cases before us. Kolbo could not carry the burden of litigation alone. One of the other partners in the Maslon firm, Larry Purdy, had been chosen to join him; they came often to Ann Arbor together. Purdy was not the lead attorney in these cases, but he gave strong support to Kolbo and to the plaintiffs. He was and is intellectually deep and conscientious. He believed, perhaps even more passionately than did Kolbo, in the moral rightness of the plaintiffs' cases. After the cases had concluded he wrote a good book responding to arguments that had been famously put forward to defend race preference.[6] On occasion I would meet with him and his family in Minneapolis; still today I treasure his friendship.

Selecting clients of the right sort was exceedingly important to Kolbo and Purdy. It had to be done with great care because we would long be saddled with the consequences of that selection. Kolbo wanted clients that would look right, sound right, and be rightly motivated. He wanted clients who would be stalwart for the long haul, who could stand the spotlight with grace, and who would not wither in the face of likely public criticism. He found just the people he was looking for in those interviews in Detroit.

The first person they interviewed, Jennifer Gratz, became the lead client in the undergraduate case. She was—she is—quite wonderful. Calm, clearheaded, and well organized, Jennifer had thought a good deal about taking legal action against the university. She was sure the admissions process had discriminated against her. The possibility of legal action had been discussed with her parents (her father was a police officer in a Detroit suburb) the day she learned that she had been denied admission to the University of Michigan. A federal case could not help her personally, because she had entered another Michigan institution and would almost certainly graduate from it before any suit against the university could conclude. Nevertheless, she was determined to proceed, and she assured Kolbo and McDonald that she would stick with them for as long as it might take. They explained to her that she might pay a price for being a litigant—her criticism of the University of Michigan might later be thought a serious mark against her in the judgment of some potential employer. She replied that she wasn't a bit worried about that; if an employer couldn't understand her detestation of racial discrimination she wouldn't want to work for him anyway. Kolbo and McDonald were *taken* by Jennifer Gratz from the first moments of their meeting. She was the client they were looking for, and she never let them down.[7]

Days later, in East Lansing, Kolbo and McDonald enlisted a second undergraduate litigant, Patrick Hamacher, then enrolled at Michigan State University as a first-year student after having been rejected at the University of Michigan. Patrick Hamacher also was resolute. He had an impressive history of extracurricular activities and athletics in high school:

the Quiz Bowl team, the football team, the baseball team. Most important, Patrick Hamacher, like Jennifer Gratz, had high test scores and had
amassed fine grades in high school; he was an applicant any university
should have been happy to admit. I never got to know Patrick Hamacher
well, but when I did meet him I liked him. He was understandably disappointed to learn that even if the suit were eventually successful it would
be unlikely to help him in his continuing desire to transfer to our university. Nevertheless, he proceeded with enthusiasm.

I learned that the day after they spoke with Jennifer Gratz (and her
mother) in that interview room at the airport, Kolbo and McDonald met
a third potential plaintiff, the most impressive of all, Barbara Grutter
(pronounced "Grooter"). Barbara Grutter and I have since become good
friends, and I think it almost impossible to praise her too highly. She was
forty-three years old at that time. In a solid, traditional, nuclear family,
she was the mother of two boys, whom she had homeschooled. She was
running her own small health-care consulting firm out of her home in
Plymouth, a town about halfway between Ann Arbor and Detroit. She
had hoped to build a career in health-care law. Much later I met the boys
at her home. We talked and played chess; untrained, they played quite
well. Barbara Grutter and her family were as impressive in manner as
they were in intellect. She was a graduate of Michigan State University,
where her undergraduate GPA was 3.8. Her LSAT score, 161, put her in the
eighty-sixth percentile of all test takers. A more attractive candidate for
law school admission would have been difficult to find. Her application
to the University of Michigan Law School, however, had been rejected.

Like Jennifer Gratz, Barbara Grutter is an extremely self-possessed
person, perceptive and gracious. Her voice is always soft and her spirit
always reasonable. In gatherings (I later invited her to my home with
other guests and also to speak to one of my university classes) she would
say, in the calmest and most winning way: "I have always taught my children that color of skin shouldn't really matter in passing judgment, and
I was disappointed to learn that Michigan paid so much attention to skin
color. Had I been black, would I have been rejected by the Michigan Law
School?" Never was there a question more purely rhetorical than that
one. Had Barbara Grutter's skin been black she would have been admitted to the University of Michigan Law School the moment they opened
her application folder.

Kolbo and McDonald had done a superb job in selecting their plaintiffs. Jennifer Gratz, Patrick Hamacher, and Barbara Grutter were ideal
representatives of the class of persons whose complaint was soon to go

before the courts. They had demonstrated all-around excellence, but their skin was the wrong color; they had quite evidently been discriminated against on the basis of race. I was proud of them and became ever more proud of them as the cases moved slowly forward.

I did not know at first that the CIR had long planned to file the two federal suits at different times. On 14 October 1997, at the federal courthouse in Detroit, the first case was filed: *Jennifer Gratz and Patrick Hamacher v. Lee Bollinger and the Regents of the University of Michigan.*

Almost immediately I became involved in debates and discussions within the university and also in Ann Arbor and nearby communities about what came to be known as the *Gratz* case. One of the central administrators of the university, Walter Harrison (who subsequently became, and remains today, the president of the University of Hartford, in Connecticut), was given the job of presenting the university's position in many of the public debates about the *Gratz* case. Local organizations, wanting to be fair and to present both sides of the issue, would call upon him, and upon me, to argue the case for the benefit of their members. We met in public argument on several occasions. I didn't mind the repetition. Locally there is a great deal of loyalty to the University of Michigan, of course, and I wanted neighbors and colleagues to see that race preferences, even if honorably motivated, were in substance really quite shameful. So Walt Harrison and I developed a sort of dog-and-pony show (each of us, of course, believing he had the better part) that we would put on at various places.

It happened that on 2 December 1997 we argued the matter once again at the Detroit Press Club. In spite of our disagreements he and I had become quite friendly, and on this occasion we were having a drink together in the Press Club lounge before the meeting was to begin. I remarked to him that I was surprised that the CIR had not yet filed suit against the Law School, which (one could see from the documents I had received the year before) discriminated by race much more egregiously than did the Office of Undergraduate Admissions. He leaned over and told me, sotto voce, what I did not know. "Don't announce the matter tonight, please," he said, "but the Law School case is to be filed against us tomorrow morning." How he had learned this I never found out. But so it was. On 3 December 1997 in the federal courthouse the second suit was filed: *Barbara Grutter v. Lee Bollinger and the Regents of the University of Michigan.* The Michigan cases were formally in court.

CHAPTER 14

The Climate of Opinion at Michigan

On the campus of the University of Michigan, long before the *Gratz* and *Grutter* cases were filed in federal court, I had begun to express openly my strong objections to the admissions preferences we were giving. In February of 1997 I published a short essay, "Race in University of Michigan Admissions," in the administration organ, the *University Record*. I reported there some of my troubling findings from the Freedom of Information Act (FOIA) request of the year before and condemned the university's reliance upon racial classifications in admissions. Racial discrimination was and always will be wrong, I wrote, and we are not permitted to dabble in it. When our university engages in deliberate discriminatory practices and then seeks to hide them, we on the faculty are right to be appalled. Moreover, advantages given to persons of some races but not others do great damage—to the university as a whole, but especially to those who were supposed to have been helped.

Spokespersons for our university, I observed, repeatedly said, "We consider race as one among many other factors." That is true but deceptive. Race was used in our admissions as no other nonintellectual criteria were used. All applicants were classified by race *first*, we counted by race at every turn, and we established "affirmative action goals" and "timetables" that could be satisfied only by racial numbers. Our admissions systems were saturated by racially preferential devices, whereas our proper "goal," I insisted, is the complete elimination of all preference by race, and the proper "timetable" for reaching that goal is *now*.

Although the quest for diversity was the university's formal claim to justify its uses of race preference, the underlying key to its rhetoric was the justice of *compensation* for the historical oppression of minorities. In the *University Record* I emphasized what the Supreme Court has repeatedly affirmed: rights are possessed by persons, not by skin-color groups. When a remedy is due, it is due to the person damaged, not to the racial group to which that person belongs.

Moreover, I wrote, whether some person or persons have in fact been injured in a way that justifies a racial remedy is a matter that certainly does not lie within the competence of the university or its admissions officers to determine. If some competent court were ever to find that unlawful racial injuries had been inflicted by our university, the authority to fix a compensatory remedy certainly would not rest in our hands.

The admissions preferences we gave at the University of Michigan had, as their objective in practice, enrolling minority students in numbers *proportional* to their numbers in the population at large. One could see this from the nature of the reports made, constantly comparing the percentage of black students with the percentage of blacks in the Michigan population. By this standard every selective university must fall short, so university officers were always promising to "do better" next year. Racial discrimination that has proportionality as its objective is indefensible. It would come to an end before long, I contended, because most citizens of Michigan, when they learned what we were doing, would not tolerate it. I was later proven right about that.

The contrast between our professed "commitment to a policy of non-discrimination" and our knowing but hidden practice of discriminatory admissions practices would provoke, I wrote, "resentment and hostility gravely damaging to us. If we continue to engage in those practices, and to deceive the public about them, we will not deserve to be excused."[1]

Lee Bollinger had recently become president of our university. Under his leadership there was no likelihood that our preferential policies would soon be altered. Nevertheless, I continued to register strong criticism openly; the university, to its great credit, never sought to silence me. The administration had no obligation to publish my essay in the *University Record* as one "faculty perspective," but it did. On a number of occasions after that I published letters and comments in the *University Record* or the *Michigan Daily* with the same critical objective. President Bollinger could have sought informally to block or discourage such vocal dissent, but he did not. His commitment to robust debate on the campus was honest and serious; moreover he believed confidently that his defense of admissions preferences was sound and that, when all the arguments had been fairly weighed, the university would come out on top.

One consequence of my pressing sharp criticism publicly and repeatedly was this: I began to receive email messages from my colleagues on the faculty, many of whom I did not know personally, expressing their appreciation and hearty agreement. But open support I did not receive. This raised questions, in my mind, concerning the duty to speak out on moral issues.

University professors, we know, generally disfavor the uses of race in admission. The National Association of Scholars reported the results of a Roper Survey in 1996 that a "solid majority" (about 60 percent) of faculties nationwide opposes race preferences in admissions.[2] In 1998 the Delaware Association of Scholars conducted a similar survey of faculty at the University of Delaware, finding that *seven in ten* opposed race preferences.[3] This report of widespread faculty antipathy was confirmed in 2002 in a large-scale study of many campuses conducted by Prof. Stanley Rothman and others.[4] The faculty at the University of Michigan, where the justice of "affirmative action" was part of the conventional liberal wisdom, would probably have been more inclined to tolerate racial devices than faculties on more conservative campuses. Even so, it must have been the case that a significant fraction of our faculty, if asked, would have opposed the use of race preferences. Our university's teaching and research faculty is large, numbering in the thousands. There must have been hundreds among us, perhaps many hundreds, who agreed in whole or in part with my criticism of our admissions practices. But they did not speak out. The number of Michigan faculty members who publicly expressed agreement with me during this period, or who criticized race preferences in their own terms, could be counted on the fingers of one hand. Not all the fingers of that hand would be needed. What accounts for this silence?

I do not know the answer to this question. I can offer some hypotheses; the reader may have others. There is a natural human inclination to avoid direct conflict with a strongly prevailing opinion. The view that using race preferences in admissions was appropriate and wise had saturated the atmosphere of this university in those days. Press releases, reports, interviews, "diversity awards," and repeated suggestions, implicit as well as explicit, would cause any rational faculty member to see that on our campus affirmative action, by which was meant race preference, was the standard view, the right view, the overwhelming judgment of the community. The unqualified enthusiasm in the official statements of the university left no doubt that faculty members who opposed it here would put themselves outside of the mainstream.

In saying this I do not mean to suggest that university administrators were deliberately pressuring faculty members to agree with them. To my knowledge that was never done. There was social pressure, to be sure, but it was an unavoidable consequence of an honorably motivated campaign of enthusiastic support for the enlargement of minority enrollment. To oppose preference in admissions would appear, to many, to be opposition to that enlargement. No self-respecting faculty member could oppose increasing the enrollment of minorities here; we all shared that objective. But everyone knew that "affirmative action" was designed precisely to advance that end, so (the implicit, but invalid, argument ran) no right-thinking member of the community could comfortably express dissatisfaction with it.

Even those who privately thought the reliance upon racial criteria to be ugly were caught up in this widespread enthusiasm and trapped by it. Almost the worst imaginable public slander one might suffer was to be called a racist. There were those, mostly students, who did loudly proclaim that opponents of affirmative action were racists. People like me, they said, were seeking to resegregate the university. The zeal of these youngsters was honest; many believed that the university was not doing enough to increase minority enrollments. To oppose publicly (as I had done) one of the concrete steps that the university had taken in the right direction was, to their way of thinking, simply evil, and no one wishes to be associated, even mistakenly, with evil. That, in my view, is the chief reason for the silence.

There is another reason, I conjecture, that is also understandable and rational. The arguments about admissions preferences were not simple. The data were complicated and perhaps not altogether consistent; the contentions of conflicting parties were not easy to sort out and evaluate. Supreme Court opinions were there to read, but their correct interpretations were much in dispute. This entire controversy was, from the point of view of the faculty member not close to it, a tangled business. With careful and extended attention one might reach a clear resolution, but who has time for that? Consider the circumstances of a professor of engineering with complicated research projects under way, or a professor of art history with ancient documents to pursue and translate. For them, and for the preponderant majority of our faculty, all this argument about preferences was in other people's territory. Yes, it might seem that Cohen was right in objecting to the injustice of racial discrimination, but maybe there was more to it than could be seen on the surface. "If I speak publicly on these matters [that engineering or art history professor might have said to herself] I may then be called upon to defend an interpretation of a statute, or a Supreme Court opinion, that I haven't read and really don't know much about. This heated quarrel is not for me." I'm pretty sure many of my colleagues around the campus were thinking in just this way. "I think Cohen is right," they might have said if asked privately, "but I can't add anything to his statement of the criticism. He seems to be doing fine. I think I'd better leave the jousting to him." I would have welcomed more public support, of course—but I have to admit that this is not an irrational position for such colleagues to have adopted. I don't blame them or bear any moral grievance against them for their silence. Of course there were, among my colleagues, a fair number who were knowledgeable and who agreed with me fully, colleagues in the Law School and the History Department and the Sociology Department who need not have feared the debate but who did fear the slander. I gently fault those too-timid persons for their silence.

There may also have been some few faculty members who, in view of their personal circumstances, genuinely feared to support me openly. There are departments, in some of the nineteen colleges of our university, in which the administration is rigidly hierarchical as it is not in the College of Literature, Science, and the Arts (LSA) and in which saying publicly what is distinctly unpopular might have put one in the bad graces of an opinionated and vindictive chair. For young faculty members without tenure who may have shared my views, and for some of the nontenured research staff, silence might have seemed the safest course on a campus wracked by argument. Nothing would be lost by keeping one's head down. But if that were true for some it was mainly self-censorship, because I am convinced that neither Lee Bollinger, nor any of his subordinate administrators, encouraged or approved the punishment of members of the faculty who publicly disagreed with them. That was unthinkable and would simply not have been done here at the University of Michigan.

Those private email messages that I received from faculty colleagues were heartening, and I greatly appreciated them. One of those messages, which came from the assistant dean of one of the colleges (not LSA), was touching and worthy of report. This professor told me that some time before, while teaching one of the basic courses in his college, he had received a vociferous complaint from a minority student averring that a failing exam grade he had received was unfairly low and was the result of racial prejudice against him. The complaint was investigated and found wholly unjustified, my correspondent wrote, but he was troubled by it and took the matter to his department chairman. The chairman reviewed the exam, and the complainant's performance on it, and said to this faculty member, in effect: "Well, your grading is fair; there is no doubt about that. But now you have two alternatives. You can change his grade, which is a minor matter and will soon be forgotten. Or you can insist that the grade you assigned is correct, and fail him, which may result in a very messy set of complaints up the line. Even if your grade is upheld in the end, which is certain, you and the Department will be accused of racism, and some will believe that the accusation is justified. It's your call."

Facing those alternatives, my correspondent told me that he did what he came to believe was cowardly. He changed the grade. He recounted the story in confidence, he said, to explain why he believed, as I did, that the race preferences we give corrupt us. We enroll inferior students and then find ourselves obliged to fail them painfully or to pass them through corruptly. He thanked me warmly for my strong objections to favoritism by race. How many stories of that sort could have been told, we cannot know.

I was struck by the fact that a number of these private communications expressed the view that my outspokenness had been not only justified but "courageous." That seemed wrong to me. It may be that some were extrapolating from their own immediate working environments, perhaps more perilous than mine. I never felt threatened. I don't think that anything I said or did was particularly courageous. The matters at stake in these arguments were important to me. I was a tenured professor of philosophy; it seemed fitting for me to speak out when important philosophical principles were at issue. Making my opposition to race preferences clear and public satisfied my intellectual and moral conscience, even if I could not change what I found wrongheaded. I did feel some regret that so few of my colleagues joined me. But I was convinced (and was later proved correct) that in the body politic at large support for my position was overwhelming.

In those days (and still today in substantial degree) the atmosphere on the Ann Arbor campus at the University of Michigan was suffused with concerns about race. Race was the frequent topic of editorials in the *Michigan Daily*; the subject of reports, special features, and awards announced in the *University Record*; the concern of groups organizing meetings; of flyers advertising new initiatives; and so on and on. The orientation of new first-year students at the start of each fall term was devoted in disproportionate degree to racial affairs: the array of racial groups on campus was called emphatically to their attention, with the suggestion that one would be well advised to apply for membership to one or another. Incoming students were strongly encouraged, implicitly and sometimes explicitly by orientation leaders, to identify themselves as members of this racial group or that and to join their peers. The spirit behind this *racializing* was not malicious. It was honestly believed (and is still believed) by many students and administrators alike that racial self-identification and ethnic pride were preconditions of satisfactory interracial relations. The products of this emphasis, however, were the very reverse of what was sought. Ethnic groups have become more isolated, more exclusive. Lip service is loudly given to harmony and inclusion, but what has been encouraged in fact is racial separateness and division.

Thinking not at all about race, I once invited the president of the university, Jim Duderstadt, to come down to East Quadrangle, where I taught and had my office, to talk informally in one of the lounges with our students about whatever was on his mind or theirs. He did come, made some gracious opening remarks in our comfortable Green Lounge, and then invited questions of any sort from the undergraduates seated on the carpet around him. A black female undergraduate rose to her feet immediately and registered a forceful complaint. Said she, in effect, "You promised us a black lounge, but we have no black lounge. When are you going to keep your promise?" (I don't know if Duderstadt had ever made such a promise; I think it unlikely. In those days of the Michigan Mandate he may have done so or more likely may have said something about facilities for ethnic groups that had been interpreted as a promise.) Before he could respond two white male students leaped to their feet, angrily asking the girl who had expressed the complaint why *any* ethnic group should have its own exclusive lounge in a public university like ours. What if some lounges were exclusively for whites?

I was sitting well over on the side of the room; I feared that we were about to experience an extremely unpleasant racial incident. That was avoided, however. President Duderstadt, experienced in the techniques of group management, responded in a way (I cannot recall what he said) that disarmed the angry young students.

Then, and for years after that, our community was jiggling its loose tooth to feel the pain. Facilities, even entire *buildings*, were devoted de facto to the special interests of one minority or another, although they were not formally race-exclusive. Racial self-separation became common on our campus. On the floor above my office today is a student lounge, an "intercultural lounge" with an African name, used nearly exclusively by black students. Along with self-segregation there developed an ever-growing emphasis upon the *percentages* of minority racial groups in each department, in each college, on the campus as a whole. The need to increase those percentages is never questioned. The critique of race preferences in admissions was and is widely seen as a threat to this enterprise, a variety of closet racism.

In the winter of 2000, a committee was appointed by the provost at that time, Prof. Nancy Cantor, to search for a new associate vice president for human resources and affirmative action. Of course the person they would appoint would have to be race-conscious, an outspoken defender of the preferences the university was fighting so hard to protect.

It was probably as a jest on someone's part that my name was submitted to the search committee as a nominee for that position. I had no desire to be an associate vice president for anything. Years before I had served briefly as the interim director of the Residential College, and that experience taught me all I needed to know about being an administrator in a university. I could do it quite well, and did, but I did not find it satisfying. I recall that I returned to my professorial duties, to teaching and writing, with relief. Nevertheless, being curious to see how this nomination would be treated, I did not treat it as a joke. The correspondence that followed will give the reader a sense of the enthusiastic concern for race that permeated our campus at that time.

From the office of the provost of the university I received, on 14 January 2000, a letter advising me that I had been nominated for that post, and with it was enclosed a "Self-Identification Form" on which I was asked to report my race and the ethnic features of my ancestry.

The spirit of that inquiry offended me, although I knew that it was not intended invidiously. It called for a response. I did respond, with two letters, one to the provost's office, another to the chair of the search committee.

Acknowledging the request for racial self-identification, I first briefly recounted my experiences with the quest for racial identification when an undergraduate at the University of Miami. Photos were required then in application forms, their evident purpose being to identify unwanted blacks. My letter continued with the observation that the same spirit of racial categorization taints our admissions process now at Michigan— and even our employment practices. "Were I to be appointed to the post of Associate Vice President for Human Resources and Affirmative Action," I wrote, "one of the first steps I would take, in the interest of genuinely equal treatment of the races, would be to cease to request identification by race or nationality."

I went on to reply in advance to the objections I knew would be raised and to express my disdain for the crude racial categories the university had provided for responses to their request for ethnic identification. My letter concluded, "All of these questions are raised by your request for racial identification. I hope that I have helped you to see how profoundly *un-American* this inquiry is. I believe that the day is not long off when we will cease to make such inquiries, when we will be mortified that we once did so, and when all those who have participated in their formulation will have been properly shamed."

I sent copies of my letter to President Bollinger and to each of the regents of the university. I was quickly advised that the request for self-identification had come from the chair of the search committee. So I sent a second letter, on 21 January 2000, to Susan Ashford, professor of human resource management at the Business School and chair of the search committee. I began by again acknowledging the fact that I had been nominated to be associate vice president and the request I had received to complete the racial self-identification form. I sent her a copy of my earlier letter to the Office of the Provost and assured her that I would do all in my power to serve the University of Michigan, to which I have devoted my professional life. My letter then continued, "I would ask you, respectfully, to reflect upon the character of the inquiry you are extending to nominees. Is that an inquiry fully in accord with our largest principles? If the aim of the search is to identify a person qualified to lead in assuring the equal treatment of all *without* regard to race, are we likely to find such a person among those who respond by giving you the details of their racial ancestry?"

I was offended by the *racialism* made manifest in this inquiry. I took the opportunity to call to her attention the despicable policy of racial identification adopted in 1935 by the Nazi regime, called the Law for the Safeguarding of German Blood, and its presupposition that blood or race could have any significant bearing upon one's work or merit. "We are not Nazis," I wrote, "but in sorting applicants for a job by their racial ancestry, making detailed inquiry about that ancestry before advancing even to examine qualifications, we are doing what the Nazis did." I told her that I understood that she may have felt obliged by external agencies to conduct this inquiry. But I thought she ought, as a matter of principle, refuse to make such an inquiry and should destroy those racial identification forms. "That form," I concluded, "gave me a chill. Read it again to yourself, front and back. See if you don't get a butterfly or two in your tummy."

Professor Ashford did not respond to my letter. I was not asked to fill the position of associate vice president for human resources and affirmative action.

CHAPTER 15

The Reading Room

At this point I am obliged to report one incident, the only one, in which I was in effect penalized for my outspoken views about admissions preferences. As I begin the account of this incident I want to emphasize my belief that there was no officer of the university who sought to retaliate. I am sure that the events I report below were no more than the by-products of an unfortunate fear on the part of some midlevel administrators.

There is no way to explain what happened to me during the fall term of 1998 without first recounting the institutional background of these events. The setting is the Residential College of the university, in which I teach. That college had been planned by a group of faculty members in the years 1964–1967 as a "college within a college," a separate unit within the College of Literature, Science, and the Arts (LSA). Its classes would be smaller, its intellectual requirements and foreign language requirements more rigorous, and its atmosphere more informal. Such an environment, we thought, would be likely to result in more satisfying and more productive undergraduate careers. When the Residential College was finally approved by the parent college and opened in the fall of 1967, I was appointed one of its founding faculty and—my aversion to administrative work obviated by the excitement of the enterprise—its associate director. My office moved to East Quadrangle, an old residence hall near the center of the campus where the Residential College has been housed from that day to this. I became an active and visible member of the Residential College family and remain so still. In 1998 I was one of the few founders still alive and the only one who continued to teach actively in that college.

In 1997 the decision was made, in the light of this institutional history, to name a small reading room in East Quadrangle after me. I was gratified and greatly honored; the decision had nothing whatever to do with the admissions controversy in which I was then much engaged. The development office, whose charge is to encourage donations supporting the university, quite understandably used this naming to solicit gifts from my many former students in the Residential College, some of whom had by this time become prosperous professionals and businesspeople around the country. In support of the newly named Carl Cohen Reading Room gifts were solicited from current faculty members as well, not least from me. I made what was for me a substantial donation in support of that room, a standard practice when such honors are given. Over the years, before that time and since, I have contributed tens of thousands of dollars to the University of Michigan and to the City of Ann Arbor. The university receives, every month, millions of dollars in donations from alumni, foundations, and friendly corporations; the gift I made then was, from the university's perspective, of no great consequence.

My family and my friends were greatly pleased by the room naming and understandably proud. Most often one has to die before being honored by a named space on the campus. I was not only alive but professionally active in the very building in which the room named after me was located. I received a congratulatory letter from the dean. An engraved plaque was put up at the door identifying it as the Carl Cohen Reading Room. It was a small room, an extension of a large student lounge called the Madrigal Lounge, named for Jose Madrigal, a deceased employee of the housing division who had loyally cleaned the floors of that hall, every day, for many years. I was tickled, of course, when new students would ask me if I was, in truth, the very person after whom their reading room had been named. *Vanitas, vanitatum, omnia vanitas.* How could I not be pleased? Imagine my delight when I brought my two children (then aged nine and seven) to East Quadrangle and showed them the room and the plaque. The naming of the Carl Cohen Reading Room took place in 1997, at the completion of my thirtieth year on the faculty of the Residential College. I appreciated the honor deeply. Eight years later, in 2005, there was a splendid celebration of my fiftieth year on the Michigan faculty; this university has been my life.

There was to be a brief ceremony and formal dedication of the reading room on 20 November 1998. The coming event was announced widely. The reaction from some quarters was most unpleasant. Bear in mind that ours is a university comprising nineteen colleges, and that the great numbers of our students, graduate and undergraduate, if they knew of me at all, knew of me only in connection with the heated controversy, then in progress, over admission preferences for minorities. Many zealous students who knew nothing about my work in the American Civil Liberties Union (ACLU), who had not read my books or essays in defense of civil liberties, simply assumed, because I was opposing what seemed to them to be an advantage for blacks and Hispanics, that I was hostile to blacks and Hispanics. Emails began to circulate around the university asserting that a reading room in East Quadrangle was soon to be dedicated to a known racist! Efforts were made to organize a campus-wide protest, to take concrete action that would stop this dedication. Instead of naming it for a racist, let us name it for one we know to have fought against racism. Let us name it the Rev. Jesse Jackson Reading Room.

There was absolutely nothing I could do about these circulating rumors. If my activity in the ACLU of Michigan and in the Ann Arbor community and my published writings were not enough to make my views clear, no statement from me at this juncture would do anything more than provoke renewed attacks. Besides, any response I might have made would have been crassly self-serving. To all that followed in this unpleasant chapter of my life, I remained silent. I had been the honoree; I deeply appreciated the honor, but it would have been unseemly to argue in its defense. There was nothing for me to say.

Agitation grew. No one could predict what might happen on 20 November at the planned dedication of the reading room. Had that dedication ceremony taken place (it did not) there might have been no disturbance; however, something ugly could have occurred, and it would have had a racial flavor, the last thing our university then wanted. Race relations on our campus were not good at that time for a host of reasons, the admissions controversy being but one causal factor.

The conversations that ensued within the administrative hierarchy of the university I could not know, of course. So I am obliged to draw inferences from the events of which I do have direct knowledge. I inferred with some confidence that the administration of the university decided that that dedication ceremony, a possible spark for wider conflict, must not take place. If it was not to take place, there had to be a plausible reason to cancel it.

Some weeks before the planned event I learned that the university was to revoke the naming of the room in my honor. Some person or group within the administration, it appears, had become desperate to avoid a demonstration based on accusations of racism. This university concern was understandable. The administration wanted the problem to go away. To achieve this objective it canceled the honor and the dedication. This was not done, I am certain, to punish me for my repeated criticism of the admissions preferences. No one, from President Lee Bollinger on down, would have instigated or condoned such petty punishment.

The publicly announced reason for removing the plaque and de-naming the space was that the room had not been named in full accordance with established procedures. A mistake in the process obliged the nullification of the naming of the room for me. This was announced in the *Michigan Daily*. Before that explanation was announced I was asked to come down to East Quadrangle one evening for a private conference with the director of the Residential College and the dean of LSA. They wanted to explain to me first what was to happen and why (in their view) it had to happen.

At that time the interim dean of LSA was Prof. Patricia Gurin. I knew her well. Pat Gurin had been a young, liberal assistant professor of psychology in the days when I had been very active in the ACLU. Although we had not been intimate friends, a close colleague of mine also in the Michigan ACLU was her good friend as well; we were members of a group who shared a serious concern for civil libertarian causes. Now, years later, the director of the Residential College was Thomas Weisskopf, a highly respected professor of economics, learned and honorable, with whom I had had an ongoing public dispute about race preferences. He and I had engaged in lengthy, thoughtful correspondence on the issue. I had agreed, at his request, that we post our correspondence on the college bulletin boards for our students to read. Computers were not then the means that today would make such posting much simpler.

That evening meeting to which I was called proved vexing both for them and me. They had been convinced, or had convinced themselves, that the procedural error had been so serious that de-naming the Reading Room was the only possible course. The error, Dean Gurin reported, had been a failure to clear the proposed new name with a student advisory committee. They acknowledged that because in East Quadrangle I was a rather well-esteemed professor, it was highly probable that the student committee would have supported the naming enthusiastically. But because the committee had not been asked, the plaque had to come down.

This bad news was especially hard for Gurin and Weisskopf to deliver, I surmise, because they knew themselves to be my committed opponents in the ongoing admissions controversy. Professor Gurin, as it turned out, was to do some survey research among students that was later relied upon by the university to support the claim that diversity among students was a compelling educative interest—research that was subsequently shown to be less than persuasive. At this time, in 1998, their duty was to assure me that it was not a reaction to my views about race preferences but an unrelated administrative error that obliged the cancellation of the honor. I sat silent as they went on to assure me that there would be other ways, not yet determined, that the university would find to honor me and my role in the development of the Residential College.

I have never believed that a procedural error was the real reason for the action taken. I do not mean to assert that Professors Gurin and Weisskopf were lying, or dissimulating. But it is hard not to believe that a decision on other grounds had been firmly made somewhere in the central administration. I was not being asked to withdraw my name; I was being told that it would be removed. The plaque alongside the reading room door was taken down, and the revocation of the naming was announced widely. I was hurt, of course; the University of Michigan had come to mean so much to me.

The matter was far from over. One of my former students, Tony O'Rourke, whom I had not seen for more than year, decided on his own that this outcome was simply not acceptable. He devised petitions to President Bollinger with his own wording, expressing vigorous disagreement with the revocation of the naming, which he (like many others) assumed was politically motivated. Hundreds of students, many of whom disagreed with my position on admissions, signed those petitions, mostly students living in East Quadrangle who knew me or about me. I was gratified when O'Rourke showed me the petitions, although I told him I had little hope that they would do any good. Undeterred, he delivered them to the dean of LSA.

I am surprised, as I think back upon it now, that President Bollinger or others in the administration did not see how quickly and confidently the general public would assume that the university was punishing me for my opposition and using procedural error as a rationale for retaliation— which is precisely how the situation was commonly viewed.

Terry Sandalow, an old friend, called me and asked me to come to his house to talk about the situation. He is an outstanding scholar of constitutional law whom I have always admired. He had earlier been dean of the Law School and had just retired. We sat in his living room drinking scotch and talked.

Before I report what he said to me I must point out that he had long been convinced that preferences, outright preferences, must be given to black applicants to our Law School. He and I had debated the matter publicly. His reasons were straightforwardly utilitarian, and I confess they gave me pause. "Carl," I remember him saying during our earlier public debate about the policy, "go 40 miles to Detroit and see that horrific parade of black defendants coming before the criminal courts, every single day, endlessly. And now imagine, Carl, that all the judges are white, and all the prosecuting attorneys are white, and all or most of the attorneys are white, while the defendants, 95 percent of them, are black. Do you think, Carl, that we can maintain a peaceful and harmonious society in the face of such gross racial imbalance? No. There must be black judges. There must be black prosecuting attorneys. There must be a goodly supply of black attorneys, for the sake of our society and our country." Having gripped our audience, he would conclude, "If that means that we must give preference to black applicants to law school, we must accept that consequence and live with it." My position, he argued, was shortsighted, a mistaken insistence upon abstract principle in the face of the harsh realities of the criminal justice system.

Perhaps he was right. Perhaps I have been too much the theoretician. But I didn't waver. In my view those well-intentioned race preferences were deeply damaging to blacks over the long haul. My answer to Sandalow at that time was incomplete. At about that time social scientists began to doubt that preference by race in admissions had actually improved the long-term outcomes for black students. The problem uncovered was one of *mismatch.* Applicants admitted to law schools by which they would normally have been rejected as unsuited go on to perform, in those schools, much less well than their classmates. The impact of this mismatch—upon retention, upon appointments after graduation, and upon professional careers—proves to be seriously adverse *for the minority students preferred.* A University of California at Los Angeles scholar who would later become a friend, Rick Sander, wrote a law review article in 2004 demonstrating convincingly that the number of black attorneys would probably *increase* if race preferences were reduced or eliminated.[1] This outcome, which seems at first counterintuitive, has been subsequently well established by the intensive statistical analysis of the many consequences of admission based in part on race. Sander's work has now appeared in book form.[2]

Sandalow had not invited me over to rehash our old debate. He wanted to tell me how dreadful he thought the de-naming of the Reading Room had been. He was horrified by it. He cared deeply for the university, and he was sure that this response would go down as a serious mark against us. "Carl," he said to me, holding up some report of the alleged procedural error, "this *stinks.*" Those were his words, exactly. He went on to tell me that in his experience as dean there never was a case in which a naming was free of procedural errors. The University of Michigan is a great place, but we are messy in doing business, he observed, especially where honors and money are concerned. The decision to revoke the honor on the grounds of procedural error, in the context of the ongoing admissions controversy, was not believable. Procedural errors are so commonly made that to fasten on one error in this context was unacceptable. He repeated himself. "It stinks."

He wanted me to know how he felt, and he wanted me to know that he was going to write Bollinger, now the president but formerly his young protégé, telling him that this mistake must be undone, and quickly. My only contribution to his information about the affair was that my supporting gift had been $10,000. He dismissed this as inconsequential. He had received donations to the Law School and our magnificent Law Quadrangle that made the entire scene in East Quadrangle seem penny-ante. I left him, that afternoon, slightly inebriated and somewhat heartened, until I recalled that the dedication ceremony had been canceled, and there was no longer a plaque with my name on it beside the reading room door.

I learned, around this same time, of another letter sent to President Bollinger (no doubt there had been many). I cannot say here how I learned this, but the letter, whose author I do know, meant a great deal to me. It was also from one of Bollinger's former colleagues at the Law School, Peter Steiner—a distinguished professor of economics and law who had also served successfully for some years as dean of LSA. He had also been national president of the American Association of University Professors (AAUP), one of whose ongoing functions is to call attention to those universities that fail to protect the academic freedom of their faculties. Steiner supported the university's admissions preferences, but did so without much enthusiasm. "Lee," he wrote (I learned), "you simply cannot allow that Reading Room to be de-named. Whatever the claims made about procedural errors in the naming process, this is intolerable, and it will seriously mar your presidency. If I were still the Dean of LSA I would find the person who had that plaque removed and fire him."

It soon became apparent to Bollinger—a constitutional lawyer, his specialty First Amendment law and the freedom of speech—that everyone would suppose I was being punished for my views. Bollinger's new general counsel and confidant, Marvin Krislov, phoned me. He explained to me that the president had decided that the de-naming of the room was not in the interests of the university. The procedural error that had led to its being done was not a sham, he insisted, but larger concerns made that error tolerable in the long run. There was one thing the president asked in return. It had to do with the gift I had made in support of the reading room. It had been listed (as is normally done in such circumstances) as "anonymous." Would I allow them to report publicly that I had made that gift? Of course I would; I was not ashamed of the gift, so I assured Krislov that that would be fine, and he thanked me. I suppose they thought that the announcement of my contribution would deflect some attention from the president's sudden change of mind.

As general counsel to the university, Krislov soon became the adroit overseer of the university's legal battles in support of race preferences. He was drawn away from the University of Michigan, a few years ago, to become president of Oberlin College, in Ohio, where he remains at the time of this writing in 2014.

Early in 1999 President Bollinger announced formally that the reading room in East Quadrangle would be permanently named the Carl Cohen Reading Room. There had been a procedural error, as earlier reported, but there was great danger that the revocation of the honor would unsettle other benefactors as well as seem to be caving in to the critics of a controversial professor. We had to make sure that this impression was scotched. The plaque was put back up next to the reading room door.

Perhaps the most important observation to be drawn from this Carl Cohen Reading Room affair is that, as far as I know, it is the *only* case in recent years in which the University of Michigan has appeared to retaliate against those who exercise their academic freedom. I continue to speak out strongly on our campus against race preferences, encountering no harassment, no threats.

CHAPTER 16

Moving Targets

As the Michigan admissions cases moved into the courts, a new person at the Center for Individual Rights (CIR), Terry Pell, became the principal spokesperson for the plaintiffs. Pell, an important personage in what follows, was first appointed to deal with the public and the press for the CIR, to present and defend its three clients. He came to know them and admire them, and like me, to be proud of them.

Newspapers and television news programs found the stories of these litigants appealing. Jennifer Gratz was the star—poised, reasonable, and articulate. In the months after the suits were filed, there were dozens of interviews and appearances that Pell planned and supported. Jennifer Gratz's photo appeared in *Glamour* magazine and in the *Washington Post*; she appeared on the *Today Show* and was the focus of a report on the *McNeil/Lehrer Newshour*. In all of these appearances her principled opposition to preferences, her sincerity and intelligence, shone through. The character and personality of the plaintiffs the CIR had chosen reinforced the intellectual and legal position they represented.

Pell was not confident, at first, that the media would be interested in his cases, but he quickly learned that the topic, with its prominent racial theme, struck a nerve nationally. On the morning the suit was to be filed, 14 October 1997, Pell arranged for Jennifer Gratz to do an exclusive interview with the *New York Times*.

The interviewer, Ethan Bronner, is one of the paper's most highly esteemed reporters. His report was accurate and impartial and had an unusual feature that gave the story great impact. Pell had given him copies of the documents I had received from the university more than a year previously. Among them were the grids that showed, when analyzed, how blatant the racial preferences had been. As a newspaper reporter he understood how provocative those grids were and that they would enrich his story—but he also realized that, if merely summarized, they wouldn't achieve the impact of a graphic presentation. Bronner (as he told me recently in an email message) therefore gave the grids to one of the graphic artists at the paper, requesting that a chart be prepared to accompany the story, one that immediately and visually conveyed their essence. The graphic required no study or deduction and showed forcefully how much more difficult it was to be accepted as an undergraduate at Michigan if one were white than if one were black. The information in those grids was translated brilliantly in that day's *New York Times*. Two charts on the same page, one for minority applicants and the other for majority applicants, exhibited the university's preferences for minorities vividly.

The special interest of the *New York Times* in this matter merits some reflection. In the New York City metropolitan area live millions of Jews, and Jews, who commonly send their offspring to college, tend to note with great interest any important changes in the process of university admissions, which not too long ago was used as a tool to restrict their own admission to college. Among the universities of interest in the suburbs of the great eastern cities, the University of Michigan looms large. We have long had a substantial enrollment of students from New York and New Jersey. The longtime chairman of the University of Michigan English Department, Prof. Warner Rice, once pointed out to me that the New York Central Railroad had contributed mightily to the great number and fine quality of our out-of-state students. From those trains boarded in central Manhattan, young folks and their parents could disembark three short blocks from the University of Michigan campus in Ann Arbor. Tuition at Michigan, long known as a center of intellectual excellence, was low in those days (it no longer is); we offered a splendid educational bargain. Families from New York and New Jersey accepted that bargain in great numbers. I was once told—I cannot vouch for the truth of the story—that a governor of Michigan once called the governor of New Jersey, seeking ways to reduce the flood of students from that state. New Jersey long had no state university at all; Rutgers, until quite recently, was an expensive private school. The University of Michigan, as a consequence, had great appeal for up-and-coming New Jersey households. Admissions practices at the University of Michigan, in which ethnicity played a role, had certainly become of substantial interest to readers of the *New York Times* by the time *Gratz v. Bollinger* was filed in 1997.

This interest was partly the product of threat. Enrollments at a much-favored and highly selective university such as ours were necessarily limited. If there were any movement toward the proportional representation of ethnic groups (which some who supported race preferences did indeed explicitly seek), the burden of that shift might be expected to fall most heavily on the highly overrepresented Jewish contingent from eastern cities. To this day the number of Jewish students on our campus is disproportionately large. One who held that there were not enough blacks on our campus might also contend—the common opinion in some Ivy League schools decades earlier—that there were too many Jews.[1]

The university's rejection of Jennifer Gratz had become front-page news in the *New York Times*. It was plain to university administrators that the grids delivered to me in the winter of 1996, which had served as the key to the preferential system, had to be replaced. Shortly after Bollinger became our president, and before the two Michigan cases were actually heard in court, the mechanics of the system used by the university for the consideration of race in undergraduate admissions were greatly changed.

The changes, which later became a controversial issue in the courts, resulted in the elimination of all grids; there were to be no more documents showing that one set of criteria applied to minorities and a different set applied to nonminorities. University administrators continued to insist that it was essential to continue to give preference to minorities if "affirmative action goals" were to be reached. But without grids, *how* was this to be done?

In place of its grids, the Office of Undergraduate Admissions devised what it called a Selection Index. Each applicant would garner *points* from various aspects of his or her status and earlier academic performance. The maximum number of points that could be amassed was 150, but most applicants would have far fewer than that. Grade-point average (GPA) in secondary school would be the single-greatest source of points: eighty points for a perfect 4.0 (A) average, with a gradually decreasing point yield for declining averages; for a 3.0 average (B), sixty points; and so on. The number of points thus awarded would be refined by evaluating the quality of the secondary school, ten points added for graduation from the most demanding schools, decreasing gradually to zero points for graduation from the least demanding. It would be further refined by an evaluation of the difficulty of the curriculum the applicant had chosen in high school, with as many as four points subtracted for an easy path and as many as eight points added for a demanding one. Test scores—SAT or ACT—could provide as many as twelve points if they were excellent, six points if they were mediocre, and zero points if they were poor. All points having academic origins would be totaled for what was called Sub-Score 1.

Nonacademic considerations, "Other Factors," would yield Sub-Score 2. These were:

1. Geography (ten points for Michigan residents; six points for residents of an underrepresented Michigan county; two points for an underrepresented state)
2. Alumni status (four points for "legacy," parents or stepparents being Michigan graduates; one point for other relatives)
3. Essay (one point for an outstanding essay; zero points for an essay that was not outstanding)
4. Personal achievement (on the national level five points, on the regional level three, on the state level one)
5. Leadership and service (also five, three, and one for national, regional, and state performance)

The last of the "other factors" was headed "Miscellaneous," of which there were five subcategories:

1. Socioeconomic disadvantage (twenty points);
2. Underrepresented racial or ethnic minority identification (twenty points);
3. Men in nursing (five points);
4. Scholarship athlete (twenty points);
5. Provost's discretion (twenty points).

Admissions counselors would score each applicant on the basis of credentials provided in that applicant's folder. On the worksheet later provided to counselors it was noted that the total of Sub-Score 1 and Sub-Score 2 could not exceed 150 points. In practice, however, the cutoff line between admission and rejection turned out to be, each subsequent year, between 90 and 100 points on the Selection Index. So the twenty points awarded for a minority applicant's ethnic status were, in fact, equal to about one-fifth (or more) of that applicant's total if admitted and exactly equal to the difference between the point yield of an A average and a B average in high school.

The Selection Index point sources, as they were first devised, were slightly revised in subsequent years. The major sources of points, however, and the number of points awarded for each—including the award of twenty points for being a minority—remained what they were at first. The point sources chart for the year 1999 appears as Figure 16.1; the worksheet for the calculation of point totals in later years appears as Figure 16.2. The reader will not be surprised to see that that worksheet was headed "Confidential: Internal Use Only."

Anxious to get the grids behind it, the university put the new system into effect as quickly as possible; devised in 1997, it applied to admissions for the fall term of 1998. Three things had been accomplished by the switch. First, the damning grids had been eliminated. Second, the machinery of the new system applied to all applicants, so the treatment of minorities under an explicitly different set of criteria, which was obviously difficult to justify, had been transcended, or so it appeared. Third, the consideration of minority identification, although it remained consequential, was now somewhat obscured, buried among a list of "other factors" appearing at the bottom of the worksheet.

The system switch was designed to move minority preferences out of the spotlight—but it changed nothing of consequence, because minority applicants, to whom preference was still to be given, received that preference by having twenty points added *automatically* to their Selection Index scores. Twenty points was a large chunk of the whole. Racial considerations were not eliminated; they were not even reduced. Race played just as large a role in the new system as it had in the old.

This became clear when evidence concerning the switch was gathered in preparation for the later trial in federal district court. How, the CIR attorney Kirk Kolbo asked, did the admissions office decide *how many* points to assign for each factor, academic and nonacademic? The answer was revealing. The university had done a statistical analysis of applications from previous years. The points to be awarded from this or that category were settled upon by reverse engineering; the numbers were chosen in such a way that the application of the new system would yield, as nearly as possible, *the same number of minority acceptances* that the old system had produced. The university never dodged this point; its attorneys reported to the court honestly and repeatedly that the university had not changed its admission principles in any substantive way; the change was only one of mechanics.

Black or Hispanic applicants were treated differently under the old system, much more generously than majority applicants. That was the explicit instruction on the older grid. If the old system had been a violation of the Equal Protection Clause of the U.S. Constitution, as I believed, the new system, designed to achieve the identical objective, would surely be that as well. This was my view and the view of the CIR. Unfortunately this was not the view of the U.S. District Judge Patrick Duggan, before whom the *Gratz* case was heard.

Academic Factors

GPA

GPA	Points
2.5	50
2.6	52
2.7	54
2.8	56
2.9	58
3.0	60
3.1	62
3.2	64
3.3	66
3.4	68
3.5	70
3.6	72
3.7	74
3.8	76
3.9	78
4.0	80

School Factor

Quality	Points
0	0
1	2
2	4
3	6
4	8
5	10

Curriculum Factor

Difficulty	Points
-2	-4
-1	-2
0	0
1	2
2	4
3	6
4	8

Test Score (assign only larger point value)

ACT	SAT 1	Points
1-19	400-920	0
20-21	930-1000	6
22-26	1010-1190	10
27-30	1200-1350	11
31-36	1360-1600	12

Other Factors

Geography

Residency	Points
Michigan	10
Underrepresented MI County	6
Underrepresented State	12

Alumni Status (assign only 1 option)

Status	Points
Legacy (parents/stepparents)	4
Other (grandparents, siblings, spouses)	1

Required Essay

Essay Quality	Points
Outstanding Essay	1
Not Outstanding Essay	0

Personal Achievement (assign only 1 option)

Level of Achievement	Points
State	1
Regional	3
National	5

Leadership and Service (assign only 1 option)

Level of Achievement	Points
State	1
Regional	3
National	5

Miscellaneous (assign only 1 option)

Criteria Met	Points
Socio-economic Disadvantage	20
Underrepresented Racial/Ethnic Minority Identification or Education	20
Men in Nursing	5
Scholarship Athlete	20
Provost's Discretion	20

Figure 16.1

Name _____

UMID _____

Unit _____

Term _____

Selection Index Worksheet

(For LS&A and selected Schools and Divisions, other than Engineering)

Points (circle)	ACADEMIC	
40		2.0
42		2.1
44		2.2
46		2.3
48		2.4
50		2.5
52		2.6
54		2.7
56		2.8
GPA 58		2.9
60		3.0
62		3.1
64		3.2
66		3.3
68		3.4
70		3.5
72		3.6
74		3.7
76		3.8
78		3.9
80		4.0

	School Factor	
0		0
2		1
4		2
6		3
8		4
10		5

	Curriculum Factor	
-4		-2
-2		-1
0		0
2		1
4		2
6		3
8		4

Points (circle one)	TEST SCORE		
ACT/ SAT I 0	01-19	400-920
6	20-21	930-1000
10	22-26	1010-1190
11	27-30	1200-1350
12	31-36	1360-1600

Add points in this column for sub score 1

OTHER FACTORS

(Maximum 40 points)

Points (circle)

Geography

- 10   Michigan Resident
- 6   Underrepresented Michigan County
- 2   Underrepresented State

Alumni

- 4   *Assign only 1 option*   Legacy *(parents/stepparents)*
-     or
- 1   Other *(grandparents, siblings, spouses)*

Essay

- 1   *Assign only 1 option*   Very Good _____
- 2   Excellent _____
- 3   Outstanding _____

Personal Achievement

- 1   *Assign only 1 option*   Very Good _____
- 3   Excellent _____
- 5   Outstanding _____

Leadership & Service

- 1   *Assign only 1 option*   Very Good _____
- 3   Excellent _____
- 5   Outstanding _____

Miscellaneous

- 20   Socio-economic Disadvantage
- 20   Underrepresented Racial/Ethnic Minority Identification or Education
- 5   *Assign only 1 option*   Men in Nursing
- 20   Scholarship Athlete *(assigned by athletic counselor only)*
- 20   Provost's Discretion

Add points in this column for sub score 2

TOTALS			Reviewer's Initials
Sub score 1	+ Sub score 2	= Selection Index	
			Date:

Maximum = 150
Transfer Selection Index number to Sel. Ind. box on front of application folder

Figure 16.2

The two cases, *Gratz* and *Grutter*, went to two different judges within the Eastern District of Michigan. They were handled in different ways. Duggan was the judge in the undergraduate admissions case, that of Jennifer Gratz. Bernard Friedman was the judge in the Law School case, that of Barbara Grutter. Within the courthouse in Detroit there was a good deal of maneuvering in the effort to consolidate the two cases. The university believed that it would be safer with Judge Duggan, into whose hands both cases would have been placed if they were consolidated because his was the first of the two cases filed. But the finding that they were "companion cases" and thus properly consolidated would require the agreement of Judge Friedman, to whom the *Grutter* case had already been assigned. Friedman, it turned out, did not believe that the cases presented identical issues, nor did the CIR. The University of Michigan was the respondent in both cases, and the essence of the complaint, unlawful racial discrimination, was the same in both cases. However, the circumstances of the plaintiffs were different, and the admissions systems used in the two colleges of the university were very different.

In resolving this judicial conflict, the chief judge of the Eastern District, Anna Diggs Taylor, disqualified herself because her husband was a regent of the University of Michigan. She handed the matter of the assignment of the cases to two other judges in the district, John Feikens and Julian Cook. But Feikens, as Kolbo learned, was a member of the University of Michigan Law School Committee of Visitors, which evaluated all aspects of the school's operations. It smelled bad. When Feikens and Cook produced an opinion, advisory and without authority, concluding that the cases were companion cases and should be consolidated under Duggan, Judge Friedman wrote a blistering response. "It is obvious that the two of you as well as Anna are determined to direct this case as you see fit, and there is absolutely no precedent for what is taking place. This is the grossest form of judge-shopping and I intend to deal with it in the appropriate form when I return." Friedman was in northern Michigan while these maneuvers were taking place and had learned about them by telephone from his clerk. Later, Judge Friedman wrote that the opinion of Feikens and Cook had no weight at all; the case had been assigned by a blind draw. Their effort to manipulate that assignment, he said, was "an affront to the dignity and the independence of the court and an unlawful intrusion upon and interference and meddling with this court's business." The entire episode, Friedman wrote, "tarnishes this court's appearance of fairness and appears to place the court's imprimatur upon a judge-shopping practice which we, collectively as a bench, in the past always have denounced."

The university's lead attorney was John Payton, a partner in the powerful Washington, D.C., firm of Wilmer Cutler Pickering. Bollinger did not rely on the general counsel of the university, Elsa Cole; he had just asked for her resignation and had not yet appointed her successor. Bollinger had been a clerk for Justice Warren Burger at the U.S. Supreme Court. He knew the federal courts well, understood the skills needed for prolonged litigation, and was prepared to have the university pay well for the best representation he could find. John Payton was his choice. Fiercely smart, gracious, and adroit, he represented the University of Michigan superbly until—well, until a sticky problem having nothing to do with his own skill or efforts led to his removal from one of the two cases. More of that later. At this point Payton argued plausibly on behalf of the university that putting the two cases before a single judge would eliminate the possibility of inconsistent rulings. The harder the university pressed to put both cases in Duggan's hands, the surer Kolbo became that that would spell trouble for the CIR. He submitted an affidavit in support of Friedman's retention of the case. Friedman, who would surely have realized that this would be a big case, bigger than any over which he had presided before, was pleased to have it remain in his courtroom.

There were good reasons to adjudicate the cases separately. The evidence in the two cases was proving to be markedly different. Kolbo reported that in the discovery process he had received 5,000 pages of documents from the university regarding the two cases, but not one document had been offered by the university as being relevant to both cases. Kolbo had requested a list of the people with responsibility for the two admissions policies; he received two such lists, as he expected, but not a single person appeared on both lists. Judge Friedman, ultimately declining to consider the two as companion cases, emphasized the fact that the "law school and the undergraduate college operate as independent units within the University of Michigan, and it appears that their admissions policies have little, if anything, to do with one another." The two cases stayed in separate courtrooms, *Gratz* with Judge Duggan, *Grutter* with Judge Friedman. Kolbo won that round.

This was not the last time that judges within the federal court system maneuvered in what appeared to be inappropriate ways to influence the outcome of the Michigan admissions cases. At the appellate court level, as we shall see, maneuvers even more troubling were aimed directly at the outcome.

CHAPTER 17

Intervenors

Federal court cases are often complicated and time-consuming, not only because the issues may be complex but also because the parties are likely to submit various motions to the court, sometimes procedural but nonetheless of consequence, that need to be resolved before the merits of the issues can be reached. Such motions often require special hearings, and the resultant rulings may not come quickly. The Michigan admissions cases were complicated in that way—but even more complicated than most—because, in them, there were *four* parties anxious to be heard in the courts. This calls for explanation.

The legal conflict was chiefly between two strong parties: the University of Michigan, where admissions practices were under attack, and the Center for Individual Rights (CIR), which had initiated and sustained that attack on behalf of Jennifer Gratz, Barbara Grutter, and others similarly situated. The university's principal attorneys were John Payton and another partner in his Washington, D.C., firm, Jane Sherburne. They defended the university valiantly, for years spending most of their working time in Ann Arbor. Behind them with encouragement and support was President Lee Bollinger. On the other side, the principal attorneys for the CIR were Kirk Kolbo and Larry Purdy, who, likewise, spent much of their time in Ann Arbor. Behind them were Michael McDonald and then, more and more effectively, Terry Pell.

Pell became, away from the public scene, the chief pillar of support for the plaintiffs. When Michael Greve became discontented with the emphasis being given by the CIR to the Michigan cases, he and McDonald had a falling out, and eventually Greve, whom the center's Board of Directors had appointed the firm's chief executive officer, resigned. The board's choice for the presidency of the CIR was Pell.

My judgment of Terry Pell is no doubt colored by our close friendship and our agreement in all aspects of the University of Michigan cases, the focus of his interest and effort for years. As president of the CIR he gave the cases his ardent and sophisticated support. He is a graduate of the Cornell Law School and received his Ph.D. in philosophy at Notre Dame University after completing his legal studies. He is the most philosophical lawyer I have ever known.

Pell is a politically conservative man, more conservative than I am by far, but he also strongly believes that discrimination by race is an abomination, and no one knows more about the law in this realm than he. He is deep, reflective, and humane. I admire him enormously. Beyond his thoughtful lawyer-like support of the plaintiffs and their attorneys, Pell was able to express eloquently, to the press and in every public context, the philosophical spirit of their position. The Michigan cases derived their energy from him.

There were two other parties with a strong interest in the outcome of the University of Michigan cases. From one point of view they were a distraction and a nuisance, but their concerns were serious, and they pursued those concerns with legal acumen and vigor. The first of these other parties was the National Association for the Advancement of Colored People (NAACP) Legal Defense Fund (LDF). The education docket of the LDF was directed by attorney Theodore Shaw, who had grown up in the civil rights movement and who believed that special attention to the needs of blacks in colleges and universities was essential for the long-term gains sought by the LDF. No stranger to the University of Michigan, he had once been a member of the Michigan Law School faculty. As I write this in 2014, Shaw is a professor of law at the Columbia University Law School.

Long before the University of Michigan cases arose, I had been a regular contributor to the NAACP LDF. Obviously I did not share Shaw's views about preferences for minorities, but I did admire and support much that the LDF had done in securing the civil rights of blacks. I am not inconsistent in giving this support. I remain a contributor to the LDF and also to the American Civil Liberties Union (ACLU); my quarrels with these organizations pertain only to their defense of minority *preferences*.

Shaw and I had first met in 1993, when he deposed me, recording my sworn testimony in a case of a related kind at the University of Maryland. The issue in that case was also one of racial preferences, but it did not concern admission to the university. At that state university, there was then a race-exclusive scholarship program. Only African Americans were eligible for the scholarships in question. Having become known for my published opposition to ethnic preferences, I was asked to testify in that case, *Podberesky v. Kirwan.*[1] When Podberesky, a University of Maryland student, applied for scholarship aid under that program, he was told that he was not qualified because he was not black. I was gratified when the 4th Circuit Court of Appeals ultimately found this race-exclusive program to be a plain violation of the Equal Protection Clause of the Fourteenth Amendment.

Now Shaw and I were again on opposite sides. Shaw, having returned to the LDF on leave from the University of Michigan Law School, assembled a coalition of the LDF, the ACLU (which by this time had formally adopted the university's position on preferences), and the Mexican American Legal Defense and Education Fund (MALDEF). The parties represented by his coalition were black high-school students, mainly in Detroit, who had (in their view) an interest in maintaining admissions preferences at the University of Michigan because those preferences would increase the likelihood of their admission. Their formal intervention would certainly delay the progress of the cases, because they would, like the central parties, have the right to submit motions, receive documents in the discovery process, and so on. The interests of black high-school students did not appear to have a direct bearing on the central issue raised by the plaintiffs, however, which was the lawfulness of the use of race-based criteria, not the advantages that use might bestow. Shaw, an effective advocate, nevertheless wanted his clients recognized by the court as having a serious concern in the outcome of the undergraduate case, and on that basis sought their status as formal intervenors.

A fourth party having an intense interest in the cases was a group calling itself the Coalition to Defend Affirmative Action by Any Means Necessary (BAMN). It came to be known by its shortened name, "By Any Means Necessary," and by the initials of that name: BAMN. The name was fitting. It had begun at California universities two years before, mainly as a group of university students who took some pride in disruptive measures: occupying administrative offices, shutting down (by making incessant noise) the meetings of university regents, and so on. Its members knew well that their conduct was at times unlawful, and they accepted the risk of arrest. They meant quite literally what their name announced: they would "save affirmative action" *by any means necessary.* They were as passionate as they were sincere.

Their leader was a thoughtful young woman named Shanta Driver. I came to know Shanta Driver quite well during the course of the controversy here at the University of Michigan, where she opened a new chapter of the California group. There were a number of debates, on television and in other contexts, in which she and I were in sharp disagreement. She did not hesitate to admit, indeed to proclaim, that "affirmative action," as she used the term, certainly did entail preferences for blacks. She thought such preferences were essential, deserved, and overdue. The University of Michigan might seek to mollify critics by claiming that "diversity" only was the object of their preferences, but that was a cowardly euphemism as she saw it; the diversity defense elicited her contempt. Almost all of BAMN's membership consisted of students from Michigan and California; in their view U.S. universities remained bastions of racism. The fact that the University of Michigan had for some years been honestly striving to increase its minority enrollment did not appease Shanta Driver. Racism and sexism still permeate our society and its universities, she believes, and must be fought vigorously, if necessary violently, even at risk of self. The University of Michigan cases were to be the stimulus of a new, revolutionary civil rights movement, in her view the successor and culmination of the movement of the 1950s and 1960s. Nothing must be allowed to stop it. They would take to the streets in large numbers if need be. Judges and politicians would have to listen.

BAMN became a significant presence in Ann Arbor. On the diagonal walkway ("the Diag") from corner to corner of the central quadrangle of our campus, BAMN held rallies on a number of occasions, waving banners, chanting slogans, shouting condemnatory accusations. Shanta Driver and others delivered fiery speeches exhorting action that would ultimately root out the alleged racism of the University of Michigan.

BAMN found itself in the somewhat paradoxical position of wanting the university (which its members despised) to be victorious in its legal battle with the CIR. From their point of view the arguments that needed most to be made, the *real* reasons admissions preferences for minorities are morally right, would never be made by the university itself. The University of Michigan, Shanta Driver thought, had been complicit in racial oppression; one could be quite sure that its attorneys would never admit that guilt or welcome the consideration of that history in court.

One of BAMN's central contentions was that the standardized tests used by the University of Michigan in determining whom to admit, the SATs and ACTs, were themselves racist and unjust. This often-repeated claim has been evaluated repeatedly and scrupulously by independent psychologists and testing agencies and proved false. Many studies have shown that the grades blacks receive when enrolled in a university are substantially *lower* than might have been expected on the basis of their performance on those exams. The standardized exams used by the university therefore *overpredict* the performance of minorities and are advantageous to them, not biased against them.[2] This was known at the time and has been repeatedly confirmed. But scientific results in conflict with its claims were of no interest to BAMN. Its members *knew* what was right.

Shanta Driver was convinced that if the real arguments for admission preferences were to be put before the courts and the nation, arguments that appealed not to diversity but to racial justice, BAMN had to be involved, formally and actively, in the cases themselves. Formal intervention in the *Gratz* case was not feasible, because Ted Shaw had staked out that ground; a motion to have the LDF coalition recognized as a third-party intervenor, acting on behalf of black high-school students, was already before Judge Patrick Duggan.

The *Grutter* case was another matter. Shaw (as a University of Michigan faculty member) had helped to draft the Law School admissions policy at issue in *Grutter*; he could not enter there. BAMN could. Another impassioned young woman, Miranda Massie, became the lead attorney for BAMN, conducting the fight to have the group recognized formally as an intervening party in *Grutter*. She too was convinced BAMN was building a new, progressive movement that would one day cleanse society of its racism.

The University of Michigan was put in an awkward position by the efforts of BAMN to intervene. It could not support the intervention of a group explicitly hostile to the university and anxious to defame it. Yet it did not wish to oppose openly any efforts, even if unruly, purportedly aimed at improving the condition of minorities. So it remained silent, taking no position on BAMN's motion to intervene. The CIR, however, did oppose the intervention, contending that BAMN's arguments, flatly rejected in *Bakke*, could not justify the university's preferences, and moreover that those arguments, grounded in historical allegations about societal discrimination, did not bear on the central issues in the *Grutter* case.

Shanta Driver and I developed a peculiar relationship. I cannot say that we liked one another, but we did respect one another. She possesses a fine intellect and outstanding rhetorical talents. I thought her views extreme, sometimes far-fetched, but I never doubted her integrity. She was eager to have a public confrontation with some university officer, but the university would not give her or her group the credence that a public debate with some official spokesperson would engender. It would not be fair to say that university admissions folks were afraid of her, but it was plain that they did not relish an open argument with her.

That was not my case, however. I loved arguing with her on university panels, on television, anywhere at all. In my view she was wrong, not entirely wrong about the depth of racism in our country, but dead wrong about the University of Michigan, which (whatever may have been the case generations ago) had long since ceased to discriminate against minorities. In giving preferences the University of Michigan was behaving wrongly, but in general it was making serious and honest efforts to overcome the disadvantages blacks had earlier faced here. A great deal of energy and money was being devoted to this compensatory effort; I knew the folks who devised it and knew their efforts to be genuine. I was unhappy with university conduct, to be sure, but unlike BAMN's members, I thought the university had gone to the opposite extreme.

Shanta Driver and I were therefore at sword points with respect to the central issues of the Michigan cases. We were civil to one another in formal contexts. Several times she complimented me for being straightforward and willing to defend my views in public. I was the only one in the university, she would say, willing to do that. That wasn't far from the truth. I am as tenacious as she and equally intense.

The outcome of the efforts to intervene, by BAMN and by Shaw's LDF coalition, I will presently report in summary fashion. They had a substantial impact on the continuing controversy. But before that report I want to relate the events at one particularly agitating and problematic confrontation with BAMN in which I was directly involved.

I don't recall the exact date, but it was after BAMN had begun formal efforts to intervene in court. An evening panel to discuss the Michigan cases had been arranged and was to take place in the Council Chamber of the City Hall in Sterling Heights, Michigan, a suburb just northeast of Detroit. David Jaye was the legislative representative from that district, and I believe it was he who had made the arrangements to use this central location. There were to be several speakers, not all on my side.

I drove to Sterling Heights, about an hour from Ann Arbor, arriving early because I wasn't sure I would find it as easily as I did. Approaching the front doors of the building, I encountered a mass of demonstrators—BAMN folks—with banners, shouting slogans in unison, partly blocking the doors. I passed them without incident, entered the building, and found the Council Chamber, where a table had been set up with name cards for each speaker. I sat down behind the card showing my name. The demonstration outside the building was becoming louder.

The audience began to arrive. At a moment apparently signaled by their leader, some five or ten minutes before the scheduled beginning of the panel presentation, all the BAMN folks, in a thick stream, poured into the chamber and occupied most of the first three rows of chairs in the center, directly in front of the speakers' table. In unison, they began to shout slogans, the words of which I don't recall. The gist of it was that the University of Michigan was a racist institution and that affirmative action had to be saved. The shouting in the chamber was very loud. No effort had thus far been made to open the proceedings formally. I sat there silently, watching them, wondering how this was going to develop. No one had yet spoken from the podium.

The hall filled, and the noise increased; the shouting was raucous, relentless. We speakers (I believe we were four, one of whom was a minister) sat in a row, waiting for the program to begin formally. Finally someone—I think it was legislator David Jaye who had organized the meeting, but in retrospect I am not sure—moved to the center of the podium in front of us and sought to open the meeting. He was completely overwhelmed by the rhythmic shouting and could hardly be heard. The shouting grew yet louder. His repeated efforts to open the meeting were fruitless. I confess that I found the situation almost amusing; the shouting continued without a break, and we speakers looked at one another in puzzlement. Other audience members, plainly irritated, added to the tumult by shouting at the demonstrators. From the two sides of the chamber came irregular shouting; from the center came the loud chanting of slogans. It went on and on.

I had experienced a similar deliberate disruption way back in 1970. I was lecturing then, on political philosophy, in one of the very large auditoriums on our campus, called Auditorium A. A student group called the Black Action Movement (BAM) had demanded that the University of Michigan commit itself to enrolling black students as 10 percent of its student body. The university had not complied with this demand, and the group retaliated by calling a one-day strike. Students were urged not to attend classes on that day and faculty members not to hold classes. Many faculty members were quite ready to cooperate, or at least did not wish to be seen refusing to do so and therefore canceled their classes. I was not willing to cooperate. There were more than two hundred students in my class (The Philosophical Foundations of Communism, Fascism, and Democracy—Philosophy 363), many of whom had no sympathy for the strikers and who deserved to have their educational interests respected. I had announced that our class would be held as usual on that day. The class period began normally, except that the auditorium was only about half full. About twenty minutes into the hour—I was lecturing on the fascist writings of Mario Palmieri[3]—a large band of students came marching into the auditorium, banging on garbage cans, shouting that the class must be dismissed. The podium from which I was speaking, higher than the seats, dominated the hall. I quickly surmised that I could control the situation for a while, but not indefinitely. I am pleased to recall that I had sufficient presence of mind to observe to the hundred or so students seated in the auditorium that what they were experiencing on this day was precisely the pattern of conduct advocated and used by Palmieri, Giovanni Gentile, and other fascist thugs. *No theories!* was their mantra—just *force* and *action; Mussolini ha sempre razione!* Mussolini is always right! I drew the parallel as well as I could under the circumstances, expressing my outrage calmly. When the disruption had continued for ten minutes or so, the noise becoming incessant, I was forced to dismiss the class, feeling a bit defeated. That was a terrible experience and a truly shameful event in the life of any university, but I was actually proud of the fact that I had been able to use the moment, for those who could hear me, to reinforce my intellectual objectives in that course. It was an event my students would rightly associate with fascism and would not be likely to forget.

No such advantage could be derived from that BAMN demonstration in the Council Chamber in Sterling Heights, where I had no control whatever. The chairman, perhaps it was Jaye, tried again and again to open the meeting, but the moment he would begin to speak the BAMN members' shouting would increase in volume. It was plain that it was their intention to close down the meeting; they were not going to allow anyone to speak. I had not said a word.

Someone called the police. They came quickly because the municipal police headquarters were apparently in that same building, on the level below. Several officers came into the hall and told the protesters that they would have to stop their interference with the speakers of the evening. The shouting continued undeterred. They were warned again, and again continued without cessation. It was apparent that they had expected this and had decided on their tactics in advance. Again they were warned by the police. Then yet again. Two of the officers made an effort to take protesters by the arm to lead them out of the hall. They resisted, and there was a minor scuffle. The police then turned to us, on the podium, and to the rest of the audience, and told everyone they were going to use tear gas to clear the hall. The BAMN shouting continued. This was not the last time I was to witness such behavior in the University of Michigan admissions controversy.

The tear gas—I do not recall how it was released—quickly cleared the hall. We ran from the Council Chamber through the front doors of the building to the outside. I did not know—I suppose no one knew—what we were supposed to do under such circumstances, so we just hung around outside of that City Hall for quite a long while. It was not cold. No one wanted to go back into the Council Chamber, yet people were curious about how the matter would turn out, and many apparently felt that by departing we would have yielded to the demonstrators. So we just waited there, talking with one another, doing nothing. Whether the demonstrators were taken into custody by the police I do not know. They had intended to break up the meeting, and they succeeded, it seemed.

Not entirely. Quite a while later—no one seemed to want to leave—we were told that the air was clear and that it was safe to come back in, at least into the large front lobby of the building. A good many folks—audience members, speakers, some police officers, slowly filtered back into that front lobby, where there were a number of sofas and benches scattered about. The shouting had stopped when everyone fled the Council Chamber; it did not begin again, and I cannot say what happened to the demonstrators while we were out of the building. But if they were persistent, so was I along with at least one other of those who had been scheduled to speak that evening. With the audience, still reasonably numerous, now scattered about the front lobby, many members seated on the floor, some on sofas, we two were introduced at last and said our piece. There was a lively discussion afterward. That evening I presented my strong objections to admissions preferences with more than usual conviction. My adrenaline was surely running high. I have always been a civil libertarian. The silencing of a public meeting troubled me even more than the admissions preferences I had come to discuss. As I looked back upon it I did not think the meeting was a total failure. For those in agreement with me, the effort to disrupt the gathering probably intensified their support. For those uncertain, the deliberate disruption may well have pushed them to my side of the argument.

Those who were anxious to defend affirmative action "by any means necessary" seemed to have disappeared by late in the evening. I recall that I was asked by a University of Michigan student in the audience whom I did not know for a ride back to Ann Arbor. As I drove him to his apartment we talked, puzzled and unsure, about the events of that remarkable evening, strange to us both.

Two other things happened to me that evening that I must also report. One concerns my briefcase, beautifully handmade for me years before by a leatherworker in Cleveland. My papers had been in it at my feet as I sat at that speakers' table. When the police advised us that tear gas was about to be released, we all ran—well, hurried—out of that chamber, leaving everything as it was on and under the table. When the dissipation of the gas allowed us to reenter the building later, I returned to the Council Chamber (the smell of tear gas remained, but only faintly) to recover my briefcase. It was not there. I asked and looked around to no avail. In the lobby I reported the loss to one of the remaining police officers, and while I was explaining to him what it looked like—beautifully hand-sewn leather, lovingly worn—another officer, standing nearby, overheard me. He came over and told me that he had noticed just such a briefcase downstairs, where the BAMN folks had met with their attorney, Miranda Massie. He asked me to wait right there in the lobby while he checked downstairs. He soon returned, carrying my briefcase. What a relief! Who had taken it, or why, he did not tell me, and I never learned. Did I think that someone had intended to abscond with it? Yes, I did, but I never pursued the matter. That beautiful briefcase I have used with satisfaction for decades. I still have it.

The other matter of special interest that evening was my meeting with Chetley Zarco, the other speaker who had stayed late with me. How he had become engaged in these disputes I never learned. He died not long ago, sadly young. I found his conduct on occasion unwisely angry, but he was quick to speak out against injustice—he hated racial discrimination—and he had a generous heart. We became friends.

Zarco believed that the University of Michigan had been deliberately deceitful; he set out to prove this by digging up documents buried in the extensive holdings of the Bentley Historical Library, on our campus. The reports he uncovered, 1994 surveys of university students regarding their experiences and attitudes pertaining to interracial relations, were never released by the university. Those surveys, revealing substantial interracial tension, were not consistent with the administration's claims about the great benefits of racial diversity.[4]

Much later, after the Michigan cases had been settled, Zarco played an active role in our efforts to prohibit racial considerations in admissions. Some years after our first meeting Zarco pressed me to send him a copy of the article by Richard Sander, a professor of law at the University of California at Los Angeles (UCLA), I had mentioned to him.[5] I knew Rick Sander. We had corresponded, and he stayed with me when he came to

Ann Arbor. He was the father of a mixed-race son, a boy who in the United States would be called black. Sander had sought, as a statistician, to determine what the real consequences of race preferences were for black students. That inquiry brought him to the conclusion that admissions preferences for blacks were in fact hurtful, not simply to those displaced but to blacks themselves. Here follows the verbatim text of a letter (date uncertain, but sometime in 2006) that I sent to Zarco.

Chet—

Warm greetings. Here enclosed is a copy of the final version of Richard Sander's article in the *Stanford Law Review.* It is a very powerful argument, solid throughout, giving very strong empirical evidence that in American law schools the race preferences given to blacks, which have been almost universal, have also been very seriously hurtful to those who received such preference. What was intended to help minorities has been hurting them badly.[6]

The reason, of course, is *mismatch.* Preference brings blacks into schools for which they are not well prepared; they do relatively badly in those law schools, first in efforts to pass the bar exams, and then relatively badly in their careers as well. Blacks and whites with the same academic credentials (LSAT scores, GPAs, etc.) do equally well in law school. It is not blackness, but preference (and the resulting mismatch) that causes the damage, and it does so throughout the system of legal education in our country, because of what he calls the "cascade effect." Sander shows this, quite conclusively, from many different sides; his evidence is voluminous and overwhelming.

At the Michigan Law School a debate between Sander and David Chambers (a principal advocate of preference here) on Monday, 24 January 2006, was a route. Sander demolished the objections raised, which he showed to be empirically unsupportable.

There is a good deal of number crunching in this piece (Sander is a very proficient statistician), which is not easily followed by a lay audience. But Sander also writes clearly and expresses his conclusions in words that no one can misunderstand. You may find pieces and quotes here that will be very useful. Jennifer [Gratz, with whom Zarco was then working] may find a copy useful as well.

Zarco had somehow become acquainted with a case in which a University of Michigan student, a reasonable and politically active young man named Jeston LaCroix, having put up on his dorm room door some propaganda opposing the university's admissions policy, had it repeatedly torn down by persons, apparently BAMN members residing in his dorm, whom he had encountered in an unpleasant argument. He sought protection from the Department of Public Safety but was told there that such material was not permitted on room doors. When he brought his complaint to someone higher in the administration, he was told to take his complaints to the head of the Department of Public Safety—from whom it was a sure thing that no apology would be forthcoming. Zarco somehow gathered the documents in this case and sent copies of them to me, thinking I might find some relief for the student; he also sent copies to the office of the university general counsel, with an angry and pugnacious cover letter.

I was concerned for that student, but I was also troubled by the harshness of Zarco's letter to the general counsel. I had occasion to deal with the counsel's staff; I knew and respected its members, although we disagreed and argued publicly. Distressed by the inappropriate tone of his letter, I apologized on his behalf because Zarco had used my name in his correspondence. Here follows the text of the letter I sent to Debra Kowich, the assistant general counsel of the university at that time, and one of her associates, Jon Alger, a fine lawyer and a staunch defender of the university's policies, also my friend.[7]

Dear Debbie (and Jon)—

Cordial greetings. Let this be a confidential note, please.

I write to apologize for the intemperate and inappropriate language used in the letter to you from Chetley Zarco. Many of his views I do share, but I believe that you and your office do what you can to handle these matters fairly; writing in that aggressive style is, in my judgment, foolish and counterproductive.

The substance of the problem you understand very well. There is a little chap with unpopular views who is, in truth, being harassed not only by some of his political opponents who are downright brutal (the BAMN folks mean it when they say "by any means necessary"—they use very ugly means indeed), but who also does not get, from the university authorities, the sort of protection that he might hope for, the sort of protection that would surely be given to some other groups on campus. So—wanting not to flog a dead horse—you will see that it is frustrating, even infuriating, to be told that, to have one's rightful activities protected, he must go to the very people—the Department of Public Safety—who are doing some of the harassing! I am mindful of the fact that your office cannot serve as courtesy police. Still, I would ask that you advise the officers involved of their duties in this connection—some duties legal, other duties flowing from the general spirit of civil liberty on campus that we share.

I trust that you will have done that. But as I reread Chet's letter I am somewhat embarrassed, and ask your patience and forbearance. If we work together to keep the campus open and free, the substance of these matters will eventually fall out as the citizens want them to, and our university will thrive. I am a great believer in democracy. (My book, *Democracy*,[8] has just been published in Chinese! Do you have a copy—in English? If not, I will send you one.)

Thank you for your understanding.

Be well.

Carl

Here is a footnote to this matter. That complaining student had also brought his complaint to me, knowing that I, too, had been a target of BAMN. I thought his complaint justified and also troubling because his report, if true, suggested that some university officers were acting like thought police. University students have all sorts of stuff (including radical political propaganda) on their room doors, and the notion that the university forbids certain content, which I believed totally false, called for repudiation. I wrote a personal letter to the university president (at this time Prof. Mary Sue Coleman, Bollinger's successor) relating the problems and complaints of Jeston LaCroix and asking respectfully if she would make our policies clear to the Department of Public Safety. She wrote back with great courtesy, assuring me that students are indeed free to adopt any political positions whatever, and advertise them on their doors as they wished, without any interference from university authorities. She assured me also that she had made that policy clear to the Department of Public Safety.

And here is a footnote to that footnote. When President Coleman took office in 2001 I had written her a letter of welcome, and in that letter rather boldly took the opportunity to present a nomination for an honorary degree from our university. I nominated one of the truly outstanding journalists of our time, Susan Stamberg, the designer and longtime host of the program *All Things Considered* on National Public Radio. I had never met Susan Stamberg, but her vivacity and acuity had made her a heroine of mine. After explaining the grounds of my admiration I told

President Coleman that I thought there was no one more deserving of the intellectual honor we could bestow.

I did not receive an immediate response to that letter, but sometime later I did receive a confidential letter from the Honorary Degree Committee advising me that my nomination of Susan Stamberg had been carefully considered and that the decision had been made to award her an honorary doctorate of humane letters. I was gratified and delighted. Nothing happened on that front for years. I wrote a gentle letter of inquiry in 2008 and was assured these matters move along slowly. Susan Stamberg was indeed soon to receive an honorary doctorate. She was among the small group of degree recipients that included President Barack Obama in the spring of 2010, receiving her degree before a crowd of more than a hundred thousand people in Michigan Stadium.

There was a dinner for the honorary degree recipients and their nominators the night before those commencement ceremonies. President Obama did not come, but I did meet Susan Stamberg there for the first time. I was so proud of her. I also had occasion at that dinner to converse briefly with President Coleman, thanking her for the attention she had given to the nomination I had submitted years before. I had been critical of her for a speech she had given in 2006, of which I will say more shortly. But our relations remained, and remain still, entirely cordial.

I was to have a number of confrontations with the members of BAMN in the years that followed. We differed sharply about preferential admissions policies, of course, but its members' anti-intellectual conduct troubled me most. Their methods were the antithesis of democracy. In a decent society, I believe, the most bitter opponents will listen to each another, try to reason with each other, seek to persuade each other, and will at least agree upon a process for the resolution of differences, with whose outcome they commit themselves in advance to comply. The BAMN folks would not do anything like that. They did not believe they had an obligation to behave with civility. They had objectives that they were determined to advance; all who blocked their path were simply wrong and had to be cleared away *by any means necessary*. The name was absolutely fitting. What struck me then, and strikes me again as I write now about those days, is how abhorrent that name ought to have been in the ears of reasonable people. They were mainly young folks, and many of their ideals were honorable. But they were adults, and theirs was a wrongheaded spirit: dogmatic, arrogant, and at times downright ruthless. The means we employ in community action, as John Dewey explained many years ago, penetrate and saturate the ends we achieve. Zealots who brutally shout down their opponents will not achieve a decent and harmonious society.

The behavior of the active members of BAMN was often despicable. Nevertheless it was our obligation to protect their freedom to engage in debate. However ugly their style, we also had to protect their right to seek to intervene formally in the federal litigation now begun.

CHAPTER 18

The Thin Line between Permissible and Impermissible

The two judges—Patrick Duggan in *Gratz* and Bernard Friedman in *Grutter*—were eager to turn to the merits of the arguments that were to come before them, but before they could do this they were obliged to decide who had a right to be heard in those proceedings. After lengthy hearings in court and prolonged procedural maneuvering by the parties seeking to intervene, both Judge Duggan, confronted by the NAACP Legal Defense Fund (LDF), and Judge Friedman, confronted by the Coalition to Defend Affirmative Action by Any Means Necessary (BAMN), decided that formal intervention by these outsiders was not justifiable.

The chief reason for denying the intervenors was not the inconvenience and delay their participation would impose but their inability to show that they had a *right* to a role in these cases. They claimed a serious interest in the outcomes because, they said, the elimination of preferences would reduce the likelihood of their admission to the university. That interest gave them no right to participate, however, because they were not *entitled* to an admissions system that would make their admission more probable. Both Duggan and Friedman denied the motions to intervene.

That was not the end of it, not nearly. Those adverse decisions by Duggan and Friedman were appealed by the would-be intervenors to the appellate court—the 6th Circuit Court of Appeals, in Cincinnati. (This court hears all federal appeals from Michigan, Ohio, Kentucky, and Tennessee.) The procedural arguments had to be heard yet again, and again deliberated upon. More motions, more hearings. In the end the 6th Circuit Court *reversed* the two district courts and held that these would-be intervenors had interests to protect that did justify their formal participation in the proceedings. The LDF, represented by Ted Shaw, and BAMN, represented by Miranda Massie, thus became formal parties in these cases, authorized intervenors deserving procedural consideration.

Permitting an additional party in each case slowed matters down enormously. The process of discovery (in which attorneys on both sides demand and receive documents and other relevant evidence from the opposing party) was lengthened. Motions requiring repeated court hearings were submitted. Proceedings sure to be slow in any case were slowed, by the formal intervention of LDF and BAMN, to glacial speed. The intervenors didn't mind that at all; the more time they would have to reach the public with their complaints the happier they would be. The university, in an awkward position (unhappy with the intervenors' attacks on it, but unwilling, for political reasons, to appear opposed to the intervenors' apparent advocacy of minority interests) was largely silent. The Center for Individual Rights (CIR) opposed the interventions, to no avail. The mills of the federal courts grind very slowly indeed. Three years—three years!—went by before the district court judges could turn to the merits of the cases before them.

In the undergraduate case, with discovery at last completed and the sworn depositions of witnesses taken, it appeared that there was remarkably little disagreement between the parties about the facts. Each side therefore submitted to Judge Duggan a motion for *summary judgment* in its favor. Trials are held to determine the facts. If there isn't any significant conflict between the two sides about the critical facts, an attorney may argue that there is no need for a trial. The entire matter, he or she may contend, boils down to the application of law to the facts already established and agreed upon by the opposing parties. Both Kirk Kolbo and John Payton held this view; both submitted motions for summary judgment in *Gratz*—each contending that the correct application of the law to the facts would result in victory, or summary judgment, for his party. Shaw, representing the intervening coalition as third party, argued that a trial was needed; he wanted an opportunity to show that there was a history of racial discrimination at the university that justified the preferences given.

The motions for summary judgment in the *Gratz* case were heard in Duggan's courtroom on 16 November 2000. Kolbo, Payton, and Shaw argued their positions in turn.

Kolbo contended that the CIR must win on the law. The university had engaged in what was explicitly a system of racial discrimination, forbidden by the Equal Protection Clause of the U.S. Constitution. At the University of Michigan, he said, pointing to the older grids, and then to their Selection Index equivalent, one standard applies to whites and a different one to blacks. It was plainly a dual admissions system based on race.

Payton relied on the diversity defense, the argument that the use of race preferences by the university was authorized by the *Bakke* decision. That was the law. Justice Lewis Powell's controlling opinion (he argued) had allowed that a "plus factor" might reasonably be given to some applicants for the sake of diversity. This plus factor was precisely what the university had introduced into its undergraduate admissions system.

Shaw emphasized that the University of Michigan had long been an overwhelmingly white institution, and that its efforts to integrate the campus had only begun seriously thirty years ago. If affirmative action were to be struck down now, he argued, those efforts would be crippled.

Responding to those motions a few weeks later, Judge Duggan issued a decision that he explained at length. The essence of it was this: no trial was needed. The case could be decided as a matter of law. Summary judgment was granted to the University of Michigan, whose undergraduate admission system he held to be consistent with the U.S. Constitution. As Payton had claimed, the university's system (he concluded) satisfied the conditions laid down in the *Bakke* case.[1]

The Duggan opinion, immediately appealed of course, delighted President Bollinger and the university team. One feature of that opinion seemed extraordinary to me. That Kolbo was right about the law I had no doubt; the university did administer an admissions system in which rejection and acceptance in many cases depended on the race of the applicant. In his opinion Duggan explicitly agreed that an admissions system classifying flatly by race would be unconstitutional. He sharply condemned the grids with their attendant instructions because they revealed the indubitable intent to discriminate. These "facially different grids and action codes based solely upon an applicant's race," Duggan wrote, were plainly unconstitutional. That much was satisfying to me personally. What I had been contending since 1996 was explicitly affirmed in Duggan's judgment. Yet he found the new system, using a Selection Index in which twenty points were automatically awarded for minority status, *acceptable!* How could this be? Both parties had repeatedly averred that the two systems were equivalent—that the differences between them were, as Payton had earlier written for the university, "mechanical rather than substantive." Both sides had *agreed* that the new system simply used a different device to achieve the same racial result as the old system. Duggan's conclusion that the old system was indeed unconstitutional but that its equivalent replacement was not infuriated me.

Duggan's reasoning was essentially this: the old system was on its face a *dual* system. It explicitly treated minority applicants in one way and majority applicants in another. Recall that the grid with which undergraduate admissions officers were guided to respond to applicants bore the instruction to "use the top row in each cell for majority applicants and the bottom and middle rows for underrepresented minorities."[2] That was intolerable under our Constitution. But the new system was *unitary*; it simply gave different amounts of points to different applicants for assorted reasons. It may be true that the preferences given by the new system ensured that the number of blacks accepted would remain just what it was under the old system, but that (he contended) is only because of the *number* of points the university had decided to award for minority status. It was not a dual system. This change in mechanics had allowed the university, in Duggan's words, to "cross that thin line from the impermissible to the permissible."

This seemed devious to me, a distinction too frail to support the grant of summary judgment to the university. The new system, whose efficacy depended precisely upon the number of points assigned for minority status, was *designed* to do exactly what the old system had done. The number of points awarded automatically for minority status had been decided upon precisely in order to achieve the same number of minority admissions that the older grid system had produced. There was, *in substance*, no difference between them.

When the cases were first filed in 1997 the university had maneuvered, unsuccessfully, to put both cases in Duggan's hands. Its leaders probably had good reasons to believe that Duggan was solidly in their corner. Now, it seemed, he was pretty clearly reaching for some formal difference, some distinction that would allow him to condemn racial discrimination and yet decide for the university that employed it. I was convinced that in the upcoming appeal the distinction on which he had so heavily relied would not bear the weight of the conclusion he had rested upon it.

CHAPTER 19

128 Honorary Degrees and a Coat Check

The *Grutter* case was handled very differently. Argued before Judge Bernard Friedman, proceedings in his court opened in January of 2001, also three years after the case had been filed.

Each of the two principal parties again sought summary judgment in its favor. Kirk Kolbo was eloquent. The University of Michigan Law School system was not identical to the undergraduate system, but it relied upon race even more fully. The Law School plainly used an unconstitutional double standard. The quest for "diversity" cannot defend that double standard; diversity is a goal so amorphous and so undefined (as the U.S. Supreme Court had said in another case) that it could not serve as the compelling interest that might justify some attention to race. John Payton, in his turn, sought here also to reestablish the diversity defense, calling again upon the authority of the 1978 Lewis Powell opinion in the *Bakke* case.

There followed an exchange between Judge Friedman and Payton (and then later on that topic with Miranda Massie) that is interesting in retrospect because it addressed a question later of great concern to justices of the U.S. Supreme Court. If diversity is so compelling a goal for the Law School, Friedman asked, why couldn't that goal be achieved by simply expanding the pool of applicants deemed qualified, making it possible to enroll, from that expanded pool, a fully diverse class without classifying by race? But doing that, Payton replied, would oblige the Michigan Law School to change its nature, to cease to be a highly selective institution. Well, Friedman countered, if diversity is so important, why not make that change? The university has the duty, Friedman believed, to devise a race-neutral admissions system; if the achievement of its diversity goals obliged the Law School to adjust its system in a way that would make it less selective, then that consequence might be simply unavoidable. Payton bridled; even a less selective system, he observed, might not result in a racially diverse entering class without some attention to race in the selection process.

Miranda Massie argued that the depressed grades of "black, Latino, and Native American law students" were a consequence of the racism that pervaded the University of Michigan campus. She wanted an opportunity to show that in a trial. She got the trial she so desperately sought, but not for the reasons she had given.

Judge Friedman decided that a trial in this case would indeed be held. It was needed because there were important matters of fact not agreed upon by the parties, and those had to be resolved. The two principal questions of fact that cried out for definitive answers, he thought, were (1) *Did the Law School really apply a racial double standard in admissions?* (2) If so, *how heavily* did the Law School rely upon race in its admissions system? Evidence, testimony, and scrupulous attention to factual detail were needed. A trial was warranted.

That trial, which finally took place in Judge Friedman's courtroom in Detroit in January of 2001, was the substantive kernel of all the legal proceedings in the Michigan admissions cases. Kolbo, Payton, and Massie presented their arguments in turn.[1]

More than half the trial was consumed by the arguments of the Coalition to Defend Affirmative Action by Any Means Necessary (BAMN), arguments whose thrust was that the inferior performance of minority students in law school was largely a consequence of racial bias. Massie presented lengthy testimony bearing upon the alleged bias of the Law School Admissions Test (LSAT), the alleged racist atmosphere at the Law School and its feeder schools, the poverty that disproportionately affects blacks and other minorities, and other matters pertaining to the long history of racial discrimination in the United States. Friedman was patient with her, permitting the presentation of a vast quantity of evidentiary material that was not really relevant to the factual questions regarding the admissions system at the Law School. Massie then provided the setting for what was one of the most decisive moments in the trial.

One of her witnesses was John Hope Franklin, a distinguished and widely admired black historian of race relations in America. "My challenge," Franklin had written, "was to weave into the fabric of American history enough of the presence of blacks so that the story of the United States could be told adequately and fairly." He did that in many writings, most notably in his monumental *From Slavery to Freedom* (1947). He had teamed up with Thurgood Marshall (long before Marshall became a justice of the Supreme Court) and the NAACP Legal Defense Fund (LDF) in developing the sociological case for the historic *Brown v. Board of Education* decision, which brought about the desegregation of the public schools in 1954. Franklin had served as chairman of President Bill Clinton's advisory commission on race. He was a most impressive witness, able to testify authoritatively and dramatically regarding the everyday treatment of blacks in all segments of American society. The whole courtroom hung on his words.

Massie wanted the judge to understand, wanted the world to understand, the irrationality, the ugliness, the plain horror of growing up black in the American South in Franklin's time, the 1920s and 1930s. With her artful questions she led him to relate, as a witness, the painful stories of his youth. This great scholar, more than eighty years of age, told how utterly demeaning his treatment as a youth had been, first in an elementary school in Rentiesville, Oklahoma, a town just for blacks that had no electricity, no running water, not even the simplest amenities. He told what it was like to be a black student in Tulsa, and then later at the almost all-black Fisk University in Nashville, Tennessee.

He recalled that a white faculty member at Fisk, recognizing Franklin's promise, had urged him to apply to Harvard. He recounted what it was like—this recipient of more than 120 honorary degrees—when he was nineteen and went across town to the Vanderbilt University campus to take the scholastic aptitude test then required of applicants for graduate school at Harvard. The examiner came in, asked him what he might want there—and upon hearing that he sought to take the Harvard exam, threw the papers at him. Upon leaving he was asked by a black janitor if he had actually been sitting in that exam room, because he had never seen a black man sitting in that room before. Franklin recalled that the man was "full of wonder."[2]

Franklin also told, with some ironic delight, of how (while subsequently at Harvard and working on a dissertation about free Negroes in North Carolina in the late eighteenth century) he had to do some research at a library in North Carolina, where the librarian explained to him that the building had no place for him to work because the designers of the library had never supposed that anyone of his color would ever seek to work there. And—since he obviously could not sit with the whites in the library, or have books delivered to him by the white library pages—he would have to be given his own key to the stacks, find his own materials, and bring them himself to his table in a separate room. What was humorous, he related, was that white researchers were envious of his ability to get into the stacks while they had to wait for the delivery of the books they had requested. They demanded their own keys! But because not everyone could be given keys to the stacks, his was taken away.

Story after story he told. One was about the occasion on which, seeking to buy a trolley ticket in Nashville, and having on him only a $20 bill, his last bit of cash, he apologized as he handed it to the clerk and said that he could take change in singles or coins, or whatever—whereupon the clerk told him that there was no need for a nigger to give him instructions about how to make change and then set about giving him more than $19 in nickels and dimes, counting it out for him coin by coin.

When he wanted to examine the old papers of former Governor John Winston at the University of Alabama, he was told by the secretary of the director of the archives to enter her office but not to sit down. She left the office door ajar to ensure that he obeyed. When the female director arrived, giving him the needed permission to examine those papers, she added, "They tell me there's a Harvard nigger in the building. Have you seen him?" Her secretary, who had been listening to the conversation through the open door, called out, "That's him!" When the director asked, "Are you the Harvard nigger?" he didn't know what to say. She wanted to know where he'd learned such nice manners, and he told of his school in Rentiesville. "No," she said, "you didn't get those manners in Oklahoma." So he told her he went to school in Nashville, and she said, "That must be it—a good old Confederate state where good manners can be learned." Franklin told the court, in a reflective spirit, how he had wanted to tell her that his mother had taught him his manners, but he was discreet enough to let that pass. This woman concluded their conversation by saying to him that "it would be beyond the realm of possibility" for her to call him "Mister" Franklin. "Reverend, doctor, professor, maybe—but I'm not ever going to call you 'Mister,'" she said; "I don't call black men 'Mister.'"

Outrageous indignity after indignity was described. Perhaps the most appalling was his story about the night before he was to receive the Presidential Medal of Freedom in 1995. He gave a dinner party to celebrate with friends at the private club in Washington, D.C., to which he belonged; he called it a "very wealthy place." Before dinner he noted that two invited friends had not yet appeared, so he went down the grand staircase to the lobby to see if they were there. And as he entered the lobby a white woman walked up to him and presented her *coat check*. He said, "Madam, if you will present that check to one of those uniformed attendants you will get your coat." He concluded, "I walked away. I don't know if she got her coat. I didn't wait to see whether she did." No one in that federal courtroom in 2001, black or white, was left unmoved.

Franklin was a monumental witness. He had driven home the cruelty and the humiliation of discrimination against blacks in the United States in ways that no one who had heard him that day would ever forget. Kudos to Miranda Massie, the BAMN attorney, who had prepared him and drawn out his testimony. But the conduct of southern bigots in the 1930s was not at issue in this trial; the conduct of the University of Michigan Law School in the 1990s was.

John Hope Franklin was cross-examined by Larry Purdy, with gentle courtesy and evident respect. That cross-examination, about which I must say a little here, was the emotional high point of the *Grutter* trial. Purdy exhibited his understanding and penetration; Franklin exhibited his candor and honesty. The exchange was pregnant, mutually gracious, and truly moving.

Purdy began, cleverly but also honestly, by observing that having been raised as Franklin had, in Tulsa, Oklahoma, he, too, had been taught his manners strictly by his mother, and that he was genuinely touched to hear Franklin recount that story about the Alabama librarian who was puzzled by his fine manners.

Then Purdy established, expeditiously and with Franklin's emphatic agreement, that he had lived through a time of racial double standards and that those double standards, which he had reported with such humanity and wisdom, were deeply unjust. "No one," said Purdy, "would know better than you, Professor Franklin, what it would be like to be denied opportunity because of one's race. You were denied admission to the University of Oklahoma?" "Yes," Franklin answered. "They denied me admission because of my race. They didn't use race as a '*factor.*' Race was *it.*"

Purdy asked a series of questions about one of Franklin's many books, a collection of Franklin's shorter writings from 1938 to 1988, *Race in History.*[3] "It was a book," Purdy observed, "about which you, Prof. Franklin, chastised me (when I took your deposition) because I told you I had borrowed it from a library." "Yes," Franklin answered with a grin, "I think you should have bought it." "I will." Purdy promised. "And you remember one sentence in that book that we talked about, in which you were referring to Prof. Carter Woodson at Harvard? You wrote there: 'He had always insisted that men and women should be judged strictly on the basis of their work and not on the basis of their race or the color of their skin.' And I asked you then," Purdy continued, "whether you still agreed with that. And what was your answer?" "Yes," Franklin answered.

The great weight of Franklin's testimony, his well-earned moral authority, was being turned by Purdy, with delicacy and respect, but also with a sure argumentative hand, into a powerful instrument in support of Barbara Grutter's complaint.

Next, questions were put about Franklin's vast college teaching experience. "And do you believe," Purdy asked, "that it is the racial mix at a school that determines the quality of the education received there?" "Well," Franklin replied, "it would depend on the students, what kind of students they were. I'd hesitate to compare educational experiences at different colleges."

Purdy asked about his experiences at Bates College, in Maine, and at the University of Miami, in Florida, two of the 128 schools that had awarded Franklin an honorary degree.

> "At Bates there was a long and distinguished commitment to diversity, not so?"
>
> "Yes," said Franklin, "for very many years."
>
> "And you honor that?"
>
> "Yes."
>
> "In fact, you think the education at Bates, where you taught, is superb—in spite of the fact that it has had, historically, a very small African American enrollment, about 2 percent. But it was still a special place in your judgment?"
>
> "Yes."
>
> "Maybe even a better place than one in which the racial proportions are very different?"
>
> "Yes, if the students are selected with care. I think that the quality of the education students could get would depend upon the purpose for which students of different races were there. So I think that if we just talk about numbers we're missing something. The same would be true at Miami, if they had selected with care. I don't know what proportion they are here or there, but they more than likely recruit more blacks for football at Miami than they do at Bates. I'm not trying to pull Miami down. That's the reality of it. I have an honorary degree there, too."
>
> "Why would being a black athlete at Miami disturb you?"
>
> "For the same reason. Many of these institutions are one-sided as

far as the education of blacks is concerned. When they go out and recruit—they recruit athletes. Here is a university 'X' that has, let's say, forty-five blacks in its student body, and forty of them are athletes recruited for the purpose of playing on their team. I don't think that's a healthy educational institution."

"So I gather . . ."

Purdy began a new question, but Franklin interrupted him: "We're not going to talk about just numbers, and think numbers will do it one way or the other. We have to talk about the purpose of an institution, its mission. We just can't rely on numbers as such."

Another nail was being driven into the coffin of the university's argument for race preference. The drama of this constructive, courteous, probing cross-examination can hardly be conveyed on paper. Purdy continued:

"At the deposition I gave you a hypothetical example, of a young man or woman who is going to graduate from high school next year, the hypothetical case of a student from Grand Rapids, Michigan, and we talked about four colleges. It was easy because there is such a long list of colleges from which you have received an honorary degree. And one of those four is Morehouse College, which is your father's alma mater, correct?"

"Yes."

"And Hope College here in Michigan, and Kalamazoo College here in Michigan, and the University of Michigan. We can all agree that as among those four institutions Morehouse is the most racially homogenous because it's virtually all African-American. Right?"

"Yes."

"But if the young man from Grand Rapids decided he wanted to go to Morehouse—given all his qualifications, letters of recommendation, his talents, grades, test scores, athletic abilities, whatever it is he brings, and he gets accepted at all four of those schools—they are all fine colleges, are they not, Dr. Franklin?"

"Yes."

"If the young man comes to you and says, 'Dr. Franklin, I'd like to go to Morehouse, in Atlanta,' you wouldn't be critical of his decision simply because it's the most racially homogenous of the four, would you?"

"No."

"In fact, he could get an outstanding education at Morehouse, correct?"

"Yes."

"Conversely, if the young man or woman said, 'Dr. Franklin, I live in Michigan and I don't want to go that far away from home, and I want to go to Hope College, and Hope College is more than 90 percent white, you wouldn't be critical if he went there either, would you?"

"No."

"And he could get an outstanding education at any one of those institutions, isn't that true?"

"Yes, he could."

"When it comes to university and college admissions you've been clear, have you not, that you do not support the admission of less qualified minority applicants over more qualified Asian or white applicants?"

"That's right."

Purdy paused to show Franklin a report of which he, Franklin was the author, then read from it:

"'Americans share common values and aspirations. We all share the thirst for freedom, the desire for equal opportunity, a belief in fairness, and the need for a common justice.' Did I read that correctly?"

"That's right. You do well."

"You certainly oppose using different qualifications to permit athletes to come into a school from others who are non-athletes, correct? You oppose that?"

"Yes."

"You oppose using different qualifications for legacies. You don't think they should confront lower qualifications to come into their school, do you?"

"I'll come to the end that you want me to come to, that is, that *I believe in using standards that are standards.*"

"For everyone?"

"Yes. *Yes!*"

CHAPTER 20

The Heart of the Trial: 257 to 1

The central issues in the *Grutter* trial were the alleged facts of race preferences by the university, and if those facts were established, whether giving such preferences was constitutional. John Hope Franklin had been turned into a stunning witness for the case against preferences by Larry Purdy's adroit cross-examination. Even if all that Miranda Massie had claimed about the history of discrimination were true (and much of it surely was), it was not to the point. The Supreme Court had repeatedly held that societal discrimination cannot justify race preferences. Massie's eight-day presentation of an alleged justification was, in effect, a show trial. Judge Bernard Friedman could not base his decision on that account of U.S. history.

A racial double standard is repugnant to us all. Kirk Kolbo (and Purdy, and Barbara Grutter, and the Center for Individual Rights [CIR], and I) was certain that the Law School had been using a racial double standard in its admissions. But could that double standard in the Law School be shown to be a *fact*? John Payton and the university denied it. This conflict was the heart of the trial.[1] The subsequent testimony of the university president, Lee Bollinger, was an eloquent statement of his view of the educational importance of a diverse student body at the Law School. Jeffrey Lehman, dean of the Law School, testified to the same effect. Also testifying for the university was Richard Lempert, a professor of sociology and law, chairman of the committee that had devised the Law School admissions system in 1992. The system formally adopted at that time did not mention numbers or percentages explicitly. It said only that there would be an effort to enroll as many minority students as would be needed to constitute a "critical mass." But how many was that?

Kolbo, conducting the cross-examination of Bollinger, Lehman, and

Lempert, pressed repeatedly for the numerical significance of that key term, *critical mass.* Bollinger had allowed that 2 percent of a class admitted would not be enough. What would be enough? Again and again Kolbo tried to pull from university officials some concrete content for the phrase "critical mass." What really was the size of the minority contingent sought? Can we say even roughly what that number is? The Law School witnesses were canny and evasive; they avoided numbers scrupulously. Kolbo countered: Well, if numbers will not be given, how can we know what a critical mass is? How is it to be *recognized*? Their reply was that it is an amount great enough that individual minority students would not feel isolated in class. Again, Kolbo: And how many would that be? They would not proffer a number.

The original draft of Lempert's committee report had explicitly set the goal of minority enrollment between 11 percent and 17 percent; that was acknowledged, but all such numbers had been removed from the final report. Dean Lehman—a fine scholar; I had recently been his guest at a Passover Seder—came close to giving the game away. Kolbo asked him, "Could 5 percent minority enrollment constitute a critical mass?" Answer: "It is conceivable to me, but it is unlikely." Cat and mouse, around and around. The witnesses held their ground. Did they in truth have some percentage numbers in mind? Probably they did. None could be elicited.

Kolbo also presented overwhelming evidence of the actual use of race preferences by the Law School. He called as a witness the director of Law School admissions at the time of the trial; she was obliged to acknowledge that yes, the race of every applicant was considered as part of his or her file. The former director of admissions, Allan Stillwagon, had resigned when Lee Bollinger became the Law School dean. Stillwagon testified that while he held that office the law faculty had set a clear goal of *10 percent to 12 percent* minority students. Stillwagon had come over from the College of Literature, Science, and the Arts (LSA). He had been an effective leader of its Honors Program. His resignation as director of Law School admissions suggested that he was not happy with those percentage "goals," but he had been the servant of the Law School faculty at large and did not control the matter. Had he been fired as a consequence of his dissatisfaction with the preferences for minority applicants insisted upon by the faculty? That could not be ascertained.

Kolbo, Purdy, and I knew—the evidence made it perfectly clear—the Law School had long been employing a de facto quota in its minority enrollments. If it had not, the fact that each year, year after year, minority students constituted between 10 percent and 12 percent of those enrolled would have been a most extraordinary coincidence. But we did not have, for the Law School, the smoking gun, a document proving *intent*, such as that we had uncovered in the undergraduate admissions system. What we did have was, nevertheless, very powerful. We had the full reports of applications, acceptances, and admissions credentials for all students, minority and nonminority, over a period of years. Some of that information had been delivered to me in 1996, in the form of grids, in response to my Freedom of Information Act (FOIA) request. Four years later those grids were submitted to Judge Friedman's court as Exhibits 15 and 16.[2]

The Law School had apparently decided in 1996 (wisely, from its leaders' perspective) that preparing those grids was not prudent and had ceased doing so. Nevertheless, in the process of discovery before the trial, the CIR had been able to obtain a trove of information about the intellectual and other credentials of Law School applicants, those accepted and those rejected, for five successive years: 1996, 1997, 1998, 1999, and 2000. Although not delivered to us in grid form, this data had been subjected by the CIR to detailed analyses. Charts and slides were then created to exhibit what those numbers revealed. That statistical analysis was the heart of the CIR proof that the Law School not only did use race preferences but also used them to a staggering degree.

Kolbo's star witness, the third of only three, was Dr. Kinley Larntz, through whose testimony this quantitative material entered the trial record. Larntz had been for many years a professor of statistics at the University of Minnesota. He presented ineluctable proof of minority preferences in University of Michigan Law School admissions going far beyond even what we had earlier supposed. The preferential thumb pressing down on the admissions scale, we learned, was much heavier in the Law School than in LSA.

Larntz was examined and cross-examined for two days in mid-January of 2001.[3] Much of his testimony was technical and mathematically complicated, but Larntz, accustomed to teaching statistics, was able to present his conclusions clearly and vividly. He was calm, matter-of-fact, and self-confident. The data were in hand; he had no difficulty analyzing them. I will summarize his testimony here because it is central to all that follows.

Bear in mind that this was a bench trial; the findings of fact in all these matters, after reviewing all the evidence, would be determined by the judge, Bernard Friedman. Friedman is not a mathematician, but he has a keen intellect, and it was evident from his comments and his demeanor that he was following the Larntz testimony closely and grasped it fully.

He often interrupted the witness to raise clarifying questions within the statistical framework Larntz had presented. The judge's penetration as questioner was apparent. Kolbo's key conclusions were underscored by the variety of slides and graphics he had made. Among the grids were those (referred to as the "original" grids) that I had shown to the CIR years before.[4]

The power of the Larntz testimony can be readily grasped by reconsidering these original grids. Recall that the Law School had laid out a matrix of 120 cells, the vertical axis being the undergraduate grade-point average (GPA) of applicants and the horizontal axis being the performance of applicants on the Law School Admissions Test (LSAT). Grids of exactly identical design had been constructed for each ethnic group: African Americans, Native Americans, Caucasian Americans, and so forth. It was therefore easy to compare the responses of the Law School to applicants *by ethnicity*. If, on the chart for Caucasian Americans, a given cell described applicants with a GPA of *abc* and an LSAT score of *pqr*, and there were X applicants and Y acceptances, the percentage of admissions for whites in that category may be readily calculated. The percentage of admissions in that same cell for African Americans, or for Mexican Americans, can be as easily calculated. The acceptance rates by ethnicity can then be easily compared.

The contrasting rates of Law School admissions among the ethnic groups were remarkable. In cell after cell acceptance rates were 2 percent or 5 percent or 7 percent for whites but 74 percent or 85 percent or even 100 percent for blacks or Native Americans.

The disproportion was easy to see, but there was a need to *refine* the data Kolbo had accumulated so as to exhibit more precisely the weight that race preferences were given in Law School admissions. It had to be shown, with respect to applicants from different racial groups having exactly the same credentials in all significant respects, *how* differently they had been treated. How may one accurately and intelligibly *express* the difference in their treatment? This was Kolbo's objective in eliciting Larntz's testimony. There are well-established techniques, using multiple logistic regression equations, to exhibit the significance of numerical comparisons; Larntz was supremely able to present these comparisons as an expert witness. He was a knockout.

Here are his conclusions in summary. Holding all qualifications for admission other than ethnicity (e.g., GPA, test scores, etc.) constant, one may determine, from the data compiled, the probability of admission for members of a given racial or ethnic group, at a given time. Logical regression makes it possible to present these admissions data in terms of the relative *odds* of Group X being admitted as compared with the members of Group Y. This *odds ratio* exhibits the *magnitude* of the preference given to any one group relative to the treatment of some baseline group.

Kolbo's opening request of Larntz was for his general conclusions. Larntz responded, "With respect to ethnicity I found an incredibly large allowance given to members of selected minority groups with respect to their chance of admission." He reviewed the odds ratios for the admission of various ethnic groups, using Caucasian Americans as the baseline. "What I did was construct a statistical model that allowed one to calculate the composite relative odds, combining all the cells for which there is competitive information. From this we could determine the relative odds of admission of one ethnic group compared to another ethnic group."

To appreciate how stunning those actual composite odds ratios were at the University of Michigan Law School, one might consider other odds ratios commonly referenced. For example, when testing a new drug, if one were to find that the odds of success using the new drug are 2.5 or 3 to 1 (using the existing standard therapy as baseline), that ratio would be quite large and would point to a drug certainly worth producing. Any odds ratio of 7 to 1 or higher is huge. Ratios of more than 100 to 1 are simply "off the charts."

Larntz testified that he had determined, using the data the Law School had provided, that the composite odds ratio for the admission of African Americans as compared with whites at the University of Michigan Law School for the years 1996–2000 was 257 to 1. The judge was visibly affected. He asked, "Is this the case for just 1996?" "Well," Larntz answered, "the composite data are from 1996 and 1997 and 1998 and 1999 and 2000."

Kolbo asked him how the size of these relative odds compares generally with other kinds of relative odds in the work he has done as a statistician for more than thirty years. Larntz seemed almost at a loss. He replied: "These numbers are just *big*. I mean they are giant. *I cannot recall any examples of any data sets of any size where I found relative odds of this magnitude.*"[5] Friedman pressed him again: "You think these figures, 257 to 1 for African Americans, really apply in the real world?" Larntz replied, "These are a summary of the information from the grids I was given. So yes, these *are* the real world," causing the judge to sit back and go silent.

Kolbo asked Larntz to focus more closely on the year 1996, the year Barbara Grutter applied to the Law School. What are the relative odds for Michigan residents that year, as compared with nonresidents, without regard to ethnic group? Larntz replied: 6.5 to 1 overall. He then added:

"That's big. That's big relative odds." Kolbo asked whether there was an additional advantage for being a woman? Yes, said Larntz, it was a "favorable factor" but not that great: 1.9 to 1 that year. And the relative odds of the several ethnic groups being admitted *that year*? asked Kolbo. The numbers, Larntz replied with precision, get vastly bigger—257 to 1 for African Americans becomes 513 to 1! For Mexican Americans the relative odds ratio becomes 116 to 1; for Puerto Rican applicants it becomes 72 to 1. Does that hold for the years 1997–2000 also? Larntz did not have the detailed breakdown for each single year at hand, but reported they were all quite similar.

Again Kolbo asked: "What is your overall conclusion and summary from all the analyses that you have done?" Larntz answered, "What I have found is that there is an incredibly large allowance given to minority applicants. Native American and Mexican American and Puerto Rican applicants, and particularly African American applicants, as compared to Caucasian Americans, are given a very, very large preference. You can see that from the original grids for 1996. My statistical analysis quantifies what was in those grids; the original grids yield exactly the same conclusion."

The court session was adjourned. Later that day and the next day Larntz was cross-examined, and there was a continuing exploration of the Law School admissions data; no significant changes resulted. When Kinley Larntz had completed his testimony, the *Grutter* trial was essentially over. The factual questions that Judge Friedman had asked at the outset had been definitively answered.

CHAPTER 21

Vindication

Judge Bernard Friedman issued his decision in the case of *Grutter v. Bollinger* on 27 March 2001. Ninety pages long, it was a meticulously detailed document headed "Findings of Fact and Conclusions of Law."[1]

Friedman first focused on the factual questions that had troubled him throughout: Did the Law School use race in admissions? If so, how heavily had it relied on race in admissions? His answer: "The evidence shows that race is not, as defendants have argued, merely one factor which is considered among many others in the admissions process. Rather, the evidence indisputably demonstrates that the Law School places a very heavy emphasis on an applicant's race in deciding whether to accept or reject."[2]

Friedman examines patiently and then demolishes the claim that all the Law School sought was a "critical mass" of minority students. "While 'critical mass' has proved to be a concept that has eluded precise quantification, [he writes] over the years it has meant in practice that the law school attempts to enroll an entering class 10 percent to 17 percent of which consists of underrepresented minority students." Did the Law School really have specific numbers, or percentages, in mind? Prof. Richard Lempert testified that "critical mass" lies in the range of 11 percent to 17 percent. In the draft of the 1992 admissions policy, when proposed to the law faculty, that range, 11 percent to 17 percent, did appear. But in the policy as adopted those numbers had been omitted. Why? Almost certainly because the law faculty was, collectively, shrewd enough to realize that if, or when, the matter came before a court, the inclusion of percentage numbers would render the "critical mass" theory an obvious facade.

One member of the law faculty, Donald Regan, objected openly to that omission. Regan, a friend of mine and also a colleague in the Department of Philosophy, had been unhappy with the removal of the percentage numbers from the final policy when all knew that that range, 11 percent to 17 percent, was the real target, as evidenced by minutes of the meetings of the law faculty. We ought, Regan had said, retain the percentage targets *"for the sake of candor."* Almost a decade later, with the matter before the court, Judge Friedman read those minutes and noted Professor Regan's suggestion. He said he was in little doubt about the evident absence of candor on the part of the witnesses before him.

> The actual admissions and graduation statistics confirm the law school's commitment to enroll African American, Native American, and Hispanic students in the 10 percent to 17 percent range. . . . From 1973 to 1985 [Friedman refers to one of the trial exhibits], underrepresented minority students constituted approximately 9 percent to 10 percent of the graduating class, and from 1986 to 1999 students from these groups constituted approximately 12 percent to 13 percent of the graduating class. These percentages conclusively demonstrate that the law school considers race in the admissions process, because applicants from the underrepresented minority groups have, on average, considerably lower undergraduate GPAs and LSAT scores as compared to Caucasian applicants and yet, nonetheless, the percentage of applicants from these minority groups who are admitted is roughly equal to the percentage they constitute in the total applicant pool.[3]

Judge Friedman was saying, in effect, "If you won't tell us forthrightly what you mean by 'critical mass,' we can figure it out for ourselves."

Friedman then turned to the question of degree. How great were the preferences given? He wrote:

> Dr. Larntz' cell-by-cell analysis provided mathematically irrefutable proof that race is indeed an enormously important factor. In each year at issue in this case, Native American, African American, Mexican American, and Puerto Rican applicants have been admitted in significantly greater proportions than Caucasian applicants with the same or similar undergraduate GPAs and LSAT scores. As Dr. Larntz noted, this fact is apparent on the face of the Law School's admissions grids. One does not need to undertake sophisticated statistical analysis in order to see it; the statistical analysis simply confirms empirically what the grids suggest intuitively. *The court specifically adopts Dr. Larntz' analysis and his conclusion that "membership in certain ethnic groups is an extremely strong factor in the decision for acceptance."*[4]

The university statistician, Dr. Stephen Raudenbush, tried to show through his testimony that the race-conscious admissions policy in force was essential if the diversity of the student body were to be safeguarded. Friedman used his testimony to confirm the immensity of the preferences given. Evidence elicited from a university witness thus helps to make the case *against* the university. Friedman writes,

> Even the testimony and reports of the Law School's statistician, Dr. Raudenbush, supports this conclusion. [He] testified that the number of minority admissions would drop 'sharply and dramatically' if race were not considered in the admissions process. . . . The percentage of underrepresented minority applicants who are admitted would have dropped from 26 percent to 4 percent in 1995, and from 31 percent to 8 percent in 1996, under a race-blind admission system, . . . in 1997 from 33 percent to 8 percent; in 1998 from 34 percent to 9 percent; in 1999 from 37 percent to 8 percent; and in 2000 from 35 percent to 10 percent. These figures . . . may explain even more plainly than Dr. Larntz' odds ratios and graphs the extent to which race is considered in the Law School's admissions process.[5]

Judge Friedman continues,

> None of these witnesses [referring to the dean and the current and former admissions directors] acknowledged that they have a particular number or percentage in mind. But as the admissions season progresses, the written and unwritten policy at the Law School charges the admissions office with assembling entering classes which consist of between 10 percent and 17 percent African American, Native American, and Hispanic students. Over the years this target has been achieved, and even exceeded, despite the underrepresented minority students' generally lower LSAT scores and undergraduate GPAs.[6]

Friedman notes how race was used surreptitiously. "The court also finds it significant that the dean and the admissions director monitor the Law School's 'daily admissions reports,' which classify applicants by race: . . . how many students from various racial groups have applied, how many have been accepted, how many have paid a deposit. There would be no need for this information to be categorized by race unless it were being used to ensure that the target percentage is achieved."[7]

In conclusion, he wrote, the court finds that the law school "explicitly considers the race of applicants . . . to enroll 10 percent to 17 percent [minorities] in each entering class."[8]

Those are his findings of *fact*. It was next his task to apply the law to these facts. Under the law, the state's use of racial classifications can be tolerated only if the interest being served is compelling and then only if the racial devices are precisely devised to serve that compelling interest. He asks: (1) Is the achievement of racial diversity a compelling state interest, as the university claims? (2) If it is, has the Law School's admissions policy been narrowly tailored to serve this interest? Judge Friedman cites *Bakke* and related decisions in great detail, then concludes that the answer to both of these questions is no.

The upshot, he concludes, is that the university has relied very heavily upon race and has done so in a way that is not lawful. It is unlawful not only because it flies in the face of the Equal Protection Clause of the Constitution but because "it is a plain violation of Title VI of the Civil Rights Act of 1964, which explicitly forbids recipients of federal financial assistance (like the University of Michigan) from deliberately discriminating by race."

In making this last point Friedman was speaking forcefully to one of my major concerns. For years I had been arguing, on academic panels and in public debates, at my own university—even in our Law School!—and elsewhere, that what the university was doing was plainly against the law. That the university did discriminate by race (whatever its motives in doing so) was admitted; Title VI of the Civil Rights Act unambiguously forbids institutions receiving federal financial assistance from discriminating by race. In my lectures I would say, "Look, one doesn't need to be a legal wizard to see how this plainly written law applies. The university is *flouting* it!" Now, at last, a federal judge, having ascertained the facts, had confirmed my argument that the university had been breaking the law. Readers will understand the satisfaction I derived from these findings.

The district court trial of *Grutter v. Bollinger* resulted in a devastating loss for the university, an overwhelming victory for Barbara Grutter. Here follows the entire conclusion of Judge Friedman's findings of fact and conclusions of law:

IV *Conclusion*
The Supreme Court has often stated that "distinctions between citizens solely because of their ancestry [are] odious to a free people whose institutions are founded upon the doctrine of equality."[9] In our history,

such distinctions generally have been used for improper purposes. Even when used for "benign" purposes, they always have the potential for causing great divisiveness. For these reasons, all racial distinctions are inherently suspect and presumptively invalid. This presumption may be overcome only upon a showing that the distinction in question serves a compelling state interest, and that the use of race is narrowly tailored to the achievement of that interest. It does not suffice for the interest in question to be important, beneficial, or laudable; the interest must be *compelling*.

For the reasons stated in this opinion, the court concludes that the University of Michigan Law School's use of race as a factor in its admissions decisions is unconstitutional and a violation of Title VI of the 1964 Civil Rights Act. The Law School's justification for using race—to assemble a racially diverse student population—is not a compelling state interest. Even if it were, the Law School has not narrowly tailored its use of race to achieve that interest. Nor may the Law School's use of race be justified on the alternative grounds urged by the intervenors—to "level the playing field" between applicants of minority and non-minority races—because the remedying of societal discrimination, either past or present, has not been recognized as a compelling state interest.

Accordingly, IT IS ORDERED that plaintiff's request for declaratory relief is granted. The court finds and declares that the University of Michigan Law School's use of race in its admissions decisions violates the Equal Protection Clause of the Fourteenth Amendment and Title VI of the Civil Rights Act of 1964.

IT IS FURTHER ORDERED that plaintiff's request for injunctive relief is granted. The University of Michigan Law School is hereby enjoined from using applicants' race as a factor in its admissions decisions.

IT IS FURTHER ORDERED that the parties' various motions for summary judgment are denied, except that the motion of the individual defendants for summary judgment on grounds of qualified immunity are granted.

IT IS FURTHER ORDERED that the clerk schedule the damages phase of the trial.

/s/ Bernard A. Friedman
United States District Judge
March 27, 2001
Detroit, Michigan[10]

This trial was the only thorough examination of the facts of the Law School's admission system in open court, with testimony and other evidence presented at length and subjected to full scrutiny. This *was* the *Grutter* trial. By its outcome Barbara Grutter and her supporters were fully vindicated. Friedman's decision was immediately appealed by the university.

CHAPTER 22

Petitions Don't Decide Lawsuits

It was universally understood that whatever decisions were reached in the district courts, they would certainly be appealed to the 6th Circuit Court of Appeals in Cincinnati. That court was sharply split on ideological grounds, and this split resulted in a nasty conflict, the details of which I will here summarily recount. It is a complicated story. These next chapters in the saga of the Michigan admissions cases do not reflect great credit on the federal courts. This critical judgment has a threefold ground: the actual concatenation of highly irregular facts, extensive conversations with attorneys involved in the cases, and above all, the published complaints of the judges themselves, some of whom were more than ready to register, within their printed opinions, their great distress about inappropriate conduct by other appellate judges.

First, the setting: Judge Bernard Friedman's order enjoined the Law School from any further uses of race preferences in its admissions decisions. This order came down during the admissions season in the spring of 2001; some admission decisions using race preferences had already been made that spring. The university quickly petitioned Judge Friedman for a delay in the imposition of this injunction, claiming that in view of the fact that the order was to be appealed and possibly overturned, the injunction might cause it irreparable harm if immediately applied. This petition for a stay was denied. Judge Friedman added to his crisp denial, "The court has found that defendants' use of race is indistinguishable from a quota system, and there is no doubt that racial quotas in this context and for this purpose are unconstitutional. Defendants are not irreparably harmed by an injunction that requires them to comply with the Constitution."[1]

The university immediately appealed this denial of a stay to the 6th

Circuit, again on the ground that the harm to the Law School would be irreparable if applicants for admission who might enroll if the admissions system were ultimately upheld could not be enrolled. A panel of three judges (two circuit judges, Martha Daughtrey and Karen Moore, and a district judge enlisted at random) heard this appeal of the denial of the stay. The panel reversed Friedman on this matter and granted the stay. The university was off to a good start.

The appeal of Judge Friedman's decision on the merits of the *Grutter* case would normally be heard, as appeals are generally heard, by a three-judge panel. The losing party may then request a rehearing of the matter before the entire court—called a hearing en banc—but such requests are most often denied. Kirk Kolbo, representing Grutter, was pessimistic about our prospects at the 6th Circuit; this I learned when we discussed the matter privately at dinner on one of his visits to Ann Arbor. The court at that time had eleven active judges and many vacancies. Six of the eleven had been Democratic appointees who were believed to look favorably on the uses of race preferences in admission; five were Republican appointees who were believed to be more likely to condemn the preferences and support Barbara Grutter.

Kolbo and the CIR team decided to take an unusual step. They requested an en banc hearing (of the two cases together) from the outset, skipping over the panel stage. An initial en banc hearing is rare. But in this case there appeared to be a reasonable chance that the request would be granted, partly because it was highly probable that a request for an en banc hearing would eventually be made anyway, and partly because that request might be welcomed by the judges in view of the national importance of the case. From Kolbo's perspective two advantages would flow from an en banc hearing at the outset. First, it would take the case out of the hands of the three-judge panel that had granted the stay of Friedman's injunction, which was pretty surely unsympathetic to the plaintiff's case. The second point was more important. Two of the judges active on the court in the spring of 2001 were planning to retire that summer and would then not be eligible for participation in any en banc hearing—and those two, Alan Norris and Richard Suhrheinrich, were known to be sympathetic to Grutter's quest for an admissions system free of racial considerations. On 14 May 2001 Kolbo submitted a motion requesting an initial en banc hearing on the two cases, *Grutter* and *Gratz*.

The response was odd. Kolbo received what he thought to be a puzzling reply from the 6th Circuit; he was told that the court would postpone any decision on the en banc petition until the parties had filed their briefs.

David Herr, one of Kolbo's partners, who specializes in appellate practice and who was to join Kolbo in argument before the court, was troubled by this response. Delaying that decision about an en banc hearing was likely to cause unnecessary confusion and uncertainty. It smelled funny.

Relations among the judges of the 6th Circuit at this time, it was widely known, were not harmonious. The appeals of the two Michigan cases had been filed in the spring of 2001; they were scheduled to be argued on 23 October of that year. A few weeks before that, a nasty quarrel had arisen within the court concerning a matter totally distinct from our cases. Chief Judge Boyce Martin had issued an order delaying the execution of a convicted murderer earlier scheduled for 12 September. Martin alleged that he had the support of a majority of the active judges in granting this delay, but some of the judges claimed not to have been notified of the request for the stay. Martin's exercise of what some thought dubious authority caused fury in some judges' chambers. One judge accused another of outright lying and would not back down. The brouhaha didn't come to an end until the execution eventually did take place in February of 2002. This quarrel had no substantive bearing on the Michigan cases, but it reinforced an atmosphere of hostility and distrust at that court of appeals.

On 19 October, four days before the scheduled argument in the Michigan cases, Kolbo received a call in his Minneapolis office at Maslon from the clerk of the 6th Circuit. The court, he was told, had just issued an order granting his motion, submitted five months before, for an en banc hearing. That hearing was now postponed from 23 October and rescheduled for 6 December 2001. We were all baffled. Kolbo had tried to nudge the court during the summer by writing a letter; he had received no response. Terry Pell, at the CIR, was convinced that something inappropriate was going on.

The order scheduling an en banc hearing was issued after Judges Suhrheinrich and Norris had taken senior status during the summer. By delaying the order for an en banc hearing until after those retirements, that hearing of the Michigan cases—a suspicious person might suppose—was being rigged. Nine judges now remained, of whom six were widely believed to be leaning toward support of the university.

What troubled Pell also troubled me. Even John Payton, at his office in Washington, D.C., was perplexed; he had first been informed of the change of schedule (we later learned) by a phone call from a reporter! Something wasn't kosher.

Meanwhile, events around the country brightened our long-term prospects. It was becoming more and more likely that the Supreme Court of the United States would agree to hear the appeal of the Michigan cases, assuming, as we did, that we were likely to lose our appeal in Cincinnati. Sharp differences had developed among several of the circuit courts around the country, differences that could be reconciled only by the Supreme Court. The 5th Circuit Court in New Orleans, as you will recall, had ruled against race preferences in 1995 in the *Hopwood* case at the University of Texas, whereas the 9th Circuit Court in San Francisco had ruled in 2000 in support of the diversity defense of preferences at the University of Washington Law School. Then, as the date of our hearing in Cincinnati grew closer, the 11th Circuit Court in Atlanta in August of 2001 struck down the preferential admissions policy at the University of Georgia. That university, not pleased by its prospects in view of what might be called "bad facts," decided not to appeal its case. The Michigan cases thus appeared to be the only remaining available vehicle for action by the U.S. Supreme Court on a matter requiring their judgment.

On the morning of 6 December 2001, having arranged to have my classes taught by a colleague, I took the four-hour drive to Cincinnati with my friend Matt Graff. It was a gray day, raining when we got to Cincinnati. A large crowd was expected at the Potter Stewart Federal Courthouse, one much larger than the fourth-floor courtroom could possibly accommodate. I had the two tickets Pell had provided. We arrived early. The student rally organized by the Coalition to Defend Affirmative Action by Any Means Necessary (BAMN)—buses had delivered people from all over the country—had not yet gotten under way. Standing in front of the building, huddled under umbrellas, were two men I immediately recognized: Lee Bollinger and Marvin Krislov, general counsel of the university. As their tickets had not yet been delivered, we chatted for a few minutes in the rain, and then Matt Graff and I went in. Bollinger didn't actually enter the courtroom until quite a bit later. He and Krislov sat in the same row in which we were seated but across the center aisle. We were on the left, directly behind the table of the CIR team of Kirk Kolbo, Larry Purdy, David Herr, and Terry Pell. On the right side was the table of the university team, John Payton its chief. Ted Shaw, who was to present the arguments of the NAACP Legal Defense Fund (LDF), and Miranda Massie, representing BAMN and allied organizations, were also at that table. I infer that Payton controlled the distribution of the time the court had allotted to that side.

One could sense, as well as hear, the excitement of the audience. At 1:30 p.m. the nine judges took their seats on the podium before us, and

Chief Judge Martin, from the central seat, welcomed the audience. He started by expressing his own agitation about this rather extraordinary hearing. He acknowledged in his affable, Kentucky manner that this was far from an everyday affair and explained how the court session would proceed. The appeal of the undergraduate case, *Gratz v. Bollinger*, would be heard first. Herr would argue for the appellants, Jennifer Gratz et al.; Payton would argue for the respondents, the University of Michigan; Shaw would argue for the intervenor, the LDF. The court would then turn to the second case, *Grutter v. Bollinger*. Payton would argue for the appellants, the University of Michigan, Massie on behalf of the intervenors, and then Kolbo would present the argument for the respondent, Barbara Grutter.

An overflow room, to which the proceedings were being televised, had been provided. The noisy crowd of students from around the country, led by Shanta Driver, was outside the building in the rain hoping to influence the proceedings with their chants: "They say Jim Crow! We say 'Hell No!'"; "Affirmative Action is on the way! Long live the fight of MLK!" The judges in our courtroom could not hear them.

Herr, an experienced appellate litigator from the Maslon firm, started by arguing against the Duggan decision in *Gratz*. The most glaring constitutional flaw in the undergraduate admissions system, he pointed out, was its crudely mechanical nature: *twenty points awarded automatically to every minority applicant.* One of the judges interrupted him to point out that the Selection Index plan, currently in force, did not reserve seats for minority applicants as the previous system did. Was that not a step forward? Herr replied that the admissions system adopted in 1998 had the same result. It didn't really matter whether you call the seats "protected." If the system has the practical effect of a racial quota, it is no better than a quota. Herr seemed to have satisfied, or at least silenced, his questioner.

The Selection Index system, Herr argued, which awarded minority applicants twenty points automatically, was no different in practice from the grid system it had replaced. Duggan had found the grid system, revealed in the documents I had received from the university years before, plainly unconstitutional. But the overall position of the 6th Circuit Court of appeals regarding the Duggan decision, and the peculiar distinction between the two systems upon which Duggan had relied, never was made clear.

Next, Payton, defending the Duggan decision, sought to soften up the court. He did not focus on any particular feature of the undergraduate system, emphasizing instead the great merit of diversity in the large as an educational goal, even as an educational necessity, and thus a compelling state interest. Years later scientific studies were to render this claim of educational merit highly dubious. But at that time and in that appellate context, Payton's defense of the Duggan decision in *Gratz* was artful, as was his critique, later in the day, of the Friedman decision in *Grutter*. Among all these superb appellate attorneys, John Payton was the star that day. I did not agree with him. His defense of racially preferential systems offended and troubled me—but he presented that defense so reasonably, so graciously, that no one could claim that he didn't serve the university effectively. Later that day I told him so. (Much later the university repaid his dedication shabbily.)

Shaw would later become the president and chief counsel of the LDF. Payton eventually became one of Shaw's successors and in that role served well the cause of minority interests. As I was writing these pages, I received notice from the interim president of the LDF (of which I have, however inconsistently, never ceased to be a member and supporter) sadly advising me that John Payton had died. He was a splendid man, a keen and eloquent advocate.

It was Shaw's turn, representing Detroit students and the LDF. He presented the *remedial* argument in support of the preferences given by the university. They were justified, he argued, by the past behavior of the university itself. He pointed out, correctly, that when the University of Michigan began its preferential program years before, diversity was not the objective. The university announced at that time it was seeking to *compensate* for the oppression of years past. That compensatory argument was rejected by the Supreme Court in *Bakke*, but it ought not be rejected in this case, Shaw said: it is the past conduct of the university that justifies this remedy.

In my view the earnest efforts of the University of Michigan, over recent decades, to recruit minority students and to retain them, seriously undermines this compensatory argument. Even the judges, except for Eric Clay, one of the two black judges on the bench, did not seem to take it seriously.

The CIR appeal of Duggan's opinion in the *Gratz* decision was never resolved by the 6th Circuit Court. The university's appeal of the *Grutter* decision did receive a definitive result at the 6th Circuit. The sharpest conflict that day in Cincinnati was between Payton, attacking Judge Friedman's decision, and Daniel Boggs, the feistiest and perhaps the keenest of the judges. When Boggs pressed Payton about the striking numerical contrasts revealed in the Larntz testimony, Payton had a difficult set of facts to defend. He argued that what really counted was the holistic way in which each individual applicant was considered; that, he said, was the real heart of the Law School's admissions system.

Boggs asked him, Would not Barbara Grutter have been admitted to the Law School if she were black? Payton responded not by evading the question but by seeking, once again, to appeal to justice in the large. "That's probably right," he answered, and continued: "If Barbara Grutter were black she would have had a completely different set of life experiences. Then the answer to your question would be yes. . . . Race matters in the United States. If a black woman had an application that looked like Barbara Grutter's, she would be a different person, with different life experiences, one who could make a different contribution to the Law School class." Boggs was tenacious, Payton sharp.

Miranda Massie was bluntly political in her attack on the Friedman decision. She began by telling the court that she had brought with her 50,000 petition signatures in support of a reversal of that decision. It was a bad move. Judges want their decisions to be seen as based on the law and the record before them. As far as the law was concerned, her petitions were irrelevant; the consideration of them would be a violation of court rules. The chief judge interrupted her. "Petitions don't decide lawsuits, Ms. Massie. We are the judiciary. We are not a legislative body or the executive branch. Petitions are not of any benefit to us."

Massie then tried to explain that although diversity had apparently become the principle of chief interest to the courts, it is racial integration that is the truly central objective. Racial diversity is not compelling, she said, unless it is connected to racial integration. Her colleagues at the table on the right side of the courtroom, also seeking a reversal of Friedman's decision, were manifestly pained by her remarks. Success could only come, they knew, on the basis of the diversity defense.

Judge Boggs's subsequent questions brought to the surface what was a partly hidden and rarely acknowledged deficiency of preferential admissions programs. How do we know, he asked Massie, when we have attained racial integration? She answered: when "rough proportionality" between the percentage of minorities in the population at large and in the Law School have been achieved. Until we reach that goal, she said, we haven't gone far enough.

The argument concluded with Kolbo delivering an orderly, persuasive defense of the Friedman decision. He emphasized the enormous size of the preferences given by the Law School, summarizing the astounding odds ratios of the Larntz testimony. Some judges on the court, he acknowledged, would seek to defend the Law School by relying on Justice Powell's opinion in the *Bakke* case. But even if that is the law, he said, what the University of Michigan Law School had been doing was not in compliance. Justice Lewis Powell had suggested that the quest for diversity might justify a "plus factor" for some applicants; the Law School was using not a plus factor but an outright double standard by race, and the figures proved it. The educational value of diversity, which earlier in the proceedings Payton had so eloquently praised, is not enough. Even if racial diversity is a good thing, Kolbo concluded, our desire for it cannot justify a program of deliberate racial discrimination by an agency of the state.

The outcome of the hearing, as we had thought likely in view of the makeup of the Court, went sharply against us. In the case of *Grutter v. Bollinger* the decision of Judge Friedman in the district court was reversed by the 6th Circuit Court of Appeals. His injunction prohibiting the Law School from considering race and ethnicity in its admissions decisions was vacated.[2] The majority opinion was written by Chief Judge Martin and joined by Judges Eric Clay, Guy Cole, Martha Daughtrey, and Karen Moore. They held, as we had expected, that the Law School's quest for a "critical mass" of minority students was in full accord with the Powell opinion in *Bakke,* which (they said) justifies a "plus factor" for the sake of diversity. They held that this was the law of the land and that the University of Michigan Law School had not violated that law.[3]

Dissenting were Judges Alice Batchelder, Ronald Gilman, Eugene Siler, and Daniel Boggs. The fiery dissenting opinion of Boggs, joined by the others, begins with his judgment that the program at issue in the Law School was "a straightforward instance of racial discrimination by a state institution."[4] The noble motives of those who propound unconstitutional policies, he wrote, "cannot save those policies, just as some segregationists' genuine belief that segregated education provided better education for both races" could not save racial segregation in the schools.

Judge Boggs calls attention to the great weight of the Law School's preferences. "Even a cursory glance at the Law School's admissions data reveals the staggering magnitude of the Law School's racial preference."[5] After reporting many details of the system he concluded, "It is clear from the Law School's statistics that under-represented minority students are nearly automatically admitted in zones where white or Asian students with the same credentials are nearly automatically rejected. Indeed, the Law School concedes that its racial preference is sufficiently heavy that three out of four under-represented minority students would not be admitted if all students were truly considered without regard to race."[6]

Judge Ronald Gilman, whose position was less predictable than that of the others, added a sharp dissent of his own. The Law School policy, he said, could not be justified by any of the opinions in *Bakke* because it amounted to precisely what *Bakke* had condemned, a two-track system.

> The primary problem with the Law School's admissions policy is that the 'critical mass' of minority students that it seeks to enroll is functionally indistinguishable from a quota. Whether viewed as a percentage or as an absolute number, the consistency in the minority student enrollment demonstrates that the Law School has for all practical purposes set aside a certain number of seats for minority students. . . . The 'critical mass' therefore appears to be a euphemism for the quota system that *Bakke* explicitly prohibits.[7]

A two-track system is created because "the Law School gives grossly disproportionate weight to race and ethnicity in order to achieve this critical mass."[8]

No response was given by the 6th Circuit Court to the appeals in *Gratz,* which was puzzling. But there were four votes, not three, supporting Judge Friedman in *Grutter.* The closeness of this appellate decision soon became a sensitive matter for procedural reasons. Therein hangs a painful tale.

CHAPTER 23

Why It Smelled Funny

Judge Daniel Boggs, as his opinion made evident, was outraged. He was indeed unhappy about the result of the *Grutter* appeal, but that was not the cause of his outrage. The majority, by five to four, had held that the court was bound by Justice Lewis Powell's opinion in the *Bakke* case. "We find," Chief Judge Boyce Martin wrote for the majority, "that the Law School has a compelling state interest in achieving a diverse student body." That diversity defense, as presented by the University of Michigan, was in fact as Chief Justice William Rehnquist of the U.S. Supreme Court was soon to show, a facade, a sham. Judge Bernard Friedman's decision in the district court—conclusions reached after an exhaustive trial of the facts—should have been affirmed, Judge Boggs believed. It had been reversed, he thought, to advance certain ideological convictions. But decision making in which some judges are motivated by their political convictions is not rare; that also was not the reason for his outrage. He could accept defeat.

Judge Boggs was outraged because he became convinced that this defeat was *engineered*. It was apparently the product of grossly improper machinations within the 6th Circuit Court of Appeals. It was, from Boggs's perspective, a *scandal*, a shameful misuse of the powers of the court (and even a violation of the rules of the court) by Chief Judge Boyce Martin.

Here is the basis for his anger: whether a case is to be heard by the court en banc, in place of the normal three-judge panel, is a matter that, if arising, must be decided by a vote of all the judges of the court. But when Kirk Kolbo, on 14 May 2001, had submitted the motion to have the two cases heard from the start by the full court, that motion was *not* put before the judges of the court. Had it been, the two judges who planned to take senior status during the summer and who were strongly opposed to the race preferences at the University of Michigan, would probably have postponed their retirement in order to retain their entitlement to participate in the probable en banc hearing. Boggs believed that Martin had maneuvered to avoid the normal procedures that would likely have produced a different result.

Three judges (Karen Moore and Martha Daughtrey and the third randomly chosen district court judge) had heard the appeal of Judge Friedman's injunction prohibiting the continued use of race by the Law School and had vacated it. In the normal course of events that panel would have continued to hear matters related to the Friedman decision. The district court judge would normally have been replaced by one of the 6th Circuit judges, selected at random by the clerk of the court. That did not happen. What did happen was this: the district court judge on that panel was replaced by the chief judge—by an order of the chief judge himself!

Kolbo's petition had arrived on 14 May. The chief judge at that time issued an order, in the name of the court, stating that this motion had come "before the court" (although in fact only he had seen it) and would be held in abeyance until the parties' briefs had been filed, at which time the court would decide whether the case would be submitted, as normally, to the three-judge panel or to the en banc court. This was the order that had so greatly puzzled Kolbo and Terry Pell. In fact, Kolbo's petition was not circulated to the judges of the court at that time.

On 1 July 2001 Judge Alan Norris took senior status. All the briefs of the parties had been filed by 30 July, but still Kolbo's petition was not circulated. Judge Richard Suhrheinrich (whose vigorous opposition to race preferences was widely known) took senior status on 15 August. Then at last, on 23 August, Kolbo's petition was referred to that specially constituted panel: Moore, Daughtrey, and Martin. That was the first time, according to Judge Moore in her concurring opinion, that she learned of the petition for an en banc hearing.

When Martin deliberately refrained from advising the other judges of the appellate court that the initial en banc hearing was a matter to be determined, by sitting silently on that request from Kolbo until after the two more conservative judges, Norris and Suhrheinrich, had taken senior status, which meant they were no longer active on the court, the chief judge had ensured the result he had plainly wanted. With those two judges off the list of active judges, he knew that a clear majority of the remaining nine judges who would sit en banc shared his position in support of the preferential programs.

Whether there was an actual violation of the rules of the court shortly became the focus of bitter dispute. But even if there had been no technical rule violation, this chain of events pointed to the chief judge having used his powers, knowing what he knew, to manipulate the result in this case.

If the full court had retained the eleven judges active at the time the Kolbo motion had been filed in May, the outcome might have been quite different. One could not know certainly that it would have been different, but in the light of the five-to-four vote after the hearing on 6 December, it seems probable that had Norris and Suhrheinrich been participating as members of the en banc court, the appellate decision would have gone the other way. The impact on the university and on the law would in that case have been historic. Judge Boggs could hardly contain his fury.

Indeed, he did not contain it. He added to his vigorous dissenting opinion (in which he explains why the diversity defense of preferences as a "compelling state interest" must fail) a "Procedural Appendix" that created a storm of argument and counterargument. In that appendix, after reviewing the suspicious chain of events, Judge Boggs wrote: "I have been on the court for 16 years, and I do not recall an initial hearing en banc in my tenure. The concatenation of the irregular panel, the withholding, by whatever mechanism, of the motion addressed to the court, and the later granting of that motion in haste, are matters for which other members of the court"—he withholds the name of the blameworthy party—"are certainly not responsible."[1]

Judge Eugene Siler, who opposed the preferences and had also dissented, wrote separately, saying: "I concur in the dissent by Judge Boggs on the merits. I write separately for the reason that I do not concur in the addition of the procedural appendix, not because I question its accuracy, but because I feel that it is unnecessary for the resolution of this case."[2] He also expressed pained regret for the intemperate remarks that Judges Moore and Eric Clay included in their responses to Judge Boggs's procedural appendix.

Judge Moore was furious in turn. She wrote, "In publishing their Procedural Appendix, I believe that Judge Boggs and those joining his opinion have done a grave harm not only to themselves, but to this court and even to the Nation as a whole."[3] Disagreements in principle among judges are often legitimate and do not undermine public confidence in the court; such differences are unavoidable. But, she argued, Judge Boggs had gone far beyond that. He had publicized disagreements over the internal workings of the court. These procedural matters, she insisted, were peripheral to the issue before us. The only reason Judge Boggs thought it important to put these matters in the formal record was "to declare publicly the dissent's unfounded assertion that the majority's decision today is the result of political maneuvering and manipulation. Boggs believes that the decisions of this court are not grounded in reasoned argument but in power, and that the judges of this court manipulate and ignore the rules in order to advance political agendas. . . . I am concerned that my dissenting colleague's actions will severely undermine public confidence in this court."[4]

Judge Moore, troubled by the fact that the court was now obliged to wash its dirty linen in public, contended that the ability of the court to perform its judicial duties "is imperiled when members of this court take it upon themselves to 'expose to public view' disagreements over procedure. The damage done by such exposés," she argued, "is the fault of those who report them." Judge Boggs's conduct in the present case, she concludes, "is nothing short of shameful."[5]

Judge Clay, an ardent supporter of the Law School's admissions system, also replied angrily to Boggs's procedural appendix. It was, he wrote, "an embarrassing and incomprehensible attack on the integrity of the Chief Judge and this Court as a whole."[6] He accused Boggs of adopting a tactic under which the procedural issues raised would cast permanent doubt on the substantive outcome reached. This tactic did not deserve to be dignified by response, he said—whereupon he proceeded to respond. "It is ludicrous to think," he wrote, that the chief judge would "single out any one particular case and maneuver the system for a particular outcome." Nothing that he [Chief Judge Martin] did was improper, contended Judge Clay, and "it is unfortunate that the dissent has chosen to stoop to such desperate and unfounded allegations, which serve no useful purpose."[7]

What actually did motivate Judge Martin in taking the steps he took in this case one cannot know. "The Devil himself," as a famous English judge wrote long ago, "knoweth not what goes on in the heart of a man." But the series of actual events in the handling of this case are known and are there to be examined. What we ought to infer from them readers may judge for themselves.

Was Judge Boggs right to publicize this matter? In my judgment he was. As best I can make out, considering all the arguments, Judge Moore was technically correct in holding that no established rules of the court were actually violated by the chief judge. And the resulting quarrel may have indeed undermined in some degree (as she alleges) public confidence in the integrity of that court. She would have the matter remain one for internal discussion and dispute. But things surely did smell bad. I believe that Judge Boggs was right about the facts, that his fury was justified, and that his public explanation of that fury was healthy in the long run. Judge Alice Batchelder, who joined Boggs and supported him, may have put the matter most wisely in her brief dissent. She wrote:

> I concur in Judge Boggs' careful and scholarly dissent, including the exposition of the procedural history of the case. In her separate concurrence, Judge Moore expresses the belief that by revealing that history, Judge Boggs—and I, by concurring—undermine the legitimacy of the court and do harm to ourselves, this court and the nation. I believe that exactly the opposite is true. Public confidence in this court or any other is premised on the certainty that the court follows the rules in every case, regardless of the question that a particular case presents. Unless we expose to public view our failures to follow the court's established procedures, our claim to legitimacy is illegitimate.[8]

That was where matters stood in May of 2002. Shortly thereafter Kolbo, for the CIR, appealed to the Supreme Court of the United States to reconsider the case of *Grutter v. Bollinger.*

CHAPTER 24

Back on the Home Front

The Michigan cases were destined, almost from the first, to wind up before the U.S. Supreme Court. Michael Greve, president of the Center for Individual Rights (CIR) when I was first asked about the materials I had received from the university in response to my Freedom of Information Act (FOIA) request, was searching widely for a case that could be pushed to the highest level. A test of the University of Michigan admissions systems appeared a promising candidate. As *Gratz* and *Grutter* made their way upward through the hierarchy of the federal courts, it seemed ever more likely that their final resolution would come only before the High Court.

The Supreme Court did agree to hear them. They were argued before that Court on 1 April 2003; the decisions were issued on 23 June 2003. That passage and its outcome I will recount shortly. I had hoped earnestly for Supreme Court review. I believed that the tangle of opinions in the *Bakke* case had badly muddied the waters. It was inevitable that the Supreme Court would speak on the matter. When its justices did, when they confronted squarely the unmistakable conflict between the Equal Protection Clause and race preferences, I was confident that such preferences in the United States would be brought to an end. But as the cases were advancing through the courts, all I could do was continue the battle against race preference in my own way, with argument and essay. Since the story I am telling is mine as well as that of the cases, I interject into the legal report some adventures of my own in these efforts.

There were some heated arguments on television. The CBS newsmagazine *60 Minutes*, after reviewing the reports of the evidence likely to be submitted in the Michigan cases, decided to devote an episode to them. The reporter was the late Ed Bradley, who handled the entire investigation in a way neatly suited to the *60 Minutes* style, flashing back and forth from one to another point of view. His editing exhibited the combatants—mainly myself and Lee Bollinger—in a sharp intellectual conflict that could be readily appreciated by a broad television audience.

Bradley was fair; he showed Bollinger great respect and gave him the first words and the last. He included clips of interviews with Jeffrey Lehman, the Law School dean, and Elizabeth Barry, one of the university attorneys. On the other side he had the plaintiffs, Jennifer Gratz and Barbara Grutter, and me. CBS titled the segment "A Negative on Affirmative Action." It was that, surely.

I was pleased by the piece. It is likely that Lee Bollinger was not. For the first time nationally appeared these two vulnerable, highly intelligent complainants, who appealed to the television audience not only with their argument but also because they were endearing, soft-spoken, and eloquent. It was good television—controversial, fast moving, and in places even funny.[1]

The CBS team came to Ann Arbor with mountains of filming apparatus, cameras and lights and audio equipment the likes of which I had never seen before. They interviewed me in my home (first rearranging the living room furniture) and in my office. They also filmed me as I was lecturing in class (on a subject that had nothing whatever to do with university admissions), only a bit of which was included in the finished production.

Bradley supervised the entire enterprise. Was he seeking to make a political or moral point? Hard to say. Bradley was black, but no words of his gave favor to one side or the other; he allowed the disputants to speak for themselves—first Bollinger, and then I, made our cases. He gently scorned Barry, a university attorney and spokeswoman, when she sought to defend the undergraduate admissions system's use of points for various merits. Interviewing Barry, Bradley held in his hand the sheet listing the point awards, which I had given him. He noted that the applicant was awarded one point for an outstanding essay and twenty points for being a minority.

> "Is that the university's view that being a minority is twenty times more important than writing an outstanding essay?"
> "We look at all the diverse characteristics of an applicant."
> "But you do give twenty points to minorities and only one point for the essay, don't you?"

"That's just not the way we look at it."

"How you look at it is determined, I would think, by how many points you give."

Next he interviewed me and then Dean Lehman. I am seen showing Bradley the grids that demonstrate the huge advantage given to minorities in Law School admissions, the same figures that were to play so big a role in the Larntz testimony at the *Grutter* trial. The scene then changes to Lehman contending that diversity is their sole and overriding aim. "So race has nothing to do with your admissions?" Bradley asks. "No," says Lehman earnestly, "nothing at all." I then point out that cell after cell after cell in which the percentage of whites admitted is miniscule, the percentage of blacks admitted is huge. I reel off the numbers and sum up: "It's wrong, Mr. Bradley, it's morally wrong. Their motives may be good, but that does not make it right."

In the segment, Bradley then interviews a group of University of Michigan students. One of them is a young black man who reports that he had been a poor student but was now doing well at the university. He observes that he would never have had a chance to improve had he received no special advantages in the first place. "What do you say to Jennifer Gratz, who lost her chance at Michigan?" Bradley asks him. His honest reply is touching: "I'd say that it's not fair, but that's just the way it is." Another student, the white editor of one of the campus periodicals, reports that the admissions preferences contribute to the silent disrespect confronted by many black students on campus.

Bradley returns to President Bollinger, who speaks again to the importance of racial diversity. So important is it, he urges, that it justifies some deliberate attention to race. "But how much attention?" Bradley asks. "How large is the edge you give?" Bollinger waffles. "Largeness or smallness is not the important point." Bradley does not respond, but the camera cuts back to me, pointing to the grids and saying, "Look at these numbers! Come on!" That *60 Minutes* segment really was a negative on affirmative action.

Bollinger left the University of Michigan to become president of Columbia University, in New York City, in 2001. At Columbia a few years ago he named the noted journalist and staff writer at the *New Yorker*, Nicholas Lemann, dean of the Journalism School. Lemann had played an interesting role in the admissions controversy. On 18 December 2000 Lemann, whose convictions are reasoned and liberal, published in the *New*

Yorker a long and penetrating report of the struggle in progress at the University Michigan. It was titled "The Empathy Defense." He recounts at great length his interviews with Bollinger and with me.

Lemann had called me from New York, asking if he might have a conversation with me when he came to Ann Arbor, as he soon would. Having read some of his work, I knew enough about him to be confident that he was unlikely to be sympathetic to my side of the argument, but I welcomed him. One might worry, in such circumstances, about what an enterprising journalist would do with the material he gathered, how biased his accounting might be. I decided nevertheless to open myself to him completely, to show him the materials I had gathered and to take my chances.

The interview took place in my study. I cannot say that I converted him, but I believe I did make progress in persuading him that the arguments on my side of the case had genuine merit, perhaps even a great deal of merit. The essay he produced was entirely fair to me and provocative. Bollinger he likewise treated evenhandedly. The finished essay showed that he got just what he was seeking.

Just prior to his coming Lemann had published a book, *The Big Test: The Secret History of the American Meritocracy*, of which I had read reviews. The big test referred to in the title is the SAT. Lemann reports its history and its impact. He recognizes the merits of the test in predicting student performance in college but concludes that it has become a fetish and even an instrument for class segregation. Advocates of race preferences often condemn the SAT, contending that such standardized testing cannot recognize the merits of minority applicants and that the reliance placed on it in admissions by universities is an indirect bias against blacks and other minorities. The reverse is true. Repeated scientific analyses have shown the SAT and similar tests *overpredict* the performance of minority applicants and thereby give them an advantage, not a handicap, in the admissions competition.[2]

Lemann was too knowledgeable to make that claim, but he is, in the large, a supporter of affirmative action as practiced at some elite universities. He might have regarded me as his opponent, but we shared many judgments about the first-tier universities, and we certainly shared a respect for the truthful reporting of facts. So he and I got along most agreeably.

His essay in the *New Yorker* is first-rate. He gives full credit to all parties for their earnest defenses. He reports the difficulties I encountered (and have earlier recounted here) when seeking information about our

University of Michigan admissions system. He explains, with a clarity exceeding that of most reporters, why the *Bakke* decision of 1978 was so unhelpful, its tangles so likely to lead to conflicting interpretations.

About the documents I had received from the university he wrote:

> The admissions system on display in Carl Cohen's FOIA documents may not be a violation of the letter of the *Bakke* decision, since Michigan did not set aside a precise number of places for minorities. But by putting applicants into different categories of consideration on the basis of their race it does appear to violate the spirit of Powell's decision, which decries "racial classifications."[3]

Lemann was sympathetic to the university's plight in being obliged for legal reasons to rest its case on the diversity argument, although a deeper argument, "the empathy defense," is what truly moved its officers. He observes, rightly, that the fact that the diversity argument is advanced as a legal necessity "doesn't mean it's insincere." He's right about that too. Bollinger, whom he depicts with warmth and admiration, really means it when he talks about the educative importance of diversity—even if, in fact, it is a defense of preferences that in my judgment cannot ultimately succeed. Diversity does not have the many happy consequences it was then thought to have, and we now know more about its negative consequences as well.

The Michigan cases, Lemann's *New Yorker* essay observed in December of 2000, could come before the Supreme Court toward the end of the next presidential term. His prediction was dead-on.

One feature of the Lemann piece greatly tickled me. The essay included a large photo—quite a nice shot of me, I thought—relaxing on the Michigan campus. At some distance behind me, leaning against a huge segment of a Corinthian pillar, stands my dear friend Barbara Grutter. It was a nice touch.

60 Minutes and the *New Yorker* having capitalized on the University of Michigan controversy, NBC could not be far behind. I received a call from one of its producers, asking if I would come to New York for an interview with Tom Brokaw, at that time the anchor of the *NBC Nightly News* program. I was told that he was planning an extended review of the Michigan cases, which (it seemed probable) would wind up before the High Court. They would show it, I was told, on a *Dateline* special. They did so, but I have lost the videotape they sent me.[4]

That interview—just the two of us conversing earnestly in a comfortable setting—was quite satisfying. The arguments I defended were the same as those I had presented elsewhere. But one feature of this occasion stands out in my recollection.

The setting was unusual. NBC's headquarters are in Rockefeller Center in New York City, at Fiftieth Street and Fifth Avenue in Manhattan, two blocks from the Waldorf Astoria Hotel at Fiftieth and Park Avenue. My NBC host assured me that a room would be reserved for me at the Waldorf the night before the scheduled meeting with Brokaw, and I was pleased by that because having stayed at the Waldorf on many occasions, it had become a favorite hotel of mine. I invited a close friend of mine, James Lipscomb, a well-known documentary filmmaker in New York, to join me for dinner at the hotel. His home is in Tarrytown, an hour north of the city, so we agreed that he should stay over in my room at the Waldorf. He and I have sailed often together in his sloop, *Brisk Living*—in Biscayne Bay and in the Bahamas, to Martha's Vineyard and Nantucket. Reliving old times, we had a lovely evening.

Being a filmmaker, Lipscomb was interested in how NBC would handle the interview; he had asked me to ask Brokaw if he might attend the interview as a silent observer. Brokaw gave his permission without hesitation, so Lipscomb came with me the next morning to the recording studio. It was not located in Rockefeller Center but in the private tower of the Waldorf Astoria, where NBC maintained a suite for just such occasions. When the time of our appointment came, therefore, we had only to ride one elevator down to the grand lobby and walk to another portion of the lobby for an elevator servicing the luxurious private apartments.

The interview itself was entirely agreeable. The setting was comfortable, the cameras all in place when we arrived. We introduced ourselves to Brokaw when he came in, and after some small talk he and I began, with cameras on, to discuss the University of Michigan admissions systems and the cases. Whether Brokaw shared my views about race preference I could not say, but he certainly heard me out with apparent interest and sympathy. His questions were intelligent and provocative. The conversation became, on my side at least—it is in my DNA—animated. It was fun, and I came to like Brokaw very much.

Lipscomb sat silently on one side of the room the whole time, watching everything intently. When the interview had ended and all formalities concluded, we departed with good wishes to Brokaw and the filming crew and returned to our room in the hotel. We were eager to exchange our impressions of the event.

Lipscomb's observations provoked my introspection. He was emphatic in reporting that he had never, in our many years together, seen me as I was during that interview. "When the conversation turned serious," he said, "and you began to press your arguments upon him, you changed completely. It was a Carl—electrified, intense—that I had never seen. Your passion *transformed* you."

Probably a fair report. Nicholas Lemann had described me, not harshly, as a "combative intellectual." I am that. My passion is part of what makes me a good teacher, an effective lecturer. Students enjoy my classes. When I become involved in argument (as I did in that Brokaw interview) my manner becomes lively, my speech forcible. And what principle is more worthy of passionate defense than the equal treatment of the races?

Thinking about this yesterday, I dug up an old videotape. Several years before, I had gone to Washington, D.C., to testify in support of the Equal Opportunity Act of 1995. The hearing was before the U.S. House of Representatives Subcommittee on the Constitution; its chairman, Rep. Charles Canady of Florida, had invited me to give that testimony, which I did proudly. C-SPAN taped the testimony of all the witnesses, and that was the tape I watched yesterday. I had forgotten how animated I had been that day. When an argument of moral importance needs defense I change, even physically. Lipscomb was right.

Watching the testimony given that day, 7 December 1995, I had another recollection that touched me. I was seated at a long table before the subcommittee, alongside several other witnesses. I was the first to testify and was allotted fifteen minutes; I had prepared my words carefully so as to waste not a moment of that time. Sitting immediately at my right shoulder, next to testify, was a fine lawyer whom I met that day for the first time and was later to come to know much better: John Payton, of happy memory.

On the campus of the University of Michigan the argument over the uses of race preferences in admissions did not diminish in intensity. The announcement of Judge Bernard Friedman's *Grutter* decision in March of 2001, sharply critical of the university, was a cause of widespread dismay. Prof. Richard Lempert, who had been a key witness for the university at the *Grutter* trial and the chairman of the committee whose report became the controversial admissions policy of the Law School in 1992, announced in the *University Record*, in April of 2002, that affirmative action was in serious need of defense. He did this in part by attacking the critics of race preferences such as myself. I responded to Lempert in the *University Record* of 22 April 2002.

Presidents John F. Kennedy and Lyndon Johnson, I wrote, had used the term "affirmative action" to describe actions taken to *eradicate* discrimination by race. The Civil Rights Act of 1964 had precisely that same objective. Title VI of that act explicitly and unambiguously forbids institutions receiving federal financial assistance, such as our university, from discriminating by race, color, or national origin. Those like myself who find the university's race preferences immoral and unlawful do not oppose affirmative action in its original, honorable sense. We oppose preference by race.

The continuing confusion over the meaning of the words *affirmative action*, I continued, is an obstacle to clear thinking in this arena. Because the words originally referred to programs designed to *eliminate* preferences by race, using the same words now to *identify* preferences by race turns their meaning upside down! The phrase *affirmative action* is understandably agreeable in many ears; it had been kidnapped.

Many varieties of affirmative action do not involve any sort of race preference—and are morally right. For example, reconsidering employment qualifications, or the examinations given to appraise candidates for promotion, seeking to detect inadvertent discrimination are entirely wholesome forms of *affirmative* action. Establishing boards and commissions to ensure equal opportunity is realized and discriminatory activities penalized is *action* that is appropriately affirmative and morally right. But the phrase *affirmative action* is now loosely used, in conversation and the press, to refer only to deliberate preferences for minorities. When I am asked, "Do you oppose affirmative action?" how should I respond? As the term is now widely understood I do oppose it; as the term was originally understood I most certainly do not. Making this distinction clearly is a never-ending burden.

In 1995 I published a collection of essays (most of them having appeared earlier in *Commentary*), titled *Naked Racial Preference*. The publisher of that essay collection, Rowman and Littlefield, wanting the intent of that title to be more clearly conveyed, insisted upon adding the subtitle "The Case against Affirmative Action." The book was that in one sense, to be sure, but not in the other. Sharing as I do the liberal spirit of the originators of affirmative action who detested race preference, I now regret that I allowed the book to be given that subtitle.

In 2002, on the University of Michigan campus, this confusion was particularly troubling; I felt the need to clarify the matter in my response to Lempert's irritating essay in the *University Record*. Arguments in which the opponent is caricatured for easy demolition are called "straw man" arguments by logicians. Lempert wrongly claimed, in a classical straw man argument, that critics of affirmative action (such as Carl Cohen) sought admission systems based entirely on test scores and grades. I wrote, "No such views need be held by one who finds racial discrimination intrinsically wrong and hurtful to the groups preferred." Did I believe that a university might justly and wisely weigh, in considering applicants for admission, merits that could not be quantified? Yes, of course. Achievements not recognized by grades or test scores? Absolutely. Character and determination? Certainly. Nonquantitative considerations may surely be considered, if considered for all applicants equally. Deciding upon admissions in a highly selective university is a complicated business. We who object to the university's ethnic preferences do not intend to tell admissions officers how to conduct that business. We insist only that *racial* considerations must be excluded. I quoted Thurgood Marshall's brief in arguing the great case of *Brown v. Board of Education*: "*Distinctions by race are so evil, so arbitrary and invidious, that a state bound to defend the equal protection of the laws must not invoke them in any public sphere.*"[5]

What Marshall believed in 1954 I believe still. Professor Lempert and some in our university's administration, I wrote, "are prepared to invoke distinctions by race to advance results they think good. Decisions by high federal courts may one day reign in their mistaken zeal." I was confident that the Supreme Court would take the Michigan cases; that far my prediction was correct.

CHAPTER 25

Some Personal Questions

The *Journal of Blacks in Higher Education* (*JBHE*) is a periodical with which I have had a relationship for many years. Recall that it was a 1995 article in the *JBHE* that triggered my inquiries into the details of admissions preferences at the University of Michigan. When the latest issue of the *JBHE* comes to my desk, I browse through it immediately, confident that I will find some material of interest: nuggets of black history, reports of black achievements, speeches and remarks by black educators and political leaders that are sometimes thrilling, always provocative. It is a rewarding periodical in part because of its inventive inquiries and its lengthy and detailed reports of great quantities of data pertaining to the circumstances—the progress and also the defeats—of blacks in institutions of higher learning.

I have also published in this journal. The editors of the *JBHE* support what they call, following common public practice, "affirmative action"—by which they mean preferences in admission, employment, and the like. Its editors fully accept, however, that there are rational arguments on the other side. They and I have maintained good relations over the years. My outspoken public opposition to race preferences brought me often to their attention.

Early in 1997 the editors of the *JBHE* published a set of responses to a proposal that they were entertaining. A compromise had been proposed; they did not support or reject it, but asked some of those who had been writing on the topic to express their judgments. The compromise (altogether hypothetical, of course) was this: affirmative action would be "mended" by allowing race-based preferential admissions at the level of undergraduate admissions but not beyond that and not at all in graduate or professional programs. They published a number of responses, among them mine, which was critical. The proposed compromise, I wrote, is unjust. Preference by race is unfair because it gives advantage and imposes disadvantage on the basis of considerations having no relevance to the admission in question; it is unfair when the preference is given to eighteen-year-olds on precisely the same grounds that it is unfair when given to twenty-two-year-old graduates, or to anyone. The age or status of those preferred has no bearing whatever on the *justice* of using racial categories. Color of skin, I wrote, is never an acceptable ground for preference; that was certainly true when preference was given to whites, and it is no less true when preference is given now to blacks, or to anyone else. Race is simply not an appropriate factor in college admissions, at the undergraduate level or at any other level.[1]

Late in 2001, when *Gratz* and *Grutter* were moving toward consideration in the 6th Circuit Court of Appeals, the editors of the *JBHE* wrote me once again, asking if I would be willing to respond to a series of questions; my responses, they thought, would be of substantial interest to their readers. The questions they wanted to put to me, they acknowledged, were of a personal sort. Would I mind that? I would not mind that at all, I replied; I was honored by their interest and would be pleased to cooperate with them. In their winter 2001/2002 issue they published those questions and my answers under the title "About Personal Consequences in the Academy When a Professor Opposes Racial Preferences." At the top of the essay appeared this "Editor's Note": "Philosophy professor Carl Cohen of the University of Michigan is nationally recognized as a leader in the campaign against racial preferences in higher education. The *JBHE* considered that his efforts might be valuable in revealing faculty attitudes and treatment when a scholar on campus challenges affirmative action. We asked Professor Cohen to state his position on preferences and to describe the reactions of faculty and students to the controversial and often unpopular position he has taken."

I began by expressing enthusiastic support for the policy professed by the University of Michigan: "nondiscrimination and equal opportunity for all persons regardless of race, sex, color, religion, creed, national origin or ancestry in employment, educational programs and activities and admissions." I followed with a compressed version of my arguments against race preference: that it was morally wrong, that it was a violation of the Constitution and of federal law, and that it was damaging to the minority groups preferred. I expressed my appreciation for the respect shown me by the editors and then turned to each of their questions in turn (here somewhat abbreviated):

1. Do you have any regrets over your role in this case?

Yes, I have some regrets. I sorely regret that my efforts have led some to perceive me as an opponent of the civil rights movement in which I have been active for decades, or as hostile to minority enrollment at the University of Michigan. Nothing could be further from the truth. I much regret that my active support of racial justice, locally and nationally, has been obscured by heated dispute over current systems of race preference. I also regret that I was obliged to adopt a posture of opposition to the University of Michigan, which I love. What I want for it is honor; I attacked only those policies that I think bring it dishonor.

2. Why did you feel it necessary to challenge the university's admissions policies in the first place?

Preference by skin color is unjust and intolerable. When my university acts unjustly, even if meaning well, I cannot be silent. Even my great affection for the University of Michigan will not cause me to silence myself.

3. What were the reactions of fellow faculty members and friends to your efforts?

They have been mixed. Some think me deeply wrong and criticize me sharply and publicly; others think me right and express appreciation for my presentation of a civil libertarian position with which they heartily agree. Our arguments on the Michigan campus have been intense and serious, but for the most part not angry. Those who defend race preferences do so with honorable purposes, but such preferences, in my view, are inconsistent with the constitutional guarantee that no person in our country may be denied the equal protection of the laws. Judging from the quantity of public statements by faculty members, mine is a minority view. But there are a substantial number of faculty members who fear that if they were to support my criticism of minority preferences they will be called racists. If a secret ballot were taken on our campus, what would be the result? I would still be in a minority, I think, but it would not be a small one.

4. Did other members of the faculty support you in these efforts?

Some did. In public my supporters have been very few; privately they have been numerous.

5. Did you ever discuss the matter with President Bollinger, a strong supporter of affirmative action?

Yes, on a number of occasions. We have long been friends. He is a fine scholar, with deeply held moral principles. I like and respect him. We have discussed these matters, mainly by correspondence, in thoughtful and friendly spirit. In view of the litigation in progress, it is inappropriate for me to report the content of this correspondence.

6. How did black students in your classes react?

I don't discuss the matter in my classes, unless pressed by students to do so. I have had many black students, some of whom have been superb scholars. There has been (at least openly) no special response of black students to my arguments. Many students, black and white, think me wrong; many others believe I am right. This difference of view is what you would expect in a university like this one.

7. Were you ever shunned or did you face hostility on campus for what you did?

Shunned? Never. Face hostility? Yes, some, but mainly from students who did not know me and were led, by their zeal, to call me nasty names. But my record, my good name, is well known here at Michigan. I have not found such hostility to be deeply troubling. I honor the conviction and intensity with which my critics have pursued their aims.

8. Did liberals on campus think you were a Judas?

I believe not. I have defended liberal causes all my life. My liberal colleagues have not attacked my character or indicated in any way that they thought I had betrayed them. Not one of my colleagues has treated me with disdain or disrespect. My rejection of race preference, after all, is not an illiberal cause.

9. Why do you believe that you are not harming blacks, but helping them, when most black students on campus appear to have a different opinion?

When preference is given to a racial or ethnic group, the individuals who are preferred usually do benefit, of course. But the group as a whole is damaged. Performance—professional skill, scholarly attainment, and so forth—has absolutely nothing to do with race or skin color. Therefore, when race is used in judgment, the process of admission, or of appointment, is corrupted. The standards for selection that bear upon performance are inevitably diluted. The result is that those persons preferred by race (in university admissions, for example) are likely to perform less well than those not preferred. This is not because of their color, of course, but because they were selected in a corrupt way. The upshot is that the actual performance of the preferred group taken as a whole becomes, and is seen to be, relatively inferior. Outstanding minority students and scholars are undermined. The good name of the group itself is besmirched by ethnic preference. The stereotype of ethnic inferiority—which is a canard!—is thus reinforced by race preference. This is a cruel irony. The advocates of race preference mean to do good, we know, but in fact they do great harm. The damage done by race preference to minorities and to race relations will, I fear, take many years, perhaps generations, to undo.

10. Final question: Are there times when you wish you had not embarked on this project?

No. There have been difficult days, to be sure, but because Michigan has the prominent place that it does have among the public universities, the battle over preferences here is likely to lead to a great cleansing of our public institutions. I believe (although I may be badly mistaken) that these Michigan cases will lead to a ruling from the Supreme Court so forceful and so unambiguous that race preference in public universities across the country must come to an end. That prospect I do not regret.

Many honorable people believe that to overcome racism we must use race in reverse. I think that deeply mistaken. If the game is injustice, turnabout is not fair play. I believe that if we are ever to heal the wounds of racial conflict, ever to leave behind the cruelties and stupidities of racism, we must transcend racial categories, resolving, with all our hearts, backed by the force of law to the extent that is feasible, never again to allow matters of importance to be decided on the basis of skin color. We advance toward that achievement only by ending all invidious uses of race. Completely. Not someday, but now.

I admire the editors of the *JBHE* for publishing these responses as they did.

My prediction that the Supreme Court would unambiguously reject race preferences as a part of its resolution of the Michigan cases turned out to be quite mistaken, although a clear and forceful rejection of preferences by that Court may yet one day come, as I earnestly hope.

I was also mistaken, as I was to learn later from the scientific research of Richard Sander[2] and others, in accepting the common assumption that individuals who receive preference in admission are thereby benefited. In fact, the *mismatch* between the preferred applicants and the institutions—colleges and professional schools—to which they are admitted, but would not have been admitted had race not been considered, results, we now know, in substantial damage to the careers of those preferred applicants. They perform less well in their studies, rank poorly among their peers, and are hindered in professional advancement. Race preference is not only *wrong*, but also has consequences that are *bad*.

CHAPTER 26

Preparing for the Big Event

The decision of Judge Bernard Friedman in the district court sup-porting Barbara Grutter was reversed by the 6th Circuit Court of Appeals in May of 2002. In August of that year Kirk Kolbo, Grutter's attorney, submitted to the Supreme Court a petition for a writ of certiorari, the formal request that a case be reviewed by the High Court. Thousands of such petitions are submitted every year; fewer than a hundred are granted. We had long believed that our prospects for Supreme Court review were good. The issues involved were (and are still) of wide interest and con-siderable importance. Moreover, conflicts among the appellate courts on the matter of race preferences strongly suggested the need for a resolu-tion from the Supreme Court. Nevertheless, we were elated when, in the case of *Grutter v. Bollinger*, certiorari was ultimately granted.

As we pressed for this outcome, some puzzling procedural problems had been facing us. Strong as we believed our case against the Law School preferences to be, we thought our case against the undergraduate pref-erences was stronger still. Partly this was because we could show that the University of Michigan Office of Undergraduate Admissions had explicitly *intended* to grant race preferences (as the grids sent to me by the university revealed), and partly it was because in the undergraduate system there was an *automatic* award of twenty points to every minority applicant, which pretty clearly shows systematic racial discrimination. But the undergraduate case, *Gratz*, which we had appealed to the circuit court in Cincinnati, still awaited action. Why the 6th Circuit had so long sat silently on the *Gratz* case we could not know, although the internal problems of that court, which Judge Daniel Boggs had exposed, caused us to fear additional irregularities in the handling of that case. We very much wanted the two cases to be heard together by the Supreme Court.

Was this possible, even though the *Gratz* case had not yet been decided at the circuit court level? Yes, but it was a long shot. The Supreme Court has the authority to hear any cases its justices wish to hear, after they have been appealed, and they can do so even if the lower courts have not yet decided the matter. They can grant a writ of certiorari before the case has been concluded at the lower level—a process, rarely used, called "cert before judgment." Supreme Court Rule 11 warns, however, that such petitions will be granted "only upon a showing that the case is of such imperative public importance as to justify deviation from normal appellate practice and to require immediate determination in this Court." The last time this cert-before-judgment rule had been invoked was in 1974, when President Richard Nixon fought for control over the Watergate tapes and the resulting dispute over the scope of presidential power and privilege had caused the Supreme Court to intervene. Important as we thought the admissions preferences were, they hardly rose to that level of concern. But we also knew that on occasion the Court had granted cert before judgment when a case not yet decided at the circuit court level presented issues closely related to those in another case that the Supreme Court had already agreed to decide. It was certainly worth a try. Kolbo formally petitioned the justices, asking them to reach down and pull the *Gratz* case from the lap of the silent 6th Circuit and then to resolve it along with the *Grutter* case, invoking the cert-before-judgment rule. If both cases were not before the Court, we argued, the justices would not be able to see the full picture of admissions preferences at the University of Michigan.

On the other side, the University of Michigan understandably opposed the granting of certiorari in the *Grutter* case. If the Court did not grant cert in that case, the ruling in Cincinnati would stand; preferences would be permissible in the four states of the 6th Circuit—Michigan, Ohio, Kentucky, and Tennessee. But John Payton and the university, to their great credit, also agreed with the Center for Individual Rights (CIR) that if the Court were to hear one of the cases it ought to hear them both. That, Payton wrote in his petition, would give the Court the opportunity "to provide more helpful guidance" to lower courts and to universities.

On 2 December 2002 the Supreme Court resolved the matter. The Court would hear both the appeal of the CIR in the Law School case and, invoking the cert-before-judgment rule, the undergraduate case as well. *Grutter* and *Gratz*, two separate cases not consolidated, would be heard on the same day: 1 April 2003. Kolbo would argue both cases for the CIR.

That was a busy winter for me. With the two cases coming to their final resolution, I was called upon to speak and to argue about them in many contexts. In early February I gave a talk to the local chapter of the NAACP in Ypsilanti, an audience mostly black. Many blacks thought that university admission preferences were an advantage justly enjoyed by their ethnic group and therefore fought for them. I sought to persuade this audience, perhaps with partial success, that for blacks generally the preferences were hurtful, a burden and not a benefit. Some individual applicants might be helped but the cost to the group in reputation, and the cost to the society in divisiveness and hostility, made preferences a bad bargain.

Making this point, however, as a white university professor addressing a black audience, was somewhat delicate. In explaining what was not in the interest of the black community it would be easy to offend. I put the matter before my audience in the following way.

Do this thought experiment, I said. Suppose that *height* were made a critical consideration in university admissions. Suppose preferences were widely given to short applicants, to overcome the disadvantage that short stature imposes. That is absurd, but suppose it. Some short applicants, minimally qualified, would be admitted because of that extra credit given them for being short; shorts overall would, *as a group*, prove to be weaker students; many of them were plainly not as well suited for academic work as their peers selected on grounds more consistently related to scholarship. With remedial instruction, patient tutoring, some wincing and some winking, the specially admitted shorts are pushed through to graduation somehow, whereupon administrators express great pride in the improvement of their "stature numbers."

Some of the most talented applicants and graduates will of course always be short; there is obviously no conflict between shortness and intellectual excellence. But where shortness has been systematically introduced into the selection process it must, indubitably, dilute the importance of intellectual excellence in that selection. The shorts *will* be poorer students as a group, not because they are short but because they (unlike the others) are on average selected on a lower intellectual standard, by hypothesis. That is what preference by height entails. The outcome? Everyone soon learns to be suspicious of the credentials of noticeably short students, or short doctors, or short lawyers. The suspicion will apply to *all* shorts because no one can be sure—not even the shorts themselves—whether their selection for some demanding position was made in virtue of their intellectual attainments, or (in some part) because of their shortness.

Expressing suspicions of shorts publicly will, of course, be unacceptable. To recognize the inferior performance of the short group (it will be said) shows prejudice, deep-seated antipathy for shorts. But that is not true. On the premise that the selection is known to have been deliberately diluted by the consideration of some physical characteristic, members of groups in whose favor that dilution was designed are inescapably suspect.

The individual talls displaced by such preferences would harbor justifiable resentment, no doubt. But talls as a group do not suffer. Shorts as a group, however, suffer mightily. Poorly prepared shorts, marginally qualified shorts who would not otherwise have been admitted, would rarely fail to recognize their own relative unsuitability for the roles into which they had been thrust. The burden upon them would be heavy. Tall colleagues and classmates, knowing or reasonably presuming the part that shortness had played in their selection, would resent them and be silently scornful.

But *all* shorts, whatever the level of their true talent, would find themselves under an intellectual cloud, a cloud created by—could it be?—their height! Even when shorts perform extremely well, in fact that performance will be seen (by talls and shorts alike) through a veil of skeptical expectations. There is rational ground to suppose that each short had been given favor because she was short; behind her back she will be referred to as the short candidate, often with a knowing wink. Any given short actually selected can never know, for sure, what accounted for her selection. In the real world short folks may be deeply thankful that we have not done this terrible thing to them.

Black students and black professors have not been so fortunate. Skin color has no more relation to intellectual excellence than height; but the most prominent group characteristic of blacks has been made their onus; what would happen to shorts in our absurd thought experiment does happen with painful frequency to blacks in your college and mine.

At the Detroit School of Law in the spring of 2006 I gave another talk about the Michigan cases. There again I strove to call to the attention of my mixed-race audience how damaging, how *demeaning* preference had become. Stephen Carter, a law professor at Yale, in his book *Reflections of an Affirmative Action Baby* and in his earlier essays, had written with justifiable sarcasm about what he calls "The Best Black Syndrome." As a student he had been selected, as black scholars are not uncommonly selected, as the best available black. Might he have been not merely the best black, but the best—without regard to skin color? That was a merit he was given no opportunity to earn. In his essay "The Best Black, and Other Tales," he wrote:

This dichotomy between the "best" and the "best Black" is not something manufactured by racists to denigrate the abilities of professionals who are not white. On the contrary, it is reinforced from time to time by those students who demand that universities commit to hiring some pre-set number of minority faculty members . . . saying, "Go out and hire the best blacks." And it is further reinforced by faculty members who see these demands as nothing more than claims for simple justice.[1]

Speaking at this time in Detroit, where the great majority of citizens is black, I could illustrate the humiliating consequences of racial considerations with an event the members of my audience would themselves have noted. Not long before, in August of 1997, a new president was appointed at Wayne State University, in Detroit. Here is how it was reported in the *Ann Arbor News:*

> In a time when affirmative action is being criticized throughout the United States, Wayne State University has appointed its first African-American President. In December 1996, Wayne State's former President, David Adamany, announced his retirement. Seven and a half months later, at an August public Board meeting, Irvin Reid was named the university's ninth president, making history by being the first black face among his eight predecessors . . . Wayne State Board of Governors Chair Denise Lewis said. . . . "He's one of the leading African-Americans in higher education because he's been in higher education for some 30 years."

Is this not painful? Insulting? Condescending? Will the elimination of race preference be good for President Reid? Good for Stephen Carter? I'll say. Good for them and good for black scholars and administrators everywhere. Individual members of minorities may benefit from favors, of course, but the minority group is not helped; it is subverted by preference. A corrupted selection process tied to race inevitably promotes invidious racial comparisons; disparities are seen by all as the result of that race preference, so that the nasty stereotypes of racial inferiority are *reinforced* by the preferential devices that were supposed to give support to previously disadvantaged groups.

National Public Radio had (until 2008) a program titled *Justice Talking*, in which they arranged for formal debates conducted by the Annenberg Foundation. I went to Philadelphia in February of 2003 to debate another professor, Eric Dyson, who took the opportunity to give his audience a lecture on the historic maltreatment of blacks. He was certainly right about the maltreatment, but the lecture was out of place in what was supposed to have been a debate on the merits of the Michigan cases, *Grutter* and *Gratz*. Moreover Dyson was melodramatic in what I thought to be an intellectually disreputable way. His opponents, he several times remarked, were citizens of the United States of Amnesia. He was simply a demagogue.

The debate was held before a substantial audience in a hall on the campus of the University of Pennsylvania. I listened to the recording of that debate just the other day; the audience participated actively, and the resulting exchanges were quite revealing. At one point an Asian American member of the audience confronted Dyson with the claim that the preferences for blacks result in significant disadvantages for Asian Americans. The antagonism between the African American professor and his Asian American critic became heated, suffused with race on both sides. When I was given the opportunity to speak I observed that quarrels of just this sort are the almost inevitable product of programs in which government benefits are awarded to one or another ethnic group. Each group is driven by that policy to press for an enlargement of its slice of the pie, with unhappy consequences for the society as a whole. Dyson's arguments for preference, presented with great flourish, had little merit; I was cheered by the response of the audience to the case I presented against race preference. That debate was broadcast on National Public Radio on 30 March 2003, two days before the argument at the Supreme Court.

I was confident that Barbara Grutter and Jennifer Gratz would prevail at the Supreme Court. I was well acquainted with the facts, the numbers, the arguments, and the constitutional issues. Each of the nine justices of the Court had a well-known track record on these matters, and most of them were known to be hostile to racial classifications. The chief justice, William Rehnquist, and Justices Antonin Scalia and Clarence Thomas were bitter foes of race preferences, certain votes for us. Anthony Kennedy was not as passionate as they, but he, too, had voted against preferences in other contexts and never for them. He had made it clear in another case that he thought the argument for preferences based on diversity (which was anticipated) was without merit, "trivial."[2] Justice Sandra Day O'Connor was not a certain vote for us, but I had studied her opinions with care, and I was convinced that she would not tolerate the blatant preferences the university had been awarding minorities. Joining Justices Rehnquist, Scalia, and Kennedy in a 1990 case, she had agreed that the only recognized state interest so compelling as to justify racial classifications was the need to remedy the effects of earlier racial discrimination by that same agency. But the University of Michigan's preferences were not being defended as a remedy for its own earlier discrimination. Diversity was the only justification being offered, and Justice O'Connor had plainly said that diversity (in the viewpoints of radio broadcasters) is "not a compelling interest. It is simply too amorphous, too insubstantial, and too unrelated to any legitimate basis for employing racial classification."[3] In the sphere of employment her antipathy to racial preferences had been plainly exhibited in *Wygant,* the schools case recounted in Chapter 5. I thought O'Connor would pretty surely be with us.

So, in my private calculations, I counted five votes for us, and possibly a sixth or maybe even a seventh. The sixth vote might come, I conjectured, from Justice Ruth Bader Ginsburg, whom I knew. She had supported preferences in other contexts, but she was deeply committed to the support of civil liberties. Long before, in the 1970s, Ginsburg had been general counsel for the American Civil Liberties Union (ACLU). I was on the National Board in those years, and from time to time she would meet with some of us—her employers, really—to explain her views about matters potentially on our docket. She was impressive. I could not help thinking that one so sharp in so many spheres would come at last to see that the diversity defense of admissions preferences was constitutionally inadequate.

The possible seventh vote, a long shot, was that of Justice John Paul Stevens. He had expressed his agreement with much of the university's case, but he was a maverick. It was he who had written in *Bakke* that the University of California, an institution receiving a great deal of federal financial assistance, was explicitly forbidden by the Civil Rights Act of 1964 to discriminate by race, which its admission preferences at the U.C. Davis Medical School had certainly done. It seemed possible, though not at all probable, that he would revert to this position when the matter came before him once again.

Those sixth and seventh votes were vague possibilities, but the five votes of justices who could not tolerate racial discrimination seemed solid to me—so much so that during those weeks and months in early 2003, when called upon to discuss these highly controversial cases coming soon before the Court, I would say forthrightly that I was indeed quite confident that *Grutter* and *Gratz* would prevail. I would sometimes say that I would be happy to wager a steak dinner on the outcome.

I made that offer in a debate at our own Law School about six weeks before the scheduled argument at the Supreme Court. My opponent at that time was Jonathan Alger, an attorney from the university counsel's office.[4] Far more sophisticated than Dyson, my younger colleague had argued with me in defense of race preferences on more than one occasion. This time, in a great hall known as 100 Hutchins, our audience consisted mainly of law students and faculty, with whom the exchanges were thoughtful and penetrating.

In front of this large audience I offered my wager once again: a steak dinner to you, Jon Alger, if the university prevails, and a steak dinner to me if it does not. How confident of the university's victory he really was I cannot say, but with a big smile he accepted my wager and shook my hand; the audience was delighted.

The former dean of the Law School, Terry Sandalow, with whom I disagreed about the wisdom of preferences (as I explained earlier), did on one occasion express his prediction of the likely outcome, the two of us being alone in his house. He, who had been a clerk to Justice Potter Stewart at the Supreme Court long ago, opined correctly that my speculative hopes about votes six and seven were quite unlikely to be realized. He observed that all the justices are lawyers and are by long training sympathetic to the needs of lawyers and the concerns of good law schools. He thought the justices would have too respectful an opinion of the University of Michigan Law School to find against it. The Law School will win, he said. But the system of preferences at the undergraduate level is difficult to defend. The Court, he predicted, would split the cases, deciding *Gratz* for the CIR and *Grutter* for the university. I told him I thought that highly improbable. No steaks this time; we were just speculating over a drink.

As the date of the Supreme Court argument came closer, I faced the problem of gaining access to the courtroom when our cases would be argued. There are about 350 seats in that courtroom in the Supreme Court Building, but most of them are designated for particular persons or persons of special status: members of the press, members of the justices' families, members of the Supreme Court Bar, members of the U.S. Senate and House of Representatives, and others. The number of seats remaining for the general public, when cases as controversial as *Gratz* and *Grutter* are to be argued, is well under one hundred. I wanted one of those seats.

One can be reasonably sure of getting a ticket if one gets into the queue early enough. But that line outside the Supreme Court building begins to form, in circumstances like these, more than two days before the tickets are to be distributed. Day and night, rain or shine, one must wait in line. I would not do that.

The CIR, as one of the principal parties in the cases to be heard, would surely be given a small number of tickets. I planned to go Washington, D.C., for the day, hoping (but having no assurance) that my ticket would be provided by the CIR. I did get a ticket, but not from them. It happened like this.

Some weeks before the scheduled day of argument I received by telephone an invitation from Langley High School, in McLean, Virginia, a suburb of Washington, D.C. Langley takes advantage of controversial Supreme Court cases to enrich the education of its students by having, each year, a series of discussions and lectures about some important Supreme Court case pending. Seniors study and research the issues and even stage their own mock argument before nine judges—local lawyers who assume that role. The arguments, discussions, and lectures all come to a head on what is called Case Day. For the year 2003 the cases selected were, understandably, *Gratz* and *Grutter*. Case Day would be 31 March, the day before the actual hearing at the Supreme Court.

The caller asked if I would be coming to Washington, D.C., for the argument. If I were, they would appreciate it if I would participate in the Case Day activities by giving a talk about the cases and discussing them with students. Others would be coming as well (including former solicitor general Kenneth Starr and the wife of Justice Scalia); there would be a big reception that evening, and they were confident that I would find Case Day at Langley an exciting event. They could not provide an honorarium, however, nor could they pay for my plane fare to Washington, D.C. But they could provide a ticket to the courtroom! As I recall, the school had been given two tickets by the Court, and the students had agreed to use one of those tickets to bring me to Langley. I was honored and lucky. I would have accepted the invitation without the promise of a ticket; with that promise I was absolutely delighted to accept. I could make the trip to Washington, D.C., as I did, with a ticket to the courtroom assured.

Case Day at Langley High was indeed a stimulating occasion. I enjoyed it, and (bearing in mind that I was quite confident of our ultimate success) it gave me the opportunity to rethink and to reformulate the issues to be heard formally before the Supreme Court the very next day.

I had never before been to a session of the U.S. Supreme Court. As a tourist, long before, I had visited the courtroom—but this was to be the real thing. The atmosphere that morning—1 April 2003—was electric. Judges Patrick Duggan and Bernard Friedman were there, of course, and

Senator Carl Levin, whom I had long known as a member of the ACLU of Michigan. By this time the ACLU had swung fully behind the university position on preferences and Senator Levin with them. Believing, mistakenly in my view, that the preferences were beneficial to minorities, the officers of the ACLU had submerged their commitment to universal equality with the honorable intention of doing good. Jennifer Gratz's family was also in the courtroom, but only because her relatives had the stamina to wait in line for forty-eight hours, under a tarp in the cold rain, for tickets. Also in the audience—every seat was taken, of course—was Roger Clegg, my much-respected friend and colleague from the Center for Equal Opportunity, who was then and remains today a penetrating and tenacious critic of race preference. I was seated roughly in the middle right of the large courtroom. Two rows directly in front of me sat Lee Bollinger.

CHAPTER 27

The Big Event

Grutter v. Bollinger was heard first. The Center for Individual Rights (CIR) was the appellant in that case, so Kirk Kolbo opened the argument crisply: "Barbara Grutter applied for admission to the University of Michigan Law School with a personal right guaranteed by the Constitution that she would not have race counted against her. The Law School intentionally disregarded that right by discriminating against her on the basis of race, as it does each year in the case of thousands of individuals who apply for admission."[1] The University of Michigan is an arm of the State of Michigan and therefore has, Kolbo said, "a solemn obligation to treat all members of our society equally" and without preference for some on the basis of race.

In the course of his presentation Kolbo was interrupted by Justices David Souter, John Paul Stevens, Ruth Bader Ginsburg, and Stephen Breyer, all of whom signaled, by their questions, their inclination to support the university's quest for racial diversity. That was to be expected; those justices were never thought likely to take Barbara Grutter's side. Much more troubling were the questions and responses of Justice Sandra Day O'Connor, whom everyone knew to be the critical, central member of the Court. Early during Kolbo's argument she expressed her discomfort with his strong position. "You are speaking in absolutes," she complained, observing (what Kolbo would never have denied, of course) that there are some remedial settings in which the use of race had been approved by the Court. It was a bad sign.

Second to argue was the solicitor general, Theodore Olson, who presented the position of the U.S. government, under President George W. Bush. That position did support Barbara Grutter, but was somewhat wishy-washy. Olson himself was strongly opposed to race preferences of any kind. Long before becoming solicitor general, he had been the lead attorney for the CIR in the *Hopwood* case, in which he had successfully attacked race preferences at the University of Texas. The position of the Bush administration, not categorically opposed to the use of race, did not permit Olson to make the identical arguments in the *Grutter* case. Nevertheless he was a polished and effective advocate for Grutter's cause.

When it was time for the university to defend its Law School preferences, John Payton did not argue. He, who had so loyally and so effectively advanced the university position from the outset of the litigation, had been replaced. Why? For both sides it was essential to win the central vote of Justice O'Connor. Lee Bollinger and Marvin Krislov had apparently decided that they would stand a better chance of success in that if their case were presented by a female attorney. They chose Maureen Mahoney, a fine litigator whose many successes before the Supreme Court suggested that she would be better able to read the moods and reactions of the justices. Her great skill in oral argument was widely acknowledged. But she was new to this case, a complicated struggle in which Payton had been absorbed for nearly six years. Mahoney was an insider. She had been deputy solicitor general; years before that she had been Justice William Rehnquist's clerk—at one point in the argument Rehnquist addressed her as "Maureen"! The university sought every possible advantage in the battle, of course, but this replacement of their lead attorney was an apparent effort to benefit from personal connections and from gender. Allowing such considerations to outweigh the years of sterling service on Payton's part seemed to me to be less than handsome. Payton was retained to argue the *Gratz* case, which the university had little chance of winning.

Mahoney did well. She did encounter some tough questions. Justice Antonin Scalia was fierce on the concept of "critical mass."

> "Is 2 percent a critical mass, Ms. Mahoney?"
> "I don't think so, Your Honor."
> "Four percent?"
> "No, Your Honor. What—"
> "You have to pick some number, don't you?"
> "Well, actually what the—"
> "Eight? Is 8 percent?"
> "Your Honor, the—"
> "Now, does it stop being a quota because it's somewhere between

8 and 12, but it is a quota if it's 10? . . . Once you use the term 'critical mass' you're into quotaland."

"Your Honor, what a quota is under this Court's cases is a fixed number. And there is no fixed number here."

"As long as you say 'between 8 and 12' you're okay? Is that it? If you said 10 it's bad, but between 8 and 12 is okay because it's not a fixed number. That's what you think the Constitution says?"

He was also flatly unwilling to accept Mahoney's claim that the diversity the university sought (as he responded) "is a compelling state interest, compelling enough to warrant ignoring the Constitution's prohibition of discrimination on the basis of race. . . . The problem [said Scalia] is a problem of Michigan's own creation. It has decided to create an elite law school. True, it is one of the best law schools in the country." But if the University of Michigan really cares so much about racial diversity, he asked,

"Why doesn't it do as many other state law schools do: lower the standards, not have a flagship elite law school? Solves the problem."

"Your Honor, the Law School surely need not make a choice between academic excellence and racial diversity."

"If diversity is important enough to override the Constitution's prohibition of racial discrimination, it seems to me it's important enough to override Michigan's desire to have a super-duper law school."

"Your Honor, the question is whether this is discrimination. What Michigan is doing benefits—"

And at this point we received one of the most comforting signals of the morning. Justice Anthony Kennedy broke in, quite evidently on Scalia's side in the matter:

"No, no, no. The question is whether or not there is a compelling interest that allows race to be used."

"That's correct, Your Honor."

"And Justice Scalia's question is designed to put to you the fact that this isn't a compelling interest because it's a choice that the Michigan Law School has made to be like this."

Kennedy, we inferred rightly, was going to cast his vote for Barbara Grutter.

Justice O'Connor raised a concern that she found especially troubling, the fact that this system under which preferences were given to support minorities apparently had no end. Where racial considerations in other contexts had been approved there was always a fixed expiration date. But not here. "There is no fixed expiration date in this, is there?" she asked. Mahoney responded by expressing the hope that one day an improved minority applicant pool would make the consideration of race unnecessary. O'Connor was plainly uneasy. "Have we approved any other affirmative action program with such a vague, distant termination date?" Her question was a favorable sign.

Rehnquist asked Mahoney if more minorities were now being admitted to the University of Michigan without quotas—and then grinned as he used the word "quotas." "They're not quotas, Your Honor. They are *aspirations.*" She grinned back. Very much an insider she was.

In response to a question from one of the justices, Mahoney said that at the University of Michigan, when whites apply for admission, "They are considered on their merits, just like every other applicant." Scalia jumped in again: "But they *aren't* just like every other applicant. Some applicants are given a preference because of their race." Justice Ginsburg, now plainly on the university's side, entered with a question putting forward the often repeated refrain of the university that race is just one factor in admission. She asked, "Don't universities look at a wide range of factors in addition to race?" Scalia became agitated once again. Some factors are permissible and some are not, he pointed out:

> "Does the Constitution prohibit discrimination against oboe players as opposed to flute players?"
> "No, Your Honor."
> "Does it prohibit discrimination on the basis of alumni status?
> "No, Your Honor, but—
> "But it does prohibit discrimination on the basis of race?
> "But the question is whether this is prohibited discrimination. . . . A minority applicant brings something special."

She did her best.

In responding to a question from Justice Breyer, Mahoney pointed out that if the system had been totally race-blind, only an additional 80 of the 2,500 applicants rejected each year would have gained admission. That, she said, "is a very small and diffuse burden, and limited in scope." Scalia was disdainful. "I don't know any other area where we decide the case by saying, 'Well, there are very few people who are being treated unconstitutionally.' I mean, if this is indeed an unconstitutional treatment of this woman because of her race, surely it doesn't make any difference whether she is one of very few who have been treated unconstitutionally." Rehnquist smiled at Mahoney, protecting her: "I think you can regard that as a statement rather than a question." The audience laughed; Mahoney sat down.

Because the *Gratz* case had been decided against us in the district court, and there had been no action on it at the appellate level, we were again the appellants when that case was heard, immediately afterward. Kolbo was again the first to address the Court.

He sought to drive home the proposition that, even if laudable, the desire to increase diversity in an entering undergraduate class could not be *compelling*. Justice Stevens asked, Did Kolbo contend that the only truly compelling interest could be the obligation to give remedy for past identified discrimination? No, Kolbo replied, there might be other reasons, but they would have to be extraordinary and rare. Justice Breyer pressed him again. In a large and diverse nation is there not an extraordinary need for diversity among the elites? How can you say that that is not compelling? "Because, Your Honor," Kolbo replied, "there are important constitutional rights at stake. Those are the rights to the equal protection of the laws. A social benefit—having more minorities in particular occupations or the schools—simply doesn't rise to the level of compelling interest."

Justice Kennedy put Breyer's question in another way. If that great need for diversity were put to you by the university president or dean, would you tell him or her there is nothing you can do about it? Kolbo answered eloquently: "I would say, Your Honor, that racial preferences are not the answer. If minorities are not competing at the same level as other racial groups, then we should take steps to solve that problem. But racial preferences, because they injure the rights of innocent people, and because of the prohibition contained in our Constitution, simply are not permissible to solve that problem."

Olson, defending the government's position in support of Jennifer Gratz, emphasized the fallacious distinction upon which Judge Duggan's opinion had relied: the supposition that although the grids that the university had earlier used were admittedly unconstitutional, the Selection Index system that replaced them was not. The new system was intended to produce, and did produce, the same outcome as the earlier one. The changes were no more than cosmetic. Justice Kennedy broke in to agree: "Yes, the stipulation is that the replacement did not change the substance of how race and ethnicity were considered." There was little doubt in our minds that Kennedy would be with us.

Olson, who had been so successful in the *Hopwood* case in Texas almost twenty years before, went on to attack the undergraduate preferences at the University of Michigan with the same argument. "What this Court has said," Olson spoke with some passion, "is that racial preferences, racial stereotyping which it is, is stigmatizing, it's divisive, it's damaging to the fabric of society, it's damaging to the goal of ultimately eliminating the problems that racial discrimination has created. . . . The one thing that the University of Michigan may not do is change its admission requirements for one race and not another. That is forbidden by the Equal Protection Clause of the Constitution."

John Payton had his chance to address the Court at last. His was the toughest job of all; he was obliged to defend an admittedly mechanical system of preferences in a process designed to sort a huge body of applicants, while making it appear that the individual merits of every applicant were thoughtfully weighed. The automatic award of 20 points to every minority applicant in a system in which 100 points would assure admission was impossible to hide. "It looks to me," Justice Kennedy made the point, "like this is just a disguised quota. You have a minority student who works very, very hard, is very proud of his athletics. He gets the *same* number of points as a minority person who doesn't have any athletics. That to me looks like an overt quota." No, said Payton, because every application gets read by a counselor who considers a wide range of factors. Scalia broke in: "None of that matters. If you're minimally qualified, and you're one of the minority races that get the twenty points, you're in. The rest is really irrelevant."

The mechanical character of the system could be obscured by insisting that applications might end up before the admissions review committee, which had the authority to ignore the point system. Justice Breyer gave Payton a boost. "I want a clear answer to this: That review committee can look at the applications individually and ignore the points?" Payton answered: "It does. The answer is yes."

Scalia was not mollified. The review committee had been given that authority because there was often a desire to admit minority students who, even *with* the automatic award of twenty points, did not have a total sufficient to win admission competitively. The university had announced, back in 1995, that *all* minority applicants thought potentially able to do the work were to be admitted. Scalia broke in: "Mr. Payton, it's easy to say that they can ignore the points, easy to say. Do you know of any case in which a minority applicant, one of the minorities favored in your program, who was minimally qualified, got the twenty-point favor and was rejected?" Payton was against the wall. "I don't know, Justice Scalia."

Payton also had a somewhat painful exchange with Chief Justice Rehnquist, who first asked him how Michigan decides that some ethnic group is "underrepresented."

Payton: "They are underrepresented in our applicant pool."

Rehnquist: "Compared to what?"

Payton: "Underrepresented groups are those with so few applicants that a critical mass wouldn't exist if race were not taken into account."

Rehnquist: "When you say 'underrepresented' it sounds like something almost mathematical, that you're saying, 'We only have a certain percentage of them, and we should have this percentage of them.' Well, what is this percentage?"

Payton: "It's actually not a percentage at all. It's driven by the educational benefits that we want from our diverse student body. If we had in our applicant pool sufficient numbers of minority students—"

Rehnquist: "What is a sufficient number?"

Payton: "African Americans, for example—"

Rehnquist: "I asked you, what is a sufficient number? Would you answer it?"

Payton: "A sufficient number so that when we made our selections we were achieving the critical mass of students that we need for the benefits I described."

The chief justice was rigid in enforcing the time limits for the disputing parties. Thirty minutes was given to each side, in each of the two cases. For the appellants a portion of that time was divided between Kolbo and Olson, the latter with fewer minutes allotted.

The university team elected to retain all of its time; none of it had been allotted to the intervenors, who were frustrated by having no opportunity to address the Court. The hearing had begun sharply at 10:00 a.m.; it ended almost exactly at noon. I left the courtroom and went to watch the scene on the steps of the Supreme Court Building.

Reporters were interviewing Jennifer Gratz and Barbara Grutter. Miranda Massie and others were giving spontaneous speeches to groups of supporters assembled on or near the steps. Marvin Krislov, John Payton, Maureen Mahoney, Jeffrey Lehman, and more than a dozen others gathered to cheer the university, singing the Michigan fight song, "Hail to the Victors," at the foot of the steps. The crowd of demonstrators who had gathered before and during the hearing was breaking up. The sidewalks around the building were littered with the signs and leaflets that had been paraded during the demonstrations, which had, I believe, not the tiniest bit of impact on the business of the Court.

On our side there were no placards or organized demonstrations, no busloads of students, no singing in the streets. The CIR had arranged a splendid lunch for our party: Patrick Hamacher, Jennifer Gratz, Barbara Grutter, and their families; Kolbo and Larry Purdy and others from Maslon; the lawyers and staff members of the CIR; and myself. Terry Pell, who surely deserved to be honored at that lunch, decided that he would have to go immediately to his office to deal with an expected flood of requests from the media.

The lunch was held at a French restaurant about five blocks from the Supreme Court building. It was a warm day with brilliant sunshine. We walked over to the restaurant to find that one long table had been set for us. We were all bubbling with comments and predictions and observations about the proceedings of the morning. I remained confident that we would prevail, although somewhat troubled by the exchange between Justice O'Connor and Kolbo at the opening of the argument in *Grutter*. Yet I did not think it likely that the Court would support any system of unvarnished racial discrimination in a state university.

Most of us were seated around that long table when Kolbo came through the doors of the restaurant. There was a spontaneous burst of applause for him, richly deserved. The large and ebullient company was welcomed, in Pell's absence, by Michael Rosman, legal director of the CIR. There were no long speeches.

Many of those seated around that long table were unknown to others. The first thing Rosman did was to ask each member of the company to introduce himself or herself, and so they did, going down one long side of the table and then up the other long side. I was seated about halfway down the table, next to Jennifer Gratz, of whom I am very fond. I was asking about her life, now newly married, in California.

Then an extraordinary thing happened. The self-introductions had moved around the table and reached me. I was about to introduce my-self as a professor of philosophy at the University of Michigan. I barely managed to voice my name, which was greeted by the most enthusiastic and long-lasting applause for me that I have ever heard. That was totally unexpected; I was dumbfounded. I suppose I had not appreciated how widely my participation in these battles had been witnessed. I recall the circumstances vividly. It was a profoundly satisfying moment.

CHAPTER 28

The End of Litigation

We lost. The U.S. Supreme Court issued its decisions in the Michigan cases on 23 June 2003. In the case of *Grutter v. Bollinger* the Court, by a vote of five to four, held that the use of race preferences as a factor in student admissions by the University of Michigan Law School is not unlawful.[1]

The rationale for this decision was, in one word, *diversity*, precisely what the university had put forward. The majority of the Court agreed: using race in admissions decisions furthers a "compelling interest" in obtaining the educational benefits that flow from a diverse student body. This use of race, the Court held, is therefore not prohibited by the Equal Protection Clause or by Title VI of the Civil Rights Act.

For Barbara Grutter, for Kirk Kolbo and Larry Purdy, for Terry Pell and the Center for Individual Rights (CIR), and for me, this was profoundly disheartening. I'll report what we did in response to this decision shortly, but the reality that day was depressing and inescapable. There is only one Supreme Court. When it speaks, even if by a narrow majority, it lays down the law. Under this authoritative interpretation of the Constitution of the United States, race preferences in college admissions were authorized. There is no appeal from that decision. The only hope for its emendation would be some action by the Supreme Court itself in some later case not then on the horizon.

Two Michigan cases were before the Court. On that same day, 23 June 2003, the decision in the case of *Gratz v. Bollinger* was also handed down, and that case we won.[2] Terry Sandalow had predicted a split result, and that was indeed the outcome. There was no doubt, however, that the University of Michigan had triumphed. *Grutter* was decided first, and in that majority opinion the governing principles were set forth. Among the criteria specified in that decision for the permissible use of race was the demand that the racial instrument employed be "narrowly tailored," that is, carefully limited to steps designed to serve the objective of diversity. *Gratz* was decided in the light of that holding; Jennifer Gratz won her case because the Court found the system of racial preferences used in the undergraduate college to be mechanical, awarding twenty points to all minority students without exception—a system that was plainly not narrowly tailored.

The vote in *Gratz* was six to three. "We find," Chief Justice William Rehnquist wrote in the majority opinion, "that the manner in which the University considers the race of applicants in its undergraduate admissions guidelines violates constitutional and statutory provisions."[3] Holding that the *manner* in which race had been considered was crude, which it surely was, constituted only a minor defeat for the university. The larger principle that race preferences could henceforth be used, that doing so was consistent with the Equal Protection Clause, was the central and overriding result of the two cases. The university could and soon did change the preference system at the undergraduate level to mirror the procedures at the Law School.

The approbative language the Court used in *Grutter*—"The Law School engages in a highly individualized, holistic review of each applicant's file, giving serious consideration to all the ways an applicant might contribute to a diverse educational environment"[4]—would soon be duplicated by the University of Michigan at all levels and was quickly incorporated into admissions guidelines at universities around the country. Whatever the admissions procedures would be in fact, the needed *descriptions* of them were set forth clearly by the Supreme Court. The University of Michigan had prevailed.

The author of the majority opinion in *Grutter* was Justice Sandra Day O'Connor; her swing vote, which I had been confident would swing to our side, swung fully to the other side. Justice O'Connor had been a close friend of the late Justice Lewis Powell, whose opinion in *Bakke* had first introduced the notion of diversity as a possible ground for race preferences in admissions. Her admiration for Powell is evident; much of her opinion is devoted to reporting Powell's views and concurring with them. She leaves forever undecided the question of whether Justice Powell's sole opinion in *Bakke* did in fact authorize the university to use race preferences as it did. But now, without any doubt, Justice Powell's views are formally adopted. O'Connor writes, "Today we endorse Justice Powell's view that student body diversity is a compelling state interest that can justify the use of race in university admissions."[5] Her opinion was joined by Justices John Paul Stevens, David Souter, Ruth Bader Ginsburg, and Stephen Breyer.

Two features of that majority opinion are worthy of special notice. The first is its great emphasis upon the alleged merits of diversity. The majority was convinced that a diverse student body produces results so highly beneficial that they justify the treatment of diversity as a compelling state interest. These alleged merits, and the grounds claimed for them, are in fact much in dispute. But anyone reading the briefs submitted by the parties in this case will see immediately where O'Connor learned of these great benefits. Her effusive praise for the role of diversity is strikingly close to the account of diversity presented by the university itself. A group of scholars, some from the University of Michigan faculty, some paid at the rate of $200 an hour, had been marshaled by the university administration to write essays in support of diversity. Those essays were compiled and issued in book form by the university under the title *The Compelling Need for Diversity in Higher Education.*

This is a peculiar book. I do not recall how I acquired my copy. No publisher, no author, and no editor is identified. No date of publication is given. There are nine essays, each containing scores of references having little, and in most cases nothing, to do with the role of diversity in higher education. It is a package of essays in social science designed to impress the layperson.

The extraordinary claims for the role of diversity are epitomized by President Lee Bollinger. For a well-rounded education, he said, diversity is "as essential as the study of the Middle Ages, of international politics, and of Shakespeare." When Justice O'Connor writes for the majority she is more restrained in her praise of diversity, but not much more.

Those claims about the alleged benefits of diversity in university enrollment are dubious; some are probably false. Even before the time of the *Grutter* decision empirical claims about the consequences of diversity had been given intensive examination; social scientists applying the most rigorous methods and standards have more recently rejected most of those claims. On some matters scientific findings about diversity turn out to be the *reverse* of what the University of Michigan claimed for them.

This complicated set of empirical issues cannot be dealt with adequately here. To give the reader a sense of how badly Justice O'Connor and her colleagues were misled about the actual consequences of diversity, I will briefly recount two studies whose outcomes fly in the face of the majority opinion.

The first is a huge study of a random sample of 1,600 students and

2,400 faculty members at 140 U.S. colleges and universities—one of the most comprehensive studies of diversity ever undertaken, by scholars of the first rank.[6] Subjects were asked to give their evaluation of the quality of education at their institution, of the academic preparation and work habits of their student body, and of the state of race relations on their campus. Then separately, using government statistics, the investigators determined the proportion of black and other minority students at each institution involved. If diversity had the great benefits claimed for it, institutions with higher proportions of minority students should certainly have been rated more highly than those with lower proportions. The reverse was the case.

Every benefit claimed for campus diversity was contradicted by the results of this study. Students, faculty members, and administrators all responded to increasing racial diversity by registering increased *dis*satisfaction with the quality of education at their institution and the work ethic of their peers. Controlling for the race, gender, economic background, and religion of respondents, controlling for institutional selectivity and for public or private status, *a higher level of diversity was found in every case to be associated with less educational satisfaction and worse race relations among students*. Of all the university administrators surveyed about one-third believed that race preferences have an impact on academic standards—and by fifteen to one these administrators say that this impact is negative. If this very large scientific study is essentially correct, the assertions of great benefit that underlay the university's alleged compelling need for diversity are at best not warranted. Some of those assertions are simply false.

Finally, I call the reader's attention to a recently published book by a fine scholar at Princeton, Russell Nieli, who has gathered and studied a great number of scientific studies of many different affirmative action programs. The upshot is the conclusion, almost inescapable, that the *damage* done by race preferences to individuals in both the minority and the majority, and to the institutions giving preferences, is great and long lasting, outweighing any benefits diversity may provide.[7]

What the University of Michigan asserted to be true was accepted as true by the *Grutter* majority without qualification; it was taken to be the empirical justification of race preferences. Those claims have been gravely undermined. The Supreme Court has repeatedly insisted that in examining government uses of a suspect classification such as race, "strict scrutiny" is required. In this case strict scrutiny was forgotten. Worse, all scrutiny was forgotten! Never was an important judicial standard more blatantly flouted.

The university team—President Mary Sue Coleman, General Counsel Marvin Krislov, former dean Jeffrey Lehman, and their supporters were understandably delighted by Justice O'Connor's opinion. But the supposed benefits of diversity, and the alleged need for it, are highly dubious. Had the justices looked closely at the claims made and considered the evidence given for them, they could not have concluded, as they did conclude, that racial diversity is a benefit so overwhelming as to be compelling. The very words and phrases of the university brief reappear over a different signature. Justice O'Connor and her four concurring colleagues were hornswoggled by the University of Michigan.

Long before, as preparation for the *Grutter* trial in Judge Bernard Friedman's district court was getting under way (1998–1999), there was a growing body of evidence that the claims for the educational benefits of diversity were at least exaggerated and perhaps even false. Why, one may ask, did Barbara Grutter's attorneys not seek to exhibit that exaggeration and dubiety at trial? Kolbo and the CIR team, of which I was a member, several times did discuss the strategic question of whether we should argue at trial that the university's claims about the great benefits of diversity were not scientifically well grounded. The claims were certainly disputable, but the body of evidence against them was not as weighty then as it later became. The huge Rothman study, recounted just above, was not yet in hand. Kolbo wanted to avoid a battle of competing social science testimony, which seemed likely to prove indecisive. He thought we could prevail without reaching the question of the actual consequences of diversity. We ought to win decisively, he believed, on the ground that, *even if all they say is true,* such benefits cannot constitute the "compelling state interest" that would be required to justify the use of racial classifications. In effect Kolbo was seeking to "cut them off at the pass."

That was and remains my view as well. This strategy should have worked; our understanding of the adjective *compelling,* as it is used in applying the standard of strict scrutiny, was intellectually sound and fully in accord with Supreme Court precedents. But the strategy did not succeed at the Supreme Court in 2003 because the majority, Justice O'Connor its spokesperson, was thoroughly *taken* by the effusive praise of diversity in the briefs of the university and its amici. The language used by some was gushing. Justice O'Connor's ardent admiration of Justice Lewis Powell—from whose speculative opinion in *Bakke* in 1978 the entire diversity argument had arisen—was evident. Explicit deference to his views is manifest in the *Grutter* majority opinion.[8] Powell's ghost was triumphant.

A second puzzling feature of the majority opinion concerned the question of when university race preferences would come to an end. In her questioning of university attorney Maureen Mahoney, Justice O'Connor had revealed that she was troubled by the fact that the race preferences in this program had no apparent end point. In response, Mahoney had assured her only that the university was earnestly looking toward its termination one day. In her majority opinion O'Connor returns to this concern, with a passage whose meaning has never yet been entirely clear. She wrote, "We take the Law School at its word that it 'would like nothing better than to find a race-neutral admissions formula' and will terminate its race-conscious admissions program as soon as practicable. . . . It has been 25 years since Justice Powell first approved the use of race to further an interest in student body diversity in the context of public higher education. . . . We expect that 25 years from now, the use of racial preferences will no longer be necessary to further the interest approved today."[9]

How will that come to pass? Ten of those twenty-five years have elapsed. There is no sign that the highly selective law schools and colleges in our country now lean less upon race preference than they did when the *Grutter* opinion was written. In 2010 the University of Michigan Press published a book, edited by Krislov and others, titled *The Next 25 Years*.[10] It is an instrument with which officers, attorneys, and other representatives of the University of Michigan argue strenuously for the *retention* of preferences in the years to come. Krislov (now president of Oberlin), President Coleman, and Prof. Patricia Gurin all appear again in this book, presenting the same arguments offered in 2003. They take satisfaction in quoting the *Grutter* opinion of the Supreme Court, in which the need for diversity had been held compelling. They are quoting themselves.

Former Justice O'Connor likewise contributes to this recent University of Michigan volume. She reflects upon the force of her specification of a twenty-five-year period at the close of her *Grutter* opinion.[11] It could not have been a deadline; that was not in her power to lay down. It was, she reports with emphasis, an "expectation." The expectation of the Court majority? Or perhaps the expression of her own hope? In 2010 O'Connor, now retired from the Court, urges *study* so that, in the years remaining of those twenty-five, scientists may establish the benefits of preferences and thus, somehow, enable universities to eliminate them. The underlying supposition appears to be that race preferences are essential and beneficial and that through their use some permanent balance of the races will—in some way not disclosed—be achieved. This position verges on the self-contradictory.

A natural and uncontrived proportionality of the races is not advanced by preferences. The continued use of race preferences to boost minority numbers makes it less likely rather than more likely that universities will soon find such preferences unnecessary. Racial hostilities are not healed but are intensified by preferences. Ethnic polarization is not reduced but is exacerbated by preferences. *Preferences reinforce the racial stereotypes they were put forward to overcome.* But the Court has spoken, and the damage has been done.

Dissenting responses to the majority opinion were powerful. Justice Antonin Scalia is caustic. He frankly doubts the integrity of the universities supporting preferences, "universities that talk the talk of multiculturalism and racial diversity in the courts but walk the walk of tribalism and racial segregation on their campuses—through minority-only student organizations, separate minority housing opportunities, separate minority student centers, even separate minority-only graduation ceremonies."[12] Scalia's view: "The University of Michigan Law School's mystical 'critical mass' justification for its discrimination by race challenges even the most gullible mind. The admission statistics show it to be a sham to cover a scheme of racially proportionate admissions."[13] What really turns out to be compelling for the university, he observes, is its interest in maintaining a "prestige" law school whose normal admissions standards exclude most blacks and other minorities. Disgusted, he adds, "If that is a compelling state interest, everything is."[14]

Justice Clarence Thomas is appalled by the carelessness of the majority argument, by its complete failure to scrutinize, not to mention scrutinize strictly, the evidence in support of the diversity argument. He writes, "The Constitution does not countenance the unprecedented deference that the Court gives to the Law School, an approach inconsistent with the very concept of 'strict scrutiny.'"[15]

There are only two circumstances, Thomas observes, in which "pressing public necessity" or a "compelling state interest" can reasonably justify racial discrimination by agents of the state. National security is one—and even in pursuit of that objective the government's use of race must be narrowly tailored to achieve the critically needed outcome. The other compelling interest may be the obligation of a state to remedy the past discrimination for which it is itself responsible. In sum, Thomas writes, "The Constitution abhors classifications based on race. Every time the government places citizens on racial registers and makes race relevant to the provision of burdens or benefits, it demeans us all."[16]

He adds a powerful argument: no state has a pressing public need to maintain a public law school of *any* sort; a number of states have long declined to do so, including Alaska, Delaware, Massachusetts, New Hampshire, and Rhode Island. Michigan has no compelling interest in having a law school *at all*, much less an elite one, with standards that exclude blacks and thus create the Law School's alleged "need" to discriminate by race.[17]

Thomas concludes with a quote from Justice John Marshall Harlan, the lone dissenter when, in 1896, the doctrine of "separate but equal" was announced: "Our Constitution is color-blind, and neither knows nor tolerates classes among citizens."[18]

But it is Chief Justice Rehnquist, joined by all the other dissenters (Scalia, Anthony Kennedy, and Thomas) who utterly demolishes the majority opinion. Analyzing the figures the Law School provided, he demonstrates what the Law School has been doing in fact. That its objective was a "critical mass" of minority students he shows to be no more than a facade. His analysis is unmerciful and contemptuous. Each year (from 1995–2000), the Law School admits between 91 and 108 African Americans, allegedly to achieve "critical mass" and thereby to prevent black students from feeling "isolated, or like spokespersons, for their race." But of Native Americans they admitted between 13 and 19, many of whom did not ultimately enroll. And of Hispanics between 47 and 56. How can these numbers possibly constitute a "critical mass" of Native Americans and Hispanics if so many more are needed to constitute a "critical mass" of African Americans? "One would have to believe," writes Rehnquist, "that the objectives of 'critical mass' are achieved with only half the number of Hispanics and one-sixth the number of Native Americans." No explanation is given of why more individuals are needed from one minority than from others to create a critical mass. He continues, "The Law School's disparate admissions practices with respect to these minority groups demonstrate that *its alleged goal of 'critical mass' is simply a sham.*"[19]

Can this disparate treatment of the several minorities be given some other explanation? Yes—there is a precise correlation between the percentage of minorities from each group *applying* and the percentage of those minorities *enrolled* as students in the Law School. Rehnquist provides a set of statistical tables that leave little doubt about what is really going on. The Law School's admission system is, in practice, "*a carefully managed program designed to ensure proportionate representation of applicants from selected minority groups.* The Law School has managed its admissions program not to achieve a 'critical mass,' but to extend offers of admission to members of selected minority groups *in proportion to their representation in the applicant pool.* This is precisely the type of racial balancing that the Court itself calls 'patently unconstitutional.'"[20] What the Law School has been doing, Rehnquist concludes, "is forbidden by the Equal Protection Clause of the Constitution."

Chief Justice Rehnquist's demolition of the majority opinion in *Grutter* is so thorough that the members of that majority ought to have been embarrassed by what his analysis of the figures so starkly revealed. The decision is more than normally vulnerable to eventual reversal. The sham quest for "critical mass," and the frailty of the defense of diversity as an allegedly compelling need, invites attack. But that must await another Supreme Court review of the matter, in a different case, on another day.

In *Gratz v. Bollinger* the petitioner (that is, the CIR, in support of Jennifer Gratz) argued, as Barbara Grutter had argued, that diversity could not serve as a need so compelling that it would warrant an exception to the Equal Protection Clause. Chief Justice Rehnquist plainly agreed, but he was obliged to recognize that "for the reasons set forth today in *Grutter v. Bollinger* [reasons he had exposed as spurious], the Court has rejected these arguments of petitioners."[21]

For other reasons the program of race preferences in the undergraduate college was struck down. The decision in *Grutter* establishes the principle that for any program of race preferences to withstand "strict scrutiny analysis" it must ensure that applicants be considered as individuals, not as group representatives. But individualized consideration is abandoned by the undergraduate program. The College of Literature, Science, and the Arts (LSA) policy "automatically distributes 20 points to every single applicant from an underrepresented minority group," which "has the effect of making the factor of race decisive for virtually every minimally qualified underrepresented minority applicant."[22] It is plain, the majority in *Gratz* concludes, that the university's undergraduate race preferences program is not narrowly tailored to achieve its purported objective, does not withstand strict scrutiny, and thus violates the Equal Protection Clause of the Fourteenth Amendment as well as Title VI of the Civil Rights Act.

Some of the justices who had supported the university in *Grutter* changed sides and supported the CIR in *Gratz*. Not changing sides, however, was Justice Ginsburg, whose dissenting view led to a remarkable exchange with Chief Justice Rehnquist. The conflict between those two was somewhat vexing for me. Ginsburg, whom I had known many years before and for whom I have great regard, was dead wrong in my view, while Rehnquist, a cool fish of whom it was hard to be fond, was dead right.

The byplay arose because of the tension between the two cases, *Grut-*

ter permitting race preferences in the Law School, *Gratz* rejecting race preferences in the undergraduate college. The Law School at Michigan admits some 350 students each year; it can truthfully claim that each of the competitive applicants is individually evaluated, all merits weighed. This individualized process led the Court to permit the consideration of race by the Law School. But the undergraduate college can make no such claim. Some *forty-nine thousand* applications for undergraduate admission were received by the University of Michigan for the academic year 2014–2015. When Jennifer Gratz applied in the 1990s the number was not that great, but tens of thousands were applying each year even then. The university had granted candidly, in *Gratz*, that "the volume of applications and the presentation of applicant information make it impractical for the undergraduate college to use the admissions system of the Law School." This is obviously true. Picture a gymnasium in which those fat application files are stacked in piles ten feet high. There will be more than 350 of such piles, stuffing the imagined gymnasium and spilling over into the showers. Any claim that each applicant to such a university is weighed "holistically," her merits considered individually without mechanical classification, is certain to be a falsehood. But, under *Grutter*, race may be considered only if it is one factor in an individualized appraisal. Constitutional strictures may not be bypassed. A university, said the Court in *Gratz*, may not employ whatever means it desires to achieve diversity. "The fact that the implementation of a program providing individualized consideration might present administrative challenges [does one detect sarcasm here?] cannot render constitutional an otherwise problematic system."[23] So, under *Gratz*, the university is forbidden to do—to give applicants points automatically, by race—what it had earlier admitted it must do to achieve the racial objective it proclaims. This invites, almost obliges, cheating by a large university.

Justice Ginsburg saw this clearly. Dissenting in *Gratz*, writing in candid support of the point system found unlawful, she frankly acknowledged that universities have long been sly in this arena, resorting to "camouflage" by encouraging minority applicants and their supporters to convey their ethnic identification deviously and backhandedly in personal essays and letters of recommendation. Justice Ginsburg then concluded, "If honesty is the best policy, surely Michigan's accurately described, fully disclosed college affirmative action program is preferable to achieving similar numbers through winks, nods, and disguises."[24] It would be better to weaken or eliminate the demand for an individualized admissions system, she is saying in effect, than to fake it. A nonindividualized program, assigning a fixed number of points for skin color, she thinks is the best available solution. If we do not permit it, the result will be widespread cheating.

She was certainly right about the cheating, which is now common at selective universities. Such cheating was virtually ensured by glib talk in *Grutter* about "holistic" and "individualized" consideration, terms that are utterly unrealistic to describe most university admissions contexts. Code words and code phrases—"winks, nods, and disguises," as Justice Ginsburg describes them shrewdly—pervade the world of undergraduate admissions at selective universities. Honesty is not paramount.

Chief Justice Rehnquist, again with a devastating reply, shames her in a footnote. He remarks that Ginsburg's observations about the behavior of universities are "remarkable" and then continues: "First, they [her remarks] suggest that universities—to whose academic judgment we are told in *Grutter* we should defer—will pursue their affirmative action programs whether or not they violate the United States Constitution. Second, they recommend that these violations should be dealt with not by requiring the universities to obey the Constitution, but by changing the Constitution so that it conforms to the conduct of the universities."[25]

In this footnote, destined to be long remembered, Rehnquist goes to the heart of the tension between the two cases: discriminatory conduct found unacceptable in *Gratz* is made inevitable by the demands of *Grutter*. But it must not be detectable. The "compelling need" for diversity thus renders deception (by the undergraduate admissions offices of the great universities) a practical necessity. Doublespeak and duplicity are to be rewarded. That is the sad note on which the litigation of the Michigan cases comes to an end.

CHAPTER 29

From Legal Battles to Political Battles

The Michigan Civil Rights Initiative Is Born

In September of 2003, just months after the Michigan cases were concluded, I published an essay in *Commentary* in which I lamented the dreadful outcome of *Grutter* and explained the tension between *Grutter* and *Gratz*.[1] I was disheartened, but I was determined to press for some way to eliminate preference by race—if not universally, at least at my own university.

The controversy, I predicted in that essay, would move from the courtroom to the ballot box. That prediction I could make with some confidence because I was one of a small group of people who began immediately to prepare for that shift in the battlefield. The Supreme Court had decided that race preferences might lawfully be given by the University of Michigan; although it was permissible it certainly was not obligatory. The people of the State of Michigan (and every other state) might now give special consideration to persons in certain ethnic groups—but citizens remained free to decide that their state ought not give such preference, now or ever. In California, a statewide vote in 1996 had resulted in just that outcome. What was called Proposition 209—the California Civil Rights Initiative—amended the California Constitution to forbid explicitly all preference by race. We were determined to follow that same path. I wrote in 2003, "In Michigan every effort will be made, by the time of the presidential election of 2004, to place on the ballot a Michigan Civil Rights Initiative (MCRI), the equivalent of California's Proposition 209."[2] In a statewide election Proposition 209 had been successfully supported by more than 54 percent of California voters.

Because Michigan circumstances differed importantly from those of California, our initiative had to be formulated somewhat differently. Like the Californians we sought to amend our state constitution by adding provisions that would permanently forbid the State of Michigan itself, and its agencies, to discriminate. In our state the chief instrument of that discrimination had been the University of Michigan, a state institution, giving race preferences. But in Michigan three public universities (the University of Michigan in Ann Arbor, Wayne State University in Detroit, and Michigan State University [MSU] in East Lansing) have special status because they are formally recognized in the Michigan Constitution. The regents of the University of Michigan are not appointed by the authority of the state legislature; they are elected by the people at large. Their full authority is established by our constitution and is not subordinate to the state legislature. The University of Michigan (like Wayne State and MSU) is therefore not an agency of the state in the same way that the various branches of ordinary state government are. To prohibit the award of ethnic preferences by the constitutionally recognized universities, which was our objective, it was therefore essential that the constitutional prohibition we proposed address those state universities explicitly.

To ensure this, the language of our initiative had to be somewhat repetitive. The MCRI, if adopted, would amend the Michigan Constitution by adding a new section, Section 26, to Article I. The full text of that new section, having nine paragraphs, may be found in Appendix C of this book. The central prohibitions of the initiative were clearly stated in the first two of those nine paragraphs; the remaining seven concerned only remedies for violation and some technical matters regarding definitions, dates, and the like.

Here follows the exact text of the first two paragraphs of the new Section 26, of Article I of the Michigan Constitution, which we put forward for statewide vote:

Civil Rights.

(1) The University of Michigan, Michigan State University, Wayne State University, and any other public college or university, community college, or school district shall not discriminate against, or grant preferential treatment to, any individual or group on the basis of race, sex, color, ethnicity, or national origin in the operation of public employment, public education, or public contracting.

(2) The state shall not discriminate against, or grant preferential treatment to, any individual or group on the basis of race, sex, color, ethnicity, or national origin in the operation of public employment, public education, or public contracting.

The nature of the prohibition set forth in each of the two paragraphs is the same, but the first paragraph is addressed specifically to public universities and colleges in Michigan, while the second paragraph is addressed to the State of Michigan itself and its several agencies. This initiative became a focus of great controversy in Michigan, which I will describe. Before discussing its subsequent history, however, I call attention to three of its special features.

First, the language of the MCRI closely tracks the language of the Civil Rights Act of 1964, which sought to eliminate racial discrimination more broadly. The state and its universities were again forbidden to discriminate against anyone on the basis of race, sex, color, ethnicity, or national origin. This was not new. What was new was the inclusion of five words that had not previously appeared in the constitution: "or grant preferential treatment to." These five words are the core of the MCRI. I had long argued that the constitutional demand that everyone be treated equally under the law without regard to race necessarily entails the prohibition of all preferential treatment by race. Those five words I had earlier believed not to be needed. But the Supreme Court, as we have seen, had held in *Grutter* that some race preferences at the University of Michigan are consistent with the Equal Protection Clause of the U.S. Constitution. We wanted to be clear that in Michigan race preferences would remain a form of racial discrimination. Hence those five critical words, "or grant preferential treatment to."

Second, the MCRI prohibits conduct of certain kinds by the state and its agencies, but not by private parties. In the third paragraph (see Appendix C for the exact text) the "state" is defined so as to include the state itself of course, but also any city, county, public college, school district, or any other political subdivision or governmental instrumentality.

Third, the MCRI specifies three spheres of state action concerning which its prohibitions do apply: (1) public employment, (2) public education, and (3) public contracting.

1. In appointments to jobs in state government, in police forces and fire departments and all Michigan civil service—and in all promotions within such state agencies—preferential treatment by race or ethnicity would be forbidden in Michigan.
2. Public education covers all the activities of all schools, colleges, and universities run by the State of Michigan. Admission preferences would therefore no longer be permitted.
3. Preferences given in public contracting commonly take the form of

set-asides, or bonuses, for certain firms doing business with the state because they are owned by persons of some specified color or ethnicity. They, too, would be prohibited. The range and force of the prohibitions set forth in the proposed amendment to the Michigan Constitution were clear.

We had reason to be optimistic about the fate of our initiative. The success of Proposition 209 in California in 1996, and then the subsequent success, in the year 2000, of a statewide vote in the State of Washington (not amending the state constitution there, but having universal effect in that state) assured us that dissatisfaction with preferential programs was widespread. Affirmative action had honorable origins and good repute—but when it takes the form of outright preference, it loses popular support. Michigan is a socially liberal state, its population highly diverse. Our spirit has been one of inclusion and fairness in racial matters. But outright ethnic preferences had been meeting here with widespread dissatisfaction. We believed that an initiative that would forbid preference in public employment, education, and contracting had an excellent chance of success.

We did not appreciate, in those early days of 2003 and 2004, how excruciatingly difficult it would be to get our initiative on the Michigan ballot. An education in that process lay before us. I became engaged in a political campaign as never before in my life.

Many years before I had been moderately active in the Democratic Party in Michigan, serving for a short while on its Executive Committee here in Washtenaw County, where the University of Michigan is located. I was encouraged and supported by Neil Staebler, a friend and adviser to our Democratic governor at that time, G. Mennen Williams. Williams (called "Soapy" because he was the heir to the Mennen shaving cream fortune) had been a successful governor long before I came to the university as a young instructor in 1955. Staebler was a native of Ann Arbor and a graduate of the University of Michigan; his dedicated service to the people of Michigan impressed me greatly. He was a conscientious and vigorous participant in the democratic process—as fine a *citizen* as I have ever known. He had become chairman of the Democratic Central Committee in Michigan. University regents win their office through partisan, statewide elections. At the Democratic Party State Convention in Grand Rapids in 1960 I was asked to join a committee of three charged with interviewing and appraising the merits of those who sought the Democratic nomination for regent of the University of Michigan.

Our committee was scrupulous and thorough. One of the aspirants for the regental nomination we found to be vastly superior to the rest in intellect and vision; we urged his nomination by our party. This man, Ellis Wunsch, was indeed nominated, but lost to his Republican opponent in the November election. I later came to know him well. Wunsch had been an administrator at Northwestern Michigan College in Traverse City. As a scholar he moved to Ann Arbor (after his election defeat) and was appointed to the faculty of the Michigan English Department. An outstanding teacher and administrator, Ellis Wunsch became, in the late 1960s, my fellow associate director of the Residential College of the university; we remained close friends until his death in 1980.

My political experience in that period had been marginal. Staebler and others had brought me to the edges of the political fray, but I had not myself run for office or been fully involved in electoral campaigns. I did not know what a serious political battle was like; in the struggle over the MCRI from 2004 to 2006 I was to learn.

There are two distinct phases of an initiative campaign. The first is getting the proposed amendment on the ballot. The second is winning the needed votes for the change that the initiative proposes. For us (and I think often for others also) the first phase was more arduous and more frustrating than the second.

The wording of the initiative—a delicate and critical matter—must first be approved in form by the office of the secretary of state. We had the California model to lean upon; the wording of their Proposition 209 was more than helpful; we largely copied it.

In California we had some wise and supportive colleagues. The California Civil Rights Initiative (CCRI) had been first devised by two California academics, Glynn Custred and Tom Wood. After the success of the CCRI, Wood maintained, for years, a fruitful website that served as a central repository for online commentary and the collection of documents, reports, and records pertaining to the campaign against race preferences. He gave us unfailing support and became my good friend.

The cochair of the CCRI campaign was Prof. Gail Heriot of the University of San Diego School of Law. Heriot (who currently serves as a member of the U.S. Commission on Civil Rights) has a superb legal mind and has proved an effective defender of the CCRI in its subsequent legal battles. She has been a personal heroine of mine.

Most helpful of all was Ward Connerly, a businessman in Sacramento who had been appointed by Governor Pete Wilson as one of the regents of the University of California. I never learned the details, but I was told that when the campaign for Proposition 209 was floundering, Connerly entered the picture belatedly. With political wisdom, force of intellect, and superabundant energy Connerly led the CCRI campaign to decisive victory. Connerly became, and has remained, a leading national opponent of race preferences. I came to admire him and will say more about him as I report the events surrounding the MCRI. He gave us great help and good advice; from his own pocket he made substantial financial contributions to the MCRI campaign. But he was—for the Michigan campaign—always an outsider. The battle for the MCRI would have to be won by Michiganders. All the help in the world from California could not replace the enthusiasm and the hard political work of Michigan citizens.

We announced the opening of our campaign on the central campus of the University of Michigan, on the Diag (a diagonal walkway between the corners of the central quadrangle of the university) in front of the Graduate Library. There were to be four speakers: Connerly, Jennifer Gratz, Barbara Grutter, and myself. My remarks were to follow immediately after Connerly's. The crowd of students surrounding us was quite large and was for the most part unsympathetic. Students often supposed that the MCRI, by eliminating preferences, was designed to hinder minority enrollment. We were therefore bad people in many eyes, and Connerly, who had famously led the fight for the CCRI, was treated as the leading villain.

That day brought back my memory of the raucous meeting in Sterling Heights I described earlier, but now the silencing of speech was to take place at the heart of my beloved university, which was shamed on that sunny afternoon. Wardell—Connerly's full first name, which I sometimes use—had been a key organizer for us; he sought to make some opening remarks. A band of hostile students that had massed directly in front of the platform on which we were sitting shouted in unison whenever he began to speak. He tried again and again without success. Some of the shouters I recognized. One of them had been a witness for the university in the *Grutter* trial; another was a young member of the faculty. I cannot conceive of any activity more directly antithetical to the role of a university faculty member than shouting down a speaker at a public gathering. I was embarrassed for him and for my institution.

After Connerly had given up in disgust I rose to speak. I was treated much more generously by the crowd, although there were a few hecklers during my brief talk. Most of the audience remained quiet, apparently content with the fact Connerly had been silenced. My message was exactly what his would have been: the people of Michigan ought not tolerate, and we think *will* not tolerate, deliberate discrimination by our university, which is what admission preference by race indubitably is. We aim to put the matter before the voters for their explicit judgment. A few people applauded; most in that crowd thought me just another one of the villains. Jennifer Gratz and Barbara Grutter then spoke briefly. The gathering broke up soon afterward.

In The *Ann Arbor News* of the next day appeared a photo taken as the audience began to disperse. In that photo I am seen ushering Jennifer Gratz and Barbara Grutter from the center of the crowd. I was indeed a little concerned for their well-being in so hostile a setting. That photograph catches quite perfectly the spirit of that day..

On our campus the MCRI was then and remains still an unpopular cause. Among Michiganders in general, however, it was not unpopular. We formally opened the petition drive before a supportive audience in Lansing shortly afterward. At that gathering I was asked—and honored—by Jennifer Gratz, who was presiding, to come to the front of the hall to be the first signatory on the first petition.

Our main challenge in the first phase of the campaign was to collect the needed number of Michigan signatures on petitions in order that the proposal might be placed formally on the ballot. This was a far more difficult and burdensome task than I had previously supposed it would be. We aimed to get the MCRI on the state ballot in 2004. We tried hard, but it soon became clear that we could not collect the needed number of signatures in time, and that we would have to try again, with more preparation, before the next statewide election, in 2006.

Our opponents raised objections that, whatever their merit, forced the expenditure of weeks and months in legal proceedings before signatures could actually be sought. Chief among these obstacles was a move to keep the proposal off the ballot on the ground that its wording did not satisfy one of the conditions every initiative must meet. The condition in question was this: every ballot proposal must put no more than one single question before the voters. This is entirely reasonable. If two or more issues are conflated in some proposal, voters who might wish to say yes to one of these questions and no to the other would be caught in an intolerable quandary. But this single-issue condition was surely satisfied by our proposal. It asked voters only whether they did or did not wish to forbid state-authorized preferential treatment by race in our state. Our opponents contended that because the initiative addressed different spheres of state activity—employment, education, and contracting—it presented more than one question to be answered and was therefore unsuitable as a ballot proposal. A court hearing was unavoidable, and more hearings followed. Then came the wait for the judicial determination. Months rolled by. The MCRI was ultimately found to satisfy the critical condition; it did indeed present a single issue for the voters.

The legal maneuvering against it continued. One Michigan judge found in a puzzling opinion that the MCRI petition failed to "reflect the language of the state constitution" and ordered the State Board of Canvassers to rescind its approval of the entire petition effort. That highly politicized court order was appealed, of course, and the appeal was successful—but more time was consumed. The assortment of moves, designed by opponents of the MCRI to delay the gathering of signatures, proved effective. By mid-June of 2004 it had become clear that there simply was not enough time to get MCRI on the ballot for that fall. Our election target date was changed. Some four thousand petitions already in circulation had to be withdrawn. I was disheartened and frustrated. I feared—mistakenly, as it turned out—that the result of the postponement would be waning enthusiasm for the initiative, that the effort begun with high hopes in 2003 would wither and collapse. But we had no alternative. If ever the MCRI was to be on the ballot it would be in 2006.

Our opponents, intense and tenacious, were of two sorts. On the one hand there were the relatively sophisticated supporters of the University of Michigan administration and its legal teams, who contended that the educative value of diversity was indeed a compelling state interest and could be achieved at our university only if some preferential treatment for minorities were sustained. Their public campaign was polished; they employed every available device to discourage support for the MCRI and to delay its advance. University administrators, however, could not interfere *directly* in the signature-gathering process.

Others could. They were opponents of a different sort, who thought of themselves as grassroots "defenders of affirmative action"—mainly students and their leaders, most from the Detroit area. The Coalition to Defend Affirmative Action by Any Means Necessary (BAMN) was typical. These groups thrived on excitement, direct action, and sometimes demagoguery. These members of our opposition became more and more troubling to us because they operated out on the street—and on the street is exactly where we had to go to collect the needed signatures on our petitions. A huge number of completed signature sheets were absolutely essential if the MCRI were ever to appear on the Michigan ballot.

To appreciate the difficulties we confronted one must understand the technical demands we were obliged to satisfy. Proponents of an initiative submit a draft petition form to the Bureau of Election (in the department of the secretary of state), and that in turn is submitted to the Board of State Canvassers for approval. After the form of the petitions has been approved, as ours was, petitions in that exact form must be circulated for the signatures (with addresses) of Michigan voters. Signatures must be solicited in person. Those who request the signatures (the "circulators") may be volunteers or they may be paid, but they must be Michigan citizens. Rules governing the preparation and completion of petition sheets are exacting and must be meticulously obeyed; any deficiency results in the sheet being voided and the signatures on it held invalid. There are also strict time limits: petitioners have a window of no more than 180 days to collect the needed signatures.

The *number* of valid signatures needed is the truly burdensome matter. The Michigan Constitution provides that for a proposed amendment to the constitution to be certified, the number of valid signatures required is 10 percent of the number of votes cast for governor in the preceding statewide election. In the Michigan gubernatorial election preceding 2006, the number of votes cast for governor was 3,177,565. We therefore needed to deliver to the Michigan Board of Canvassers *317,756 valid Michigan signatures*—the signatures of persons who affirmed, by signing, that they wanted our proposed constitutional amendment to be on the ballot in 2006.

This is a huge number. Money had to be solicited with which the drive for signatures could be organized and conducted. An executive director of the MCRI had to be appointed; we were fortunate to be able to appoint Jennifer Gratz, still passionate about the matter that had brought her as litigant to the U.S. Supreme Court, to serve in this critical role. I contributed $10,000 to the MCRI organizing committee. Some money came from outside Michigan. Ward Connerly, our adviser and supporter from California, contributed some $355,000. But ours was a Michigan campaign; the citizens of Michigan would cast the deciding votes. They were the ones who mainly sought an amendment that would prohibit race preferences. Across the State of Michigan (which stretches nearly a thousand miles from the copper country near the western end of Lake Superior to the Ohio border at the western tip of Lake Erie), we enlisted some 1,700 volunteer circulators and many paid circulators as well.

Direct interference with the signature-collecting process, by the members of BAMN and similar organizations, made this difficult task yet more difficult. BAMN members followed our circulators on the street and in shopping malls, shouting at them, heckling them, seeking to intimidate them and to frighten away passers-by who might indicate a willingness to sign the petition sheets. Our circulators were called "racists" and "deceivers." They were reviled for allegedly seeking to end all affirmative action; there were even some efforts at physical intimidation. Without the efficient organization of the MCRI Executive Committee, overseen by Jennifer Gratz and undergirded by her great energy, it is not likely that we would have succeeded.

One issue in particular became a sensitive matter of dispute, on the street and then later in the courts. BAMN and other opponents of the MCRI contended that circulators were gathering signatures fraudulently, deliberately deceiving members of the public from whom signatures were sought. The circulators, alleged our critics, were telling potential signers that the proposed amendment would promote affirmative action; in the streets of Detroit and its suburbs, opponents claimed, many who signed the petitions had been bamboozled by falsehoods.

I have no direct knowledge of what was said out on the streets, but our circulators were firmly instructed not to mislead, just to say clearly what the initiative sought to accomplish. I discussed this matter on several occasions with Jennifer Gratz, reviewing our procedures; we agreed that it was exceedingly improbable that any such deception played a significant role in signature collection. It is possible, of course, that some circulators, under some circumstances, made remarks—some perhaps deliberately—that resulted in confusion or misunderstanding. But even if that were true in isolated cases, the number of persons deceived could have been no more than a tiny fraction of the number of signatures we collected. Besides, it was unlikely that any adult asked to sign who read the petition would not have understood what he or she was signing. Each petition sheet, with about twenty lines for signatures and addresses, carried the following heading. The top two lines, in boldface, read: "INITIATIVE PETITION—AMENDMENT TO THE CONSTITUTION." Directly under these lines appeared, on every sheet, a paragraph with exactly the following words—in large, block, capital letters: "A PROPOSAL TO AMEND THE CONSTITUTION TO PROHIBIT THE UNIVERSITY OF MICHIGAN AND OTHER STATE UNIVERSITIES, THE STATE, AND ALL OTHER STATE ENTITIES FROM DISCRIMINATING OR GRANTING PREFERENTIAL TREATMENT BASED ON RACE, SEX, COLOR, ETHNICITY, OR NATIONAL ORIGIN." In my view, the claim that signers of these petitions were systematically deceived is not only false but also patronizing in supposing such widespread ignorance.

Our opponents were convinced that if the MCRI were eventually put before voters on a statewide ballot, it would be adopted. They did everything they could to block us, but they failed.

Long before the deadline of 31 May 2006—it was still 2005—the many boxes of petition sheets were gathered at the MCRI office in Detroit and driven to Lansing, the state capital, in a caravan. The boxes were received, identified, and registered by an officer of the Michigan secretary of state, who would later submit them to the Board of State Canvassers for review. I myself, behaving calmly and properly but internally pleased and proud, carried in my arms some of those heavy boxes of petitions into the offices of the secretary of state, where we were greeted with courtesy.

Delivering the many boxes of signatures—there were scores of boxes, but I have forgotten their exact number—is far from the end of the struggle to get an initiative on the ballot. The reason is this: every initiative drive collects some signatures on the street that turn out to be invalid. A person signing might not use his real name or might not write down his correct Michigan address. Some errors are inadvertent; some are not. Some circulators might provide sheets with signatures inappropriately collected or might have prepared the petition sheets incorrectly. Deficiencies of one kind or another are sure to be found; to overcome them the Board of State Canvassers must determine how many *valid* signatures have been submitted. The number of valid signatures we needed was 317,756. We knew that we would have to submit many more than that to be safe.

How many more? Experience in past initiative drives has shown that the number of invalid signatures on the sheets can be large, sometimes as much as 25 or 30 percent. The percentage of signatures that are valid is determined, in Michigan, using a random sample method of verification. The Board of State Canvassers does this in two stages. First, each individual sheet is checked to determine whether there are errors on it that would invalidate all of the signatures on that sheet. Sheets that pass this initial review are numbered and their signatures counted. From the total number of such counted signatures, a random sample of 500 is collected using a process developed by the Department of Statistics and Probability at Michigan State University. These 500 signatures, serving as a statistical sample, are examined closely to determine, with respect to each signature, if there really is such a person, and if he or she really does reside at the address given. The actual list of those 500 names and addresses is provided to both proponents and opponents. The percentage of valid signatures among that randomly selected sample is taken to be (with an extremely narrow margin of error) the percentage of valid signatures in the entire body of signatures submitted.

The boxes with thousands of sheets of signatures that we had delivered to the secretary of state contained, by verified count, 508,282 signatures—well over a half million. Even if our collecting standards had not been high (as our opponents claimed) we would have had well more than the needed 317,756. If the percentage of valid signatures were as low as 65 percent, we would have had enough. In fact our standards were high; the verification procedure of the Board of State Canvassers showed that the percentage of valid signatures among those we submitted was nearly 90 percent. The MCRI seemed certain to be on the 2006 ballot.

But not without a continuing struggle. The Board of State Canvassers has four members. They, it turned out, were sharply split along political party lines. The Michigan Democratic Party and Jennifer Granholm, our Democratic governor at that time, were strongly opposed to the MCRI. When the Board of State Canvassers met in July of 2005 to review the MCRI proposal for the November 2006 ballot, the evenly divided board refused to certify it. We went quickly to the Michigan Court of Appeals, and that court *ordered* the board to certify the petitions.

Despite that court order, recalcitrance by the Board of State Canvassers continued. On 14 December 2005 the board was scheduled to meet to comply with the court order to certify our petitions. I drove up to Lansing that morning; the fall term at the university had ended, and I wanted to be present at the certification. What took place at that meeting was scandalous. A large number of Detroit high-school and middle-school students had been marshaled by BAMN and bussed to the meeting in Lansing. The aim, one must suppose, was to create an atmosphere in the meeting hall in which members of the board would find it difficult to vote for certification. Disruption may have been contemplated. The students were being manipulated to ensure that the certification could not go forward. Directed by unidentifiable leaders, the students in the meeting room began to shout "No Voter Fraud," apparently believing that the deceptive collection of some signatures should invalidate all the petitions submitted. Because the number of valid signatures we had submitted was far greater than that required, those objecting on this ground would have to believe that 140,000 Michigan citizens were deceived by our circulators, led to sign petitions they did not understand. But any reading of the large heading (described above) on each of those sheets would make perfectly clear what the petition was about. Michigan citizens can read. The claim that deception invalidated the signatures submitted is preposterous.

The shouting became so loud ("They say Jim Crow! We say hell no!") that members of the board, shortly after opening the session, adjourned it until 2:00 that afternoon. The protesting crowd then surged forward, throwing over the table at which the board had been sitting. It was a shameful scene. The Lansing police were called to control the situation. Opposition to the MCRI had sunk to new depths. Members of the board who had refused to certify the petitions, as they had been ordered by the court to do, were eventually fined $250 each for contempt of court. They resigned from the board. The MCRI was at last certified for the November 2006 ballot.

CHAPTER 30

Defending the Michigan Civil Rights Initiative

We were on the ballot. I believed that voters in Michigan were offended by race preferences. When faced bluntly with the question at the polls I was quite confident that they would support our proposal to prohibit, permanently, all preferential treatment for any ethnic group for any reason. That confidence was psychologically comforting—but we had a political campaign on our hands. We had to make sure, as far as we were able, that our conviction—that *fairness* obliges the prohibition of ethnic favoritism—would register effectively in November of 2006.

We named what we had been defending the Michigan Civil Rights Initiative (MCRI). Our opponents decried that name, contending that the proposal had nothing to do with "civil rights," which they thought of chiefly as the rights of minorities that needed protection. They believed that we were capitalizing on the moral spirit of the "civil rights movement" to advance a goal inconsistent with it. Many voiced this complaint sincerely; for them "civil rights" did mean the minority rights valiantly defended during the 1950s and 1960s. But the term "civil rights" means more than that. It refers to the rights of all citizens in a body politic, not those of minorities only. *All* citizens have the right to be treated equally by the laws, to be confident that there will be no discrimination for or against whites, or blacks, or any racial or ethnic group. Our initiative, aiming to protect that fundamental and universal right to equal treatment, we justly named the MCRI.

As the political battle began, however, our initiative came to be known by a different name. On the Michigan ballot it had been given a number by state election authorities. It was Proposal 06-02; it came to be commonly called Proposition 2.

I became embroiled in the statewide political campaign in support of

Proposition 2. My work as a professor of philosophy at the University of Michigan, principally the classes I taught, remained my central activity during the months before the election of 2006. But my involvement in the campaign was intense and absorbed much of my time.

I was called on to give talks and engage in debates around the state. The universities in Michigan, and above all the University of Michigan, were vigorous opponents of Proposition 2. The great resources of the universities, in money and personnel, were marshaled in statewide attacks on the proposition. I was therefore obliged to become, and I did become in those years (2004–2006), the most vigorous public critic of my own university. In the talks I gave I rarely failed to report that I had long been, and will always remain, a loyal servant of the University of Michigan, to which I have devoted my entire professional career. I would say, proudly, that of all worldly institutions besides my family and my country, the University of Michigan is the one I love most. But the principle that all races, by right, deserve equal treatment was more important than institutional loyalty. That principle I had been defending all my adult life and with enthusiasm as the chairman of the American Civil Liberties Union (ACLU) of Michigan. The preferential policies of my university were inconsistent with that principle and morally wrong—even though a narrow majority of the Supreme Court had found them lawful.

This internal conflict, between loyalty and philosophical convictions, obliged me to resolve for myself some tangled theoretical issues concerning the proper role of universities, and university professors, in the discussion of public issues. I explain.

Many years before I had been asked to address the Southern University Conference—a group of college and university presidents from the South. My topic then was "Political Controversy and the University." There was a growing movement at that time to enlist the various institutions of higher learning as participants on one side or another in the public controversies then afoot. In that lecture I argued that for us, for the colleges and universities, there is an intellectual gyroscope that must hold us on course, and, as far as possible, keep our institutions from becoming combatants in the political wars. Learning and teaching is our mission, I said—the advancement of understanding and the accumulation of new knowledge. We serve our country and our community best by providing that precious setting in which every rational opinion—every argument, theory, or proposal—may be advocated and criticized, defended or debunked. In practice we may fall short of this ideal, but it is the ideal that justifies the support given to us and justifies our insulation from political pressures. I defended, in sum, the classical view of the university as the impartial host for argument, a role sacrificed when the university itself supports one side or another in political controversy.

The Southern University Conference in Savannah published that lecture as an essay in 1980;[1] it was later republished with warm approbation in 1983 by Williams College.[2] My argument was long and detailed. I was careful to address counterarguments, especially the argument of those who held that neutrality on controversial issues was not really possible for universities. I called this the argument from inevitability. I noted the eloquent statement of that position by philosophical colleagues Robert Paul Wolff of the University of Massachusetts[3] and Henry David Aiken of Brandeis University.[4] Wolff and Aiken were my personal friends, but their argument from inevitability was mistaken: universities *can* set themselves to pursue educational objectives while not becoming institutional actors. There are some exceptional cases, but universities can pursue and often can attain reasonable intellectual neutrality. That was and remains my view.

The exceptions arise when controversial issues before the public bear directly upon the goals and the standards of the universities themselves. When some proposed legislation threatens the freedom of inquiry, or when some public policy in dispute has a serious bearing on our capacity to fulfill our mission, universities may be obliged to speak out and certainly ought to be free to do so. Such exceptions are important, but they do not swallow the rule. My conclusion was expressed in these words: "On controversial political or moral issues a college or university should neither take official stands, nor adopt policies [that] in effect support one side or the other, *unless doing so is essential to its intellectual mission.*"

I held that view in the essay of 1980, I held it in 2004, and I hold it still. How did this considered judgment bear upon the controversy over Proposition 2? It seemed pretty clear to me that under my own principles a university advocate of admissions preferences—the president of the University of Michigan, for example—would be fully justified in bringing the university itself into the dispute as advocate, speaking out for the university as agent, expending funds, and conducting forums and meetings aimed at defeating Proposition 2. The dispute over affirmative action had become one of those exceptional cases. I might have wished it were otherwise, but I knew it was not. The University of Michigan was beyond doubt directly and centrally involved in the dispute, and had, therefore, a right to take a stand as an institution.

That was what the university did with great vigor. Large meetings for students and faculty supporting "affirmative action" were held on campus; talks given by university administrators with the same objective were directed at faculty and local citizens. The *University Record* and other periodicals published by the university carried on the propaganda battle with intensity. I argued with the provost of the university at that time, Paul Courant, in a well-attended public debate. There was no pretense of university neutrality. My university's officers were convinced that the passage of Proposition 2 would seriously undermine their efforts to achieve the racial diversity they so much wanted.

All this I found painful, of course. Many of the claims made about diversity were unfounded; some were false. But it was all part of a serious intellectual conflict, and (as a legitimate exception to the ideal of institutional neutrality that I had long defended) the university had the right to be an outspoken participant in *this* political controversy, in view of its university-oriented nature. The first paragraph of Proposition 2 began, "The University of Michigan . . . shall not. . . . " I could not have expected, and I did not expect, that the University of Michigan, as an institution, would remain silent.

The volume and the intensity of the university's campaign against Proposition 2 did, nevertheless, trouble me. There never was any doubt that as private citizens, professors as well as students had every right to engage in the argument also. No one questioned my right to do so. In the classroom, however, from the lecture platform, I thought it not my business to support or attack any position in the political wars. I teach political philosophy. When my students seek in class to have me take a stand in some political dispute, I will explore the bearing of the philosophy we are discussing on that controversy but will resist the temptation to take sides. Some of my students, learning of my views from materials in the *Michigan Daily* and the *Ann Arbor News*, would question me in ways that invited a defense of Proposition 2. I was scrupulous about not going down that path. Many of my colleagues on the other side of the issue were not so scrupulous; they had the advantage of the great echo chamber that was the university, in which the alleged evils of Proposition 2 were repeatedly and loudly denounced.

Finally I came to ask myself whether I might rightly be more forward, speak more candidly in support of Proposition 2 in my classes as well as in my community. It would go against my grain to do so; it would be inconsistent with the impartial role I had earlier argued ought to be maintained by university professors—even though I knew that there were many on our faculty who denounced Proposition 2 in their classrooms without any hesitation. At last I decided to be somebody outspoken, not so much because I thought my voice, pretty nearly a lone voice, would have much impact from within my classes, but because I was simply fed up with the attacks on Proposition 2 that suffused the campus atmosphere and cried out for response.

Simply turning my classroom into a political platform would have been disgraceful in my eyes. The students in philosophy who had enrolled in my classes had done so with intellectual objectives and would have been unfairly used if they were forced to be a captive audience for my views. Proposition 2 was highly controversial on campus in those days. If I were to defend it openly in my classroom, that must be done, I thought, in such a way as to trap no one and to fool no one. How then was I to do it?

I decided that I would propose to my colleagues in the Residential College that I teach a course on the entire cluster of issues raised by Proposition 2, with the clear announcement at the outset that I would do so from the perspective of an advocate of the MCRI. I proposed a course (what we call a minicourse because it would meet only about half as frequently as most other university courses) titled Race and Admissions, to be offered—for academic credit—in the fall term of 2005. I laid out the topics of my lectures and discussions in that proposed course, and I brought that syllabus to the director of our college at that time, Prof. Thomas Weisskopf. We talked about it at length. I wanted to be sure he understood my intentions, and I wanted to be confident that no one would later allege or suppose that I had behaved improperly. I asked him explicitly if he thought such a course, taught from the perspective of one who openly supports Proposition 2 (as he certainly did not), would be appropriately offered in our college. I did not want to sneak my views into the classroom; I wanted my position in the matter to be fully understood by colleagues and by the students who enrolled in that class. To his great credit, he agreed to such an offering without qualm.

I knew that such a course would provoke wide interest on the campus and therefore wanted an even more widespread understanding of what I was planning to do. I sent my syllabus and explanation to the deanery of the College of Literature, Science, and the Arts (LSA), our larger college, where I knew there was virtually no sympathy for Proposition 2. Would such a formal course offering be fully appropriate? Again, from the dean's office the response was unequivocal: we understand and have no complaint. The reader will appreciate the fact that such restraint on the part of university officers was, in the light of the propaganda wars under way, honorable and worthy of respect. Well (as I often observed then and later), this is the University of Michigan.

I did teach that course in the fall term of 2005, to about thirty-five enrolled students (and often some visitors as well), and I want to say a little about how that went. It was an experience unlike any other I have had in years of teaching at Michigan. As lively discussion in that classroom went on over the weeks of the term, it became evident that the enrolled students held a variety of views, some supporting Proposition 2, some opposed to it. There was one group of about five students, always seated together, who had plainly enrolled in the course with the aim of using it to attack Proposition 2. They were prepared to disrupt the class, but disruption was not their main objective. I recognized them as members of the Coalition to Defend Affirmative Action by Any Means Necessary (BAMN) I had encountered in earlier gatherings on campus. They invariably came as a group and sat in the front row of seats in the classroom. I did not by any means object to their being there. They had every right to enroll in the course. I welcomed them; the tension that arose from their questions and comments heightened the interest of those sessions for us all.

The BAMN members and I would argue on occasion, and of course there would be no resolution of the matters in dispute. The other members of the class would be, in effect, the judges of the matter, and since I had confidence in the merit of my position in support of Proposition 2, I was quite happy to argue and leave it at that. I will admit that there were one or two occasions on which I was sharply taken aback by the character of comments from members of this group. There were two young ladies in particular whose passion in support of the university's admission system overwhelmed them at times and led them to abandon argument and condemn me personally, sometimes with language more vulgar than one would ever expect to encounter in a university classroom. That conduct redounded to my argumentative advantage, of course; the other students were offended, sometimes greatly angered, on my behalf. Some enemies can be helpful.

In this class I discussed the Michigan cases, of course, long before concluded by the Supreme Court decisions of 2003, but still of theoretical interest. Barbara Grutter, the leading plaintiff in the major case the university had won, came as a visiting lecturer to the class on one occasion, and the students gained much, I think, from hearing her. Her restrained and gracious manner, as well as her patient thoughtfulness, was exceedingly effective in that academic atmosphere.

I brought other guest lecturers as well: Terry Pell, of the Center for Individual Rights (CIR), flew up from Washington, D.C., to talk to my class on one occasion. The students were impressed by him, and I think he was equally impressed by them. Jennifer Gratz came also—and, as I had promised to do, I invited the general counsel of the university, Marvin Krislov, to conduct one of the sessions of the class—which he did, effectively. I had promised him that I would remain silent during his visit, in order that it not become a battle between him and me, and I kept my promise.

How much was accomplished by offering that course I cannot say. Students were evaluated on a credit/no credit basis; I made it plain that their thinking and reasoning, not their political views, were to be evaluated. I assigned one long paper in which some aspect of the issues was to be explored in some detail; some of those papers were quite fine. The BAMN group, having abandoned the class after Krislov's visit late in the term, did not submit papers and received no academic credit. The students learned a good deal, I believe, and their evident appreciation was rewarding to me.

The fate of our initiative would depend on the votes of citizens all across the state. So it was important for us to reach citizens far away from Ann Arbor. I received many invitations to speak or to debate, and I accepted those invitations whenever it was feasible for me to do so. This activity was facilitated, in some degree, by an organization called Toward a Fair Michigan led by a professor of political science at Michigan State University, William Allen. Professor Allen's view was that everything was to be gained, and nothing lost, if the issues raised by Proposition 2 were widely discussed and argued. He believed that the strongest presentations on both sides of the issue were in everyone's best interest, and with his wife he set out to organize such presentations statewide. Barbara Grutter, living in Plymouth, Michigan, had the same view and devoted her time and energy, with Professor Allen, to arranging for debates around the state. She was a committed advocate of the initiative itself, of course, but she was convinced that the best thing she could do in its support was to encourage open and vigorous argument on all sides. She worked as hard, I believe, to find speakers who opposed Proposition 2 as to find speakers who supported it. There were plenty of people who opposed the proposition, but outside the university context speaking on that side of the question was often not comfortable. The thrust of Proposition 2 was the elimination of preferences by race and ethnicity. Opposing Proposition 2 therefore entailed supporting those preferences—a view not so easily defended in a public talk.

Among the presentations I gave around the state, some were especially memorable. On 7 November 2005 I gave a talk at Kalamazoo College, a fine small college about a hundred miles west of Ann Arbor. The setting was a large hall that had the look of a great old chapel (which I think it had originally been); the audience, from the Kalamazoo community as well as the college, was large and much involved in the discussion that followed my talk. I took that opportunity to discuss with the audience the meaning of the term *affirmative action*. Opponents of Proposition 2 often alleged that it would, if adopted, end all affirmative action. The truth of this claim depends, of course, on what is meant by affirmative action. It first entered the current political arena when used by President John F. Kennedy in an executive order,[5] by which he established the President's Committee on Equal Employment Opportunities, in 1961. A long history of racial discrimination in government employment cried out for remedy. Part of the remedy—an important part—would be to end racial discrimination by the many private firms that hold contracts with the federal government. The president did not have the authority to tell them how to hire and fire, but he did have the authority to tell them that if they did not cease to discriminate by race, they would not qualify for contracts with the U.S. government. "All government contracting agencies," the order (which is still in force) proclaimed, "shall include in every government contract . . . the following provisions: The Contractor will not discriminate against any employee or applicant for employment because of race, creed, color, or national origin. The contractor will take *affirmative action* to insure that applicants are employed, and that employees are treated during employment, *without regard to their race, creed, color, or national origin.*"[6]

That was the original, honorable, and proper sense of affirmative action—to ensure that race and ethnicity play no part whatever in employment practices. The objective of Proposition 2 was exactly the same. Not only would our proposition not end affirmative action, it was the *realization* of the spirit of affirmative action as originally conceived.

President Lyndon Johnson, four years later, implementing and strengthening the Civil Rights Act of 1964, issued a supplementary executive order of his own, 11246, which established requirements for non-discriminatory practices in hiring and employment on the part of U.S. government contractors. By this order, contractors and their subcontractors were again prohibited from discriminating in employment decisions on the basis of race, color, religion, sex, or national origin. Contractors would, henceforth, be obliged to "*take affirmative action* to insure that applicants are employed, and that employees are treated during employment, *without regard to their race, color, religion, sex, or national origin.*"[7]

It is plain that affirmative action meant, and does mean in its proper sense, steps taken to *eliminate* preferences by race. That was the essence of Proposition 2. Subsequent loose usage resulted in the inversion of this meaning. Being a phrase with positive connotations and much appeal, it was adopted by those who wished to take race and ethnicity into account to describe their preferential programs, thereby turning the phrase *affirmative action* on its head. It was important, I believed, that as the debate over our proposition continued, this full understanding of affirmative action be widespread.

In Midland, Michigan, on 15 March 2006, in a formal debate, I argued with my friend and university colleague Tom Weisskopf. This was one of the debates organized by Toward a Fair Michigan, and a mark of its impartiality was persuading him, as an opponent of Proposition 2, to travel around the state. Weisskopf is an exceedingly sophisticated professor of economics and an effective public speaker. We knew each other well, of course, and had long argued these questions privately. I thought that debate went well from my perspective, and I enjoyed it mightily; I think he felt the same way.

There was a reunion, on 27 April 2006, of the old-time members of the debate team at the University of Miami in Coral Gables, my undergraduate alma mater. The debate coach, David Steinberg, asked me to give the principal address, which I thought a signal honor. My audience would include many of my debate teammates of decades earlier, among them a superb teacher (Ray Adkins) and a federal judge (Jerry Kogan) and others of fine intellect and happy memory. I used the occasion to reflect upon the role of intellectual debate in the life of a university professor like myself. It was on that debate team, in the late 1940s, that I found my voice. It seemed, in retrospect, as though my entire life had become, with great satisfaction, a long series of debates—about free speech, about democracy, about the uses of animals, about racial justice and the equal protection of the laws. Of course I reviewed with them the ongoing debate over Michigan's Proposition 2, not a burning issue in Miami, but much on my mind at that time.

The African American Alumni Council of the University of Michigan asked me to present my views in support of Proposition 2 at the Alumni Center in Ann Arbor on 5 May 2006. On that occasion, as also when I spoke to the local chapter of the NAACP in Ypsilanti, most of my audience was black. I welcomed this. Preferences for minorities in university admissions are particularly damaging to African Americans, although many in that community mistakenly supposed the initiative would take from them a good thing long enjoyed. In this setting I had the opportunity to explain why preferences are the opposite of a benefit for minorities. The inevitable result of race preferences, I pointed out, is the admission of minority applicants not as well prepared for college work or for professional school study as most of their classmates. The inevitable consequence is that the performance of black students, statistically, is comparatively poor. This is not because of any native inferiority in them, of course, but because of the distortion of the admission standards applied. This relative inferiority in performance by blacks (which cannot be hidden) serves to reinforce the stereotype of black intellectual inferiority. By giving preference to minorities we *forge a link* between color and inferior performance. It is the worst thing we could do for minorities, not a boon but a great and continuing burden borne by *all* those of the preferred skin color. One of the best consequences of the adoption of Proposition 2, I argued—with special intensity before black audiences—is that it would remove this scandalous burden. That blacks are intellectually inferior is a *canard* that preferences engender and support.

At the University of Michigan Law School, where the frequency of my appearances might have been causing me to lose my welcome, I was asked to speak to the Asian American Law Students Association on 11 October 2006. If they were not on my side they certainly ought to have been. Admission to selective professional schools is a zero-sum game; the number of available places (at Michigan, for example) is sharply limited. Asian American students have been greatly overrepresented. If the implicit (and sometimes explicit) objective of preferential programs is approximate proportional representation by ethnic group, Asian Americans and Jews will most assuredly carry much of the burden. Every preference in *admission* favoring blacks or Hispanics must result in a *rejection* based in part on color or ethnicity. That is just logic.

The response of the Asian American law students was mixed in a peculiar way. They saw well enough that the burden of the preferences given to underrepresented minorities would probably fall largely on their own group; most were sympathetic to the arguments I put forward for that reason among others. There was, however, an apparent reluctance on the part of some to oppose those preferences insofar as they were seen (as they were then widely seen) as a *minority* benefit. Their experiences as members of a clearly identifiable minority appeared to engender, among some Asian Americans, a sort of kindred feeling for blacks and Hispanics, tacitly supposing that the preferences were indeed beneficial for the minorities preferred.

Predominantly black audiences were those I most enjoyed addressing, like that in Benton Harbor, Michigan, on 24 April 2006. African Americans rarely fail to understand how momentous the passage of the Civil Rights Act was in 1964, how profoundly it has changed life in the United States. I could reach those audiences effectively by calling their attention to the essential spirit of Proposition 2 and the spirit of the Civil Rights Act. The very *words* of our proposition deliberately tracked those of the Civil Rights Act. "It shall be an unlawful employment practice," Title VII of the act proclaimed, to limit, to classify, or to discriminate against any individual "because of such individual's race, color, religion, sex, or national origin." Where the federal government gives financial support, Title VI of the act proclaimed, discrimination by race or color or sex will be henceforth prohibited. Not blacks alone, but "any individual," *all citizens of all colors and origins* were protected and remain protected by that great law, which we owe, in good part, to the sometimes heroic efforts of black actors and the provocation of black moral teachers. What they taught, genuine equality before the law, was precisely what we were seeking to incorporate now into the Michigan Constitution. With all my heart I could assure my audience in Benton Harbor that the fairness they have longed for was precisely the fairness that Proposition 2 would demand.

My public defense of Proposition 2 took different forms. Within the University of Michigan my voice was largely drowned out by that of the central administration, possessing many pulpits more effective than mine. Recall that Lee Bollinger had left Michigan in 2002 to become president of Columbia University. His successor was Prof. Mary Sue Coleman, an accomplished biologist who had exhibited great managerial success as president of the University of Iowa. No one could have been appointed as Bollinger's replacement who was not an enthusiastic supporter of the Michigan admissions preferences, and President Coleman was most certainly that. In the higher reaches of our university administration the rightness and necessity of admissions preferences were more than conventional wisdom; they were defended universally and sometimes with absurd hyperbole, with statements from the president asserting even that our excellence as a university was based entirely on the diversity of our student body.

I was never able to arrange a person-to-person debate with President Coleman, which would have pleased me greatly. But there was one way in which I could create a person-to-person debate. I wrote "An Open Letter to the President of My University," published that fall in *Academic Questions.*[8]

My letter to the president was courteous and respectful, of course. It did not aim directly at the support of the initiative that she so firmly opposed, although that was its purpose, as all could see. It took the form of urging her to read a recently published little book by Shelby Steele, *White Guilt,*[9] whose argument I summarized. Steele, who had long ago been one of those angry protesters presenting nonnegotiable demands to their university presidents—and who were successful because, as he points out, white racism had given way to a new age. Guilt about race had become so widespread, so enervating, that it cleared the path to power for black activists.

White guilt became, and remains, I wrote, "the central nerve of relations between blacks and whites." Steele understood that dynamic deeply. He called attention to the ways in which whites in authority, especially in the universities, are often trumped by their own feelings of guilt. They hunger to show themselves redeemed. College presidents, Steele wrote, "lose moral authority over everything having to do with race, equality, social justice." The obsequious behavior of some university presidents—and some university faculties too—can thus be understood. White guilt, I wrote to President Coleman in that open letter of September 2006, "is not a transitory phenomenon of a generation past; it is the moral theme that has come to pervade our universities."

In the letter I reported the incident (recounted in this book in Chapter 14) of a professor's reluctant change of a student's grade when confronted by the unjustified threat of the accusation of racism—and that professor's private confession to me, his retrospective feeling of shame. The impact of white guilt on the entire University of Michigan campus is made manifest, I pointed out, by the fact that, although we know that university faculties around the country, when polled secretly, oppose race preferences, here the number of faculty openly supporting Proposition 2 can be counted on the fingers of one hand. Why, I asked, is it so difficult for members of our faculty to speak out in support of the MCRI?

You and others in your administration have spoken strongly in opposition to it, because you wish to retain the ethnic preferences that this initiative would forbid. Supporters of the Initiative among our faculty, however numerous, are for the most part silent. Why? There is no fear that we would be penalized if we disagree with you. There would be no such penalty, we know. What then can explain this remarkable silence? In *White Guilt* Shelby Steele explains it very well.

The preferences we give to minorities in admission were initiated as a form of compensation for injuries earlier suffered; they were efforts to make payment for guilt. In reality those preferences impose great burdens on minorities, burdens that outweigh any benefits they appear to offer. Nevertheless the preferences are commonly viewed as instruments of redress. This compensatory intention was for many years explicit. But equal treatment under the law is plainly inconsistent with compensation by ethnicity; one is entitled to redress for injury without regard to skin color. So the compensatory justification of preference has been repeatedly rejected by the courts. Our university, defending preferences in the courts, renounced that compensatory justification explicitly, resorting to the one justification that had some hope of winning the legal battle: diversity.

That the diversity defense is no more than a stratagem is revealed by the history of this controversy. Diversity was hardly ever mentioned until the compensatory justification was thrown out by the courts. The evidence in the Michigan cases, *Grutter* and *Gratz*, exposes the ruse. If a "critical mass" of minority students (what was claimed to be our compelling need) requires, let us say, 50 blacks among an entering law school class, how can it be that only 25 are needed for a critical mass of Hispanics? And only 5 for a critical mass of Native Americans? I wish not to offend, President Coleman, but candor compels the conclusion that all our talk about using preference to achieve a "critical mass" of students of each minority is—as four members of the Supreme Court made very clear—a "sham." We resort to it because it is the only device available with which we can continue to satisfy the inner compulsions of white guilt.

Perhaps you cannot admit this, even to yourself. But I ask you to reflect. A number of the states in our country, Massachusetts among them, do not even have a state-supported law school. Can an increase in the number of certain racial minorities in the entering class of our Law School be a truly "*compelling*" need for the state of Michigan? So compelling that we must allow an exception to the Equal Protection Clause to permit it? The claim is preposterous.

That citizens must be treated equally, without regard to race or national origin and without discrimination or preference, is the fundament of the American experiment. That is the proposition, as President Lincoln rightly said, to which our nation is *dedicated*. Is that dedication now to be given up for the claimed (but very uncertain) advantages of classroom discussions in which more students of different colors are in the room? You cannot seriously believe that.

When we *give* by race it follows necessarily, in competitive contexts, that in doing so we *take* by race. The applicant displaced and disadvantaged by her color, whose name we cannot know, is real; she and all those similarly rejected are the persons who must pay for the guilt we feel and seek to expiate. Do you think that fair? The Chief Justice of the U.S. Supreme Court recently put it succinctly: "It is a sordid business, this divvying us up by race."

Madame President, our current admission practices, honorably motivated, are one form, not very subtle, of outright racial discrimination. Our conduct, well meant, is shameful. We would not behave in this shameful way were we not driven by guilt.

You have exhibited, to your great credit, a continuing concern for the happiness and satisfaction of student life in our residence halls. My office is in one of those residence halls. I am there night and day, year in and year out. Come and stay with us for a while. You will experience directly the humiliating truth of what Shelby Steele has written:

> When I visit university campuses today, black students often tell me that racism is everywhere around them, that the university is a racist institution. . . . The students feel aggrieved by racism even as they live on campuses notorious for almost totalitarian regimes of political correctness. . . . This is because their feeling of racial aggrievement is calibrated to the degree of white guilt on university campuses and not to actual racism. . . . Even announcements of a new commitment to "diversity" within an institution will very likely *increase* feelings of racial aggrievement in minorities. We blacks always experience white guilt as an incentive, almost a command, to somehow exhibit racial woundedness and animus. . . . Threatened with a stigmatization that can gravely injure businesses and ruin careers, whites can be pressured into treating the merest accusation of racism as virtual proof. . . . Texaco, Coca-Cola, and Toyota are only a few of the corporations that have paid hundreds of millions of dollars to the diversity industry to avoid stigmatization as "racist."[10]

In an atmosphere of pervasive racial guilt the race card always works. The accusation of racism leveled at a person or an institution sticks like glue and needs no proof to do its damage. Universities, like corporations, do not pay, with preferences, to the measure of any actual racism. They pay to the measure of racism's bloated reputation in the age of white guilt.

As your admirer, Professor Coleman, and your Michigan colleague, I strongly urge you to read Shelby Steel's painfully penetrating little book.
Respectfully yours,
/s/ Carl Cohen
Professor of Philosophy

No reply from the president was expected, of course, and none was received.

I really cannot remember all of the towns in Michigan, and colleges in Michigan, to which I was invited in the year before the fate of Proposition 2 would be decided in the election of 2006. But of all those events there is one in particular I remember most vividly.

It took place on the evening of 28 March 2006, on the campus of Michigan State University (MSU), in East Lansing. It was a carefully organized debate, between me and a man named Tim Wise, who condemned Proposition 2. To recount accurately what happened on that occasion, I begin by describing the setting. We argued in a large hall on that campus; our audience was huge, consisting almost entirely of MSU students. Who had organized the debate and advertised it I do not recall, but he or she had plainly done a splendid job.

This Wise is an interesting character. He is a young white man whose profession is lecturing about racism. From his website, on which there is a biography and booking information, one learns that he has lectured on more than 600 college campuses. His theme is always the same, although the contexts vary: racism in religion, racism in the schools, racism in New York, racism in the universities, racism in the age of Obama—you name the setting and he will work up a lecture for you in which the thrust is sure to be pervasive and despicable white privilege. At the time of this debate I had not yet read the book by Shelby Steele about which I was to write President Coleman some months later, but one can say, without injustice, that Tim Wise has made a career out of white guilt.

He is good at it. He is a superb public speaker. He exaggerates but he does not lie. He specializes in plucking the guilt strings of white university students, and that is what he did, with great skill, on that March evening in 2006. Usually it is the case, when I engage in a person-to-person public debate, that I am the more effective speaker. Public debate has been the substance of my work, in and around the University of Michigan and elsewhere. There are no scorekeepers in most political debates, but when the evening is over I know, usually with great confidence, who won.

I cannot say that with respect to this lively debate with Wise at MSU. I was in good form. I had important things to say, and I said them well, clearly and with punch. But the hundreds of white students in that audience began the evening on his side of the argument, and (I believe) most of them stayed with him.

The success Wise had that evening was due in part to his artful changing of the subject. We were there to argue the merits of Proposition 2, which would prohibit preference by race or nationality in the public universities and elsewhere. He used his time, very effectively, to exhibit the advantages of being white in our society. Much that he said was quite right and worth thinking about. I had no interest in denying the truths he justly called to attention. It certainly does not follow, from the fact that being white is indeed an advantage in our world, that preferences for nonwhites are morally right or beneficial. But in a debate on the initiative his hammering repeatedly on the realities of white privilege played perfectly to the sympathies, to the guilt, of his young white audience. His argument was fallacious. It was, as the classical logicians would say, an *ignoratio elenchi*, an argument in which the premises do indeed support a conclusion, but that conclusion is not the point actually at issue. Some fallacies serve their authors well.

Correctly supposing in advance that that would be the thrust of Wise's remarks, I sought in my remarks not to deny the advantages of white skin but to exhibit the *disadvantages* of giving *preference* to black skin.

Every fine black scholar, junior or senior, is sabotaged by race preferences. All the achievements of black students are put under a cloud, undone by skepticism. One of my former students, superbly qualified for legal studies, and black, told me that as he walked around the Michigan Law Quad, he felt as though he had AFFIRMATIVE ACTION stamped on his forehead. Only a few weeks before that debate a black undergraduate, Meisha Williamson, wrote in a letter to the *Michigan Daily* in December of 2005, "Whenever I ask a question in class I have to worry about being seen as the dumb black girl who doesn't deserve to be here." Humiliating. Yet painfully true because, if it is known that black students are given marked preferences in admissions—as they certainly are—every black student is assumed to have been admitted as a result of that charity, not upon her own merits. Racially oriented *disdain* is widespread on university campuses, though not publicly expressed, of course. Even black students who need no preference—and there are plenty of those—cannot know *themselves* whether they have received preference or not.

Some individuals do get, by preference, what they otherwise would not have gotten; they may be benefited. (Although if there is a resulting mismatch between that student and the school to which he or she is thus admitted, the apparent benefit may be illusory, the preference perhaps a handicap rather than a benefit.) But in any case the minority preferred, *the group as a whole,* is not benefited by the preference; he or she is *undermined.*

Preferences result inevitably in the appointment and admission of persons on grounds not relevant to their duties or their studies. Skin color has nothing to do with intelligence or academic promise. What results? Those so admitted perform less well—not because they are black or brown—that is an outrageous supposition. But if students are admitted to the university with credentials diluted by considerations having nothing to do with intellectual attainment or promise, it is a statistical certainty that those students will (as a group) do less well in their college studies. This relative weakness in their performance is publicly evident because of their color and is widely taken to be the product of that color. So the nasty stereotypes of racial inferiority are *reinforced* by the preferential devices that were supposed to give support. That minorities are intellectually inferior is false. By giving race preference we *create* and *reinforce* the links that lead to that damaging false belief.

If some demon had sought to concoct a scheme to undermine minority students and scholars, to *stigmatize* them and to *humiliate* them publicly, he could not have selected a more ingenious device than the race preference now widespread. Wherever a system results in the *regular association of inferior performance with color*—as it must when color is given weight in the selection process for university admission—those whose skin are of that preferred color become unavoidably suspect.

Preferential affirmative action has thus given maddening plausibility to the claim persons of some colors are not really capable of meeting the same standards of performance as those imposed on the majority. There is no way for minorities to cleanse themselves of the taint.

Minorities are hurt the most, but society as a whole is also damaged by preference. We seek an integrated society, but race preferences lead to *dis*integration. Those preferred and those not preferred become distrustful of one another. On the campus of the University of Michigan the open criticism of preferences risks the accusation of racism. So lips are buttoned and racial resentment boils. Resentment leads to suspicion and often to outright hostility. It is a downward spiral difficult to reverse. Jesse Jackson says, "I don't trust white Republicans or white Democrats. I want a black party." Hostility grows into hate. Hate talk becomes widely acceptable, even on the radio. "Honkey" and "whitey" are terms commonly heard, even in formal settings. Sister Souljah tells her black audience, "If black people kill black people every day, why not take a week off and kill white people?" The response is laughter and applause.

Universities offer scholarships by race; municipalities award building contracts by race. The need of each ethnic group—Puerto Ricans, Koreans, African Americans, Cubans, Haitians—to protect its portion of the spoils engenders ethnic competition—mutual distrust and dislike.

I concluded the debate with Wise by listing in summary the many kinds of serious damage done to our society by preference:

- Preference *divides the society* in which it is awarded; it separates rather than heals.
- Preference *excuses admitted racial discrimination* for the sake of achieving some political advantages.
- Preference *corrupts the universities* in which it is practiced, sacrificing intellectual values and creating pressures to discriminate by race in appointments, and in grading, and even in the award of honors.
- Preference *breeds hypocrisy within schools.* College officials hide what they are doing. At times they lie. We are corrupted by the preference we give.
- Preference *obscures the real social problem* of why so many minority students are not academically competitive, and thus it delays effective response.
- Preference *obliges us to choose among ethnic groups*, favoring some but not others.
- Preference *obliges us to devise a system for determining the membership of racial groups*. How much blood is needed? One drop? One grandparent? One great-grandparent? Some "objective" criteria for racial identification become essential, and some persons or bodies must then be given the authority to enforce them.
- Preference *reduces incentives* for academic excellence.
- Preference *encourages separatism* among racial and ethnic minorities.
- Preference *mismatches students and institutions*, greatly increasing the likelihood of failure for many minority students.
- Preference *does great injury to race relations over the long haul.*

And worst of all—as I noted at length earlier—race preferences do deep and lasting injury by *undermining the minorities they are intended to support.*

I thought long and hard about that debate as I drove back to Ann Arbor. I had put the case for the MCRI well, forcefully and rightly. But that was the least successful of the events in which I had participated. Most of that audience—white university students—would not support Proposition 2. I came to conclude that forensic argument would not be the determining factor in the election soon to come. Of course we advocates would do all we could to persuade people that preferences for some on the basis of race are unwise and unjust; that to vote for Proposition 2 was to vote for *fairness.* But the vote on the proposition, I concluded, would not be much changed by anything I could say or do.

CHAPTER 31

The Constitution of Michigan Amended

We won. When all the ballots had been counted, 58 percent of the votes cast supported the Michigan Civil Rights Initiative (MCRI). The Constitution of the State of Michigan was amended by an overwhelming popular vote, a landslide.

On the evening of Election Day, 7 November 2006, supporters of Proposition 2 gathered in Lansing to be together as the votes were counted and announced. Jennifer Gratz, the executive director of the MCRI, rented a hotel suite where we watched the television screens, ate, drank, and talked. As soon as significant chunks of the vote began to come in it became apparent the proposition was going to be adopted. Ward Connerly and I sat side by side on a sofa on one side of the large room, receiving messages, greeting friends, congratulating and being congratulated.

I have always been a democrat, a realistic but also an enthusiastic defender of participatory government. Democracy is morally right. It works. Reasonably well-educated citizens can be trusted, over the long haul, to decide wisely on the large issues that affect their lives. This conviction of mine was never more sweetly confirmed than on that occasion. As the evening went on, that apparent victory became real, concrete, and overwhelming.

It was one of the most deeply satisfying evenings of my life. Only three other days have had so great an emotional impact for me: the ending of World War II ("V-J Day"), 14 August 1945, when I was fourteen years old; the day the Civil Rights Act of 1964 passed the U.S. Senate, 19 June 1964, when I was thirty-three years old; and the day the first black man was elected president of the United States, 4 November 2008, when I was seventy-seven years old. The events celebrated on those three days, however, although vastly more important than the passage of the MCRI, had not involved me as directly. The passion I had devoted to the passage of the civil rights initiative exceeded all earlier efforts of mine in any political undertaking.

By popular vote a new section was added to Article 1 of the Michigan Constitution. It reads exactly as follows:

§ 26 Affirmative action programs.
Sec. 26.

(1) The University of Michigan, Michigan State University, Wayne State University, and any other public college or university, community college, or school district shall not discriminate against, or grant preferential treatment to, any individual or group on the basis of race, sex, color, ethnicity, or national origin in the operation of public employment, public education, or public contracting.

(2) The state shall not discriminate against, or grant preferential treatment to, any individual or group on the basis of race, sex, color, ethnicity, or national origin in the operation of public employment, public education, or public contracting.

(3) For the purposes of this section "state" includes, but is not necessarily limited to, the state itself, any city, county, any public college, university, or community college, school district, or other political subdivision or governmental instrumentality of or within the State of Michigan not included in sub-section 1.

(4) This section does not prohibit action that must be taken to establish or maintain eligibility for any federal program, if ineligibility would result in a loss of federal funds to the state.

(5) Nothing in this section shall be interpreted as prohibiting bona fide qualifications based on sex that are reasonably necessary to the normal operation of public employment, public education, or public contracting.

(6) The remedies available for violations of this section shall be the same, regardless of the injured party's race, sex, color, ethnicity, or national origin, as are otherwise available for violations of Michigan anti-discrimination law.

(7) This section shall be self-executing. If any part or parts of this section are found to be in conflict with the United States Constitution or federal law, the section shall be implemented to the maximum extent that the United States Constitution and federal law permit. Any provision held invalid shall be severable from the remaining portions of this section.

(8) This section applies only to action taken after the effective date of this section.

(9) This section does not invalidate any court order or consent decree that is in force as of the effective date of this section.

History: Approved Nov. 7, 2006, Effective Dec. 23, 2006

The saga of Proposition 2, the MCRI, was not over, as I will explain in Chapter 33. But from November 2006 it was clear and certain that the citizens of Michigan strongly disapprove of preferential treatment by race or ethnicity. Michigan is my adopted state, and I am proud of it.

CHAPTER 32

Race Preference at the University of Texas

In 2003 universities were authorized by the Supreme Court in *Grutter v. Bollinger* to consider the race of applicants for admission under some circumstances. The Michigan Constitution was amended in 2006 to forbid such consideration in this state. At other state universities, however, the consideration of race continued.

At the University of Texas circumstances were unique. Before *Grutter* the University of Texas Law School had considered race so blatantly that when its procedures were finally brought to the 5th Circuit Court of Appeals (as I explained in Chapter 13) those procedures were held (in 1995) flatly unconstitutional. Finding the diversity defense of race preferences to be without merit, that court compelled the University of Texas to abandon its discriminatory admissions procedures. The legislature of the State of Texas, demanding racial diversity, responded to that judicial decision by enacting a statute obliging the University of Texas to admit all applicants from Texas secondary schools graduated in the top 10 percent of their high-school class. This statute ensured diversity at the university, because de facto segregation in the residential patterns of Texas communities resulted in the admission of the top 10 percent of many schools whose students were almost entirely black or entirely Hispanic. The diversity argument failed in the 5th Circuit Court, but it succeeded in the Texas legislature. By the early years of the twenty-first century approximately one-quarter of the University of Texas students were minorities—a percentage greatly exceeding that obtained by ethnic preferences in the years before the *Hopwood* decision.

The statute obliging the admission of 10 percent of high-school classes was not universally admired. It resulted in the admission of many weak students from schools with mediocre standards and intensified competition among students of fine secondary schools with the highest standards. In that latter group were many of superior ability who did not quite finish in the top 10 percent of their classes. When these graduates applied for admission to the University of Texas (where the number of available places had been sharply reduced by the 10 percent statute) would it be fair, in the light of the *Grutter* decision, to consider their race? The university did so, seeking a greater percentage of minority students than the 10 percent statute had produced.

Abigail Fisher was graduated in the top 12 percent but not the top 10 percent of her class; her application, in 2008, for admission to the University of Texas was rejected. For applicants not in the top 10 percent of their class, race counted. Fisher was white; blacks and Latinos were given preference because the university sought a critical mass of minority students not only in the entering class but *in every classroom*. Believing that this was excessive and unfair, Fisher went to court, claiming that the University of Texas had discriminated against her because of her race, in violation of the Equal Protection Clause of the U.S. Constitution. In the U.S. District Court she lost. The university's admission policy was there found legal under *Grutter*. That decision was appealed to the 5th Circuit Court of Appeals; it was affirmed there by a three-judge panel. The Supreme Court agreed to review the case and heard arguments in October of 2012.[1]

Grutter v. Bollinger was the critical precedent. How extensive is the consideration of race that *Grutter* justifies? Is the "critical mass" of minority students that the University of Texas sought a critical mass in every classroom? The makeup of the Supreme Court had changed significantly from the time of *Grutter;* Justice Sandra Day O'Connor had retired and had been replaced by Justice Samuel Alito, whose disapproval of race preferences was known. It was conceivable that *Grutter* would be reversed.

Fisher did not ask the Court for that reversal. She argued that the University of Texas was not legally justified in using race preferences as it did in rejecting her because the racial diversity that might be legitimately sought under *Grutter* had already been achieved there. The 10 percent statute had produced ample ethnic diversity within its student body; the university's claim that diversity in every classroom was a compelling need (she contended) could not be sustained.

The seven-to-one decision of the Supreme Court (Justice Elena Kagan having recused herself), written by Justice Anthony Kennedy, was a partial but significant victory for Fisher. The university policy using race in considering applicants such as Fisher was not struck down, but the circuit court opinion that had upheld it was vacated, and the case was sent back to the lower courts for reconsideration under carefully refined principles.

The *Grutter* decision of 2003, binding and now applied to the University of Texas, makes it clear that "all racial classifications imposed by government must be analyzed by a reviewing court under strict scrutiny."[2] The standard of strict scrutiny has two prongs: (1) the need, for which racial considerations are introduced, must be *compelling,* and (2) the instruments in question employing race preferences must be *narrowly tailored* to meet that need. The University of Texas contends that racial diversity on its campus is a compelling need and that its admissions policies are indeed carefully designed to meet that need. Consider first the need alleged. Is it in fact compelling? In *Grutter* the Court reaffirmed the proposition, famously put forward by Justice Lewis Powell in the *Bakke* case of 1978, that "obtaining the educational benefits of student body diversity is a compelling state interest that can justify the use of race in university admissions." The University of Texas asserts that to be its objective, and the Court in *Fisher* does not question its good faith statement of this aim.

The second prong of the standard, however, is more problematic. Has the instrument designed by the university been *narrowly tailored* to achieve this objective? Only if that is true, only if the racial admissions policies of the university are shown essential for the achievement of that objective, and its use of racial classifications goes no further than is required to achieve that end, can the university policies be said to have withstood the standard of strict scrutiny.

Just here, the seven-member Supreme Court majority explains, the lower courts seriously erred. It was reasonable to defer to the judgment of the university with respect to its own objective. But it was a mistake to defer to the university in determining whether, in fact, the policies it devised were narrowly tailored to meet that need. The appropriateness of the policies devised must be scrutinized *strictly.* That is not a matter properly resolved by relying upon the good faith of the university. Kennedy wrote, "The District Court and the Court of Appeals confined the strict scrutiny inquiry in too narrow a way by deferring to the University's good faith in its use of racial classifications."[3]

What was lacking? In order for the judicial review (of a university's use of racial classifications) to be meaningful, a court "must assess whether the University *has offered sufficient evidence that would prove that its admissions program is narrowly tailored* . . . to achieve the only interest that this Court has approved in this context: the benefits of a student body diversity that encompasses a . . . broad array of qualifications and characteristics of which racial or ethnic origin is but a single though important element."[4]

This demand, now to be confronted by any university that would use racial classifications, is the one important change wrought by the *Fisher* decision. The 5th Circuit had held that Fisher could challenge only "whether the University's decision to use race as an admissions factor was made in good faith." That's just wrong. Under the ruling in *Grutter*, said the Supreme Court in 2013, the burden of providing evidence in support of its claims rests upon those who use race not upon those who contest its use. *Grutter* was not reversed by this decision, but its application was much refined. Claims previously accepted as true because universities—in Michigan and Texas—had simply asserted their truth were henceforth to be scrutinized more rigorously by the courts.

The heavier burden thus placed on the universities by the *Fisher* decision is particularly important because, as I have noted earlier, the alleged benefits of ethnic diversity, as a matter of empirical fact, are now being called into serious question.[5] Evidence from the social sciences increasingly tends to show that race preferences are not beneficial but impose a serious cost on the minority applicants to whom they are given. In his concurring opinion, Justice Clarence Thomas pointed out preferential admissions programs are doing substantial *harm* to minorities. He wrote, "Blacks and Hispanics admitted to the University as a result of racial discrimination are, on average, far less prepared than their white and Asian classmates. . . . Any blacks and Hispanics who likely would have excelled at less elite schools are placed in a position where underperformance is all but inevitable because they are less academically prepared than the white and Asian students with whom they must compete."[6] He relies in part on meticulous studies by Richard Sander and others, the results of which, explained fully in Chapter 28, turn the diversity argument on its head. In the light of what we now know about the real consequences of race preferences, the burden of proof of alleged advantages that the *Fisher* decision places upon the universities has become far more difficult to sustain.

The concurring opinion of Justice Thomas in the *Fisher* case, although it does not alter the outcome, is nevertheless remarkable. He had dissented disdainfully in *Grutter*, the case in which the universities were given license to use race, and here repeats his reasons for that dissent. He notes that the Court has repeatedly rejected assorted interests purporting to justify racial discrimination: the best interests of children, remedying societal discrimination, providing role models for minority children, and so on. Where the security of the nation is involved, perhaps this is warranted; where the government must remedy past discrimination for which it is itself responsible, perhaps this is justified. But where state action is at issue, only a social emergency rising to the level of imminent danger to life and limb can justify racial discrimination. To obtain the benefits of diversity? It is obvious, Thomas observes, that "there is nothing pressing or necessary about obtaining whatever educational benefits may flow from racial diversity."[7]

Thomas then goes well beyond those observations, comparing the benefits claimed by contemporary universities for their use of race to the benefits urgently claimed by the advocates of segregated public schools sixty years ago for *their* uses of race. School boards argued then that if the Court found segregation unconstitutional, white students would migrate to private schools, funding for public schools would decrease, and public schools would either decline in quality or cease to exist altogether. These claims were later shown to be well warranted. It was argued that the true victims of desegregation would be black students who could not afford private school. With the demise of segregation public education would receive (in many southern states) a serious setback. All true. In a very few years what had been threatened became a reality. Prince Edward County (Virginia) closed its public schools from the summer of 1959 to the fall of 1965. Thomas writes, "Unmoved by this sky-is-falling argument, we [the Supreme Court] held that segregation violated the principle of equality enshrined in the Fourteenth Amendment."[8] The fact that the schools might be closed if the order to desegregate were enforced is no reason for not enforcing it. The Court, Thomas observed, "never backed down from its rigid enforcement of the Equal Protection Clause's antidiscrimination principle. . . . If today the Court were actually applying strict scrutiny, it would require Texas either to close the university or to stop discriminating against applicants based on their race. The Court has put other schools to that choice, and there is no reason to treat the university differently."[9]

The university asserts that the diversity obtained through its discriminatory admissions program better prepares its students to become leaders in a diverse society. Segregationists made the identical claim, which in their case had some merit because segregated schools provided many more leadership opportunities for blacks. But it is irrelevant, under the Fourteenth Amendment, whether segregated or mixed schools produce better leaders. Indeed, no court today would accept the suggestion that segregation is permissible because historically black colleges produced Booker T. Washington, Thurgood Marshall, Martin Luther King Jr., and other prominent leaders. Likewise, the university's racial discrimination cannot be justified on the ground that it will produce better leaders.

The university asserts that student body diversity improves interracial relations. With this contention also the university repeats arguments once marshaled in support of segregation. Its result (the segregationists argued) has been to improve the relationship between the different races. "If segregation be stricken down, the general welfare will be definitely harmed ... there would be more friction developed.... The separation of the races has kept [racial] conflicts at a minimum."[10] Thomas responds, "We [the Supreme Court] flatly rejected this line of argument.[11] We held that segregation would be unconstitutional even if white students never tolerated blacks. It is, thus, entirely irrelevant whether the University's racial discrimination increases or decreases tolerance."[12]

Racial discrimination in admissions, the University of Texas admits, is not ideal but says it is a temporary necessity. We aspire to a color-blind society in which race does not matter, "but in Texas, [writes the university] our highest aspirations are yet unfulfilled."[13] This echoes painfully the justification long advanced for segregation in the public schools. "We grant that segregation may not be the ethical or political ideal [but] we recognize that practical considerations may prevent realization of the ideal."[14] Again, "The *mores* of racial relationships are such as to rule out, for the present at least, any possibility of admitting white persons and Negroes to the same institutions."[15] These arguments were unavailing in the 1950s, of course. Writes Thomas, "The Fourteenth Amendment views racial bigotry as an evil to be stamped out, not as an excuse for perpetual racial tinkering by the State."[16] The incisive observations of Justice William O. Douglas in his *DeFunis* dissent, cited in the first chapter of this book, Thomas quotes in his concurring opinion. "The Equal Protection Clause commands the elimination of racial barriers, not their creation in order to satisfy our theory as to how society ought to be organized."[17]

In sum, the arguments of the University of Texas, Thomas points out, are no more persuasive today than they were sixty years ago. "*There is no principled distinction between the University's assertion that diversity yields educational benefits and the segregationists' assertion that segregation yielded those same benefits.*"[18] Moreover, one should note, the claims of the segregationists were empirically much more well founded than those of the University of Texas.

"My view of the Constitution," Justice Thomas concludes, "is the one advanced by the plaintiffs in *Brown*: 'No State has any authority under the Equal Protection Clause of the Fourteenth Amendment to use race as a factor in affording educational opportunities among its citizens.' The Equal Protection Clause strips states of all authority to use race as a factor in providing education. All applicants must be treated equally under the law, and no benefit in the eye of the beholder can justify racial discrimination."[19]

CHAPTER 33

Race Preference in Michigan Is Permanently Ended

The Michigan Civil Rights Initiative (MCRI), resulting in a constitutional amendment forbidding race preference in Michigan, was overwhelmingly approved (58 percent to 42 percent) in a statewide vote in 2006. The battle did not end then. Opponents of that amendment, the exact text of which appears in Chapter 31 of this book, took their case to the federal courts. The Coalition to Defend Affirmative Action by Any Means Necessary (BAMN) first fought to keep the initiative off the ballot and then to defeat it when it was on the ballot. After it was approved decisively by the voters, the coalition contended that the amendment was unconstitutional because it violated the Equal Protection Clause of the Fourteenth Amendment.

This claim is bizarre. The Michigan amendment *forbids* discrimination by race, sex, color, ethnicity, or national origin. Its plain words *implement* the equality guaranteed by the U.S. Constitution. How could a demand for equality in the Michigan Constitution violate the requirement in the U.S. Constitution that no persons may be denied the equal protection of the laws? When the argument, seemingly paradoxical, eventually reached the 6th Circuit Court of Appeals, the fifteen judges of that court decided, on 15 November 2012 (by a vote of eight to seven) that the MCRI did violate the Equal Protection Clause. The constitutional amendment for which I had fought so long and so hard was struck down.

The attorney general of Michigan, Bill Schuette, appealed immediately to the U.S. Supreme Court, which quickly agreed to hear the matter. The case would be called *Schuette v. the Coalition to Defend Affirmative Action by Any Means Necessary*. It was argued before the Court on 15 October 2013. I wanted to be present at that hearing, but without assurance that I would gain entrance to the courtroom, I thought it would be foolish to make the trip to Washington, D.C. For this hearing there was no Case Day at Langley High. But things worked out well.

The longtime chairman of the philosophy department at the Dearborn campus of the University of Michigan was Prof. Edward Sayles (now retired). At the celebration of his ninetieth birthday I met his former student, James Bork, now an attorney and member of the Supreme Court Bar. He promised to help me gain entry and subsequently wrote the marshal of the Supreme Court, Pamela Talkin, explaining my role in the passage of the Michigan amendment. She was very cooperative. Her letter, assuring me a reserved seat at that hearing on 15 October 2013, was in my briefcase when I flew to Washington the day before.

Terry Pell, of the Center for Individual Rights (CIR), arranged a small dinner party for that evening; Jennifer Gratz, James Bork, and I were invited. Like myself, Terry Pell and Jennifer Gratz were moderately confident that the 6th Circuit Court would be reversed and the MCRI upheld. Nevertheless we were anxious. The case was scheduled for argument at 1 p.m.; shortly after noon I was ushered to my seat, which was directly in front of Chief Justice John Roberts.

As the argument unfolded, Justices Antonin Scalia and Samuel Alito made their support of our amendment clear by their questions; Justice Clarence Thomas would almost certainly join them. Justices Sonia Sotomayor and Ruth Bader Ginsburg made their opposition to the amendment evident. It was an eight-person court, Justice Elena Kagan having recused herself, presumably because she had worked on the case while solicitor general. The comments and questions of Chief Justice Roberts and Justices Stephen Breyer and Anthony Kennedy left their positions uncertain. I believed that at least two of those three would join Alito, Scalia, and Thomas in reversing the decision of the 6th Circuit Court of Appeals.

Before continuing with the drama, let me explain the intricacy of the paradoxical dispute confronting the Supreme Court. We must go back to earlier Supreme Court cases, by which the circuit courts are governed. Two such cases constituted the *entire foundation* of the 6th Circuit's condemnation of the MCRI. These two precedents must now be set forth.

The first was a 1969 case involving the City of Akron, Ohio, *Hunter v. Erickson*.[1] The Akron City Council had enacted a fair housing ordinance to prohibit racial discrimination in the sale and rental of housing in that city. Voters did not like it; they amended the city charter to overturn the ordinance and to require that any additional antidiscrimination housing ordinance be approved by referendum. Most other ordinances regulating real property in Akron were not subject to that requirement. The U.S. Supreme Court found that the city charter amendment, by singling out antidiscrimination ordinances, placed a "special burden on racial minorities within the governmental process."[2] It was constitutionally impermissible because it had been enacted with the invidious intent to injure a racial minority. Justice Harlan, concurring, argued that the city charter amendment had "the clear purpose of making it more difficult for certain racial and religious minorities to achieve legislation that is in their interest."[3] The procedural restructuring of the Akron City Charter had deliberately aggravated racial injuries earlier done. *Hunter*, central to the argument of the circuit court, rests on the principle that the state may not alter the procedures of government to target racial minorities.

The second precedent was *Washington v. Seattle School District No. 1*,[4] decided in 1982, which the 6th Circuit Court said "mirrors the [case] before us."[5] The school board in Seattle had adopted a mandatory busing program to alleviate the racial isolation of minority students in the local schools. Voters did not like the school board's busing plan; they passed a state initiative that prohibited busing to desegregate. Striking the initiative down, the Supreme Court found that the school board's plan "inures primarily to the benefit of the minority"[6] and that therefore the practical effect of the initiative was to "remove the authority to address a racial problem—and only a racial problem—from the existing decision-making body in such a way as to burden minority interests."[7] By barring the busing remedy that had been earlier devised, the initiative adopted by the voters had as its purpose deliberate injury on the basis of race, as in *Hunter*.

The 6th Circuit Court in 2012 concluded that the Michigan amendment prohibiting race preference was defective in just that way; it did deliberate injury to minorities, they said, on the basis of race. How? By making it more difficult for minorities to obtain preferential admission to Michigan universities. The MCRI amendment had moved decision making with respect to race preference, formerly in the hands of college governing boards and administrators, to the constitutional level. Henceforth, to gain the preferences they had formerly enjoyed, minorities in Michigan would be obliged to seek another constitutional amendment. Because the MCRI amendment had imposed this special burden on minorities, the court concluded, it must be struck down.

I was confident that the Supreme Court would reject this argument, and it did so decisively in *Schuette*. The alleged "burden" imposed by our amendment, if a burden at all, was imposed on everyone: no person or group was to receive preference henceforth. The decision of the Michigan voters was one of policy and applies to all; it is a decision insisting upon equal treatment, one that voters are surely free to make. The Court reversed the decision of the 6th Circuit on 22 April 2014.[8] All but the final chapter of this account of the battle over affirmative action at Michigan had been written. Now I could write this denouement.

The vote was six to two. Five opinions, totaling 108 pages, were issued. The controlling opinion was written by Justice Kennedy joined by Justice Alito and Chief Justice Roberts. Justices Scalia and Thomas joined in a separate opinion, which concurred in the outcome but differed in rationale. Justice Breyer also wrote a separate opinion, concurring in the judgment on narrower grounds. The one dissenting opinion, by Justice Sotomayor, joined by Justice Ginsburg, is a lengthy recapitulation of the argument of the 6th Circuit Court; it too relied *entirely* on the two precedents discussed above. There is no other plausible ground for striking down the Michigan amendment. All three factions supporting the amendment thus confronted the same question: How to deal with the precedents, *Hunter* and *Seattle*?

The controlling opinion (and Justice Breyer's opinion also) explains in detail why the Michigan initiative is not at all like the initiatives struck down in those two cases. The 6th Circuit Court, Kennedy points out, supposes that we can determine which political policies serve the "interests" of a given racial group and that race preferences are among the interests of the minority in Michigan. This supposition relies upon racial stereotypes that he rejects and deplores. The notion that racial groups subscribe to certain "minority views" Kennedy finds demeaning and false. "It cannot be entertained as a serious proposition that all individuals of the same race think alike. Yet that proposition would be a necessary beginning point were the *Seattle* formulation to control, as the Court of Appeals held it did in this case."[9]

The 6th Circuit Court, says Kennedy, mistakenly relies upon an interpretation of the *Seattle* case that supposes the "interests" of a minority are known and that race preferences are among them. But the outcome in *Seattle* is rightly justified by some actual injury done to minorities by the initiative in question. In Akron and in Seattle there was injury, or the aggravation of injury. But the Michigan amendment that prohibits race preference for all does no injury to anyone, let alone the racial minority. It is a policy decision that a majority of voters may choose to adopt. Our holding in this case, Kennedy writes, is simply that the "courts may not disempower the voters from choosing which path to follow."[10]

In short, the argument of the 6th Circuit Court is rejected by the plurality because what was objectively true in *Hunter* and *Seattle* is simply not true in this instance. Kennedy writes, "Here there was no infliction of a specific injury of the kind at issue in . . . *Hunter* and in the history of the Seattle schools. Here there is no precedent for extending these cases to restrict the right of Michigan voters to determine that race-based preferences granted by Michigan governmental agencies should be ended."[11]

The later pages of Kennedy's plurality opinion are an encomium to democracy. He is passionate, but more importantly, his rhetoric enriches our understanding of the issues raised by the MCRI:

> By approving Proposal 2 and thereby adding Sec. 26 to their State constitution, the Michigan voters exercised their privilege to enact laws as a basic exercise of their democratic power. In the federal system States respond through the enactment of positive law, to the initiative of those who seek a voice in shaping the destiny of their own times. . . . Michigan voters used the initiative system to bypass public officials who were deemed not responsive to the concerns of a majority of the voters with respect to a policy of granting race-based preferences that raises difficult and delicate issues.[12]
>
> Our constitutional system embraces . . . the right of citizens to debate so they can learn and decide and then, through the political process, act in concert to try to shape the course of their own times and the course of a nation. . . . Here Michigan voters acted in concert and statewide to seek consensus and adopt a policy on a difficult subject against a historical background of race in America that has been a source of tragedy and persisting injustice. That history demands that we continue to learn, to listen, and to remain open to new approaches if we are to aspire always to a constitutional order in which all persons are treated with fairness and equal dignity. Were the Court to rule that the question addressed by Michigan voters is too sensitive or complex to be within the grasp of the electorate; or that the policies at issue remain too delicate to be resolved save by university officials or faculties, acting at some remove from immediate public scrutiny and control; or that these matters are so arcane that the electorate's power must be limited because the people cannot prudently exercise that power even after a full debate, that holding would be an unprecedented restriction on the exercise of a fundamental right held not just by one person

but by all in common. It is the right to speak and debate and learn and then, as a matter of political will, to act through a lawful electoral process.

The respondents in this case [BAMN] insist that a difficult question of public policy must be taken from the reach of the voters, and thus removed from the realm of public discussion, dialogue, and debate in an election campaign. . . . [This] is inconsistent with the underlying premises of a responsible, functioning democracy. One of these premises is that a democracy has the capacity . . . to discover and confront persisting biases; and by respectful, rational deliberation to rise above these flaws and injustices. . . . It is demeaning to the democratic process to presume that the voters are not capable of deciding an issue of this sensitivity on decent and rational grounds. . . . Freedom embraces the right, indeed the duty, to engage in rational, civic discourse in order to determine how best to . . . shape the destiny of the Nation and its people. These First Amendment dynamics would be disserved if this Court were to say that the question here at issue is beyond the capacity of the voters to debate and then to determine."[13]

Having laid down these corollaries of democracy, Justice Kennedy returns to the question of the relevance of *Hunter* and *Seattle*. When hurt or injury is inflicted on racial minorities by the encouragement or command of the laws, or by other state action, the U.S. Constitution does indeed require that courts provide some redress. Those were the circumstances in *Hunter* and in *Seattle*, he agrees—but not in the present, Michigan case. In those cases the political restriction was *designed* to inflict injury by reason of race. That is simply not the case here, where government is instructed not to grant favored status to persons in some racial categories and not others. He concludes:

This case is not about how the debate about racial preferences should be resolved. It is about who may resolve it. There is no authority in the Constitution of the United States or in this Court's precedents for the judiciary to set aside Michigan laws that commit this policy determination to the voters. . . . Democracy does not presume that some subjects are either too divisive or too profound for public debate. The judgment of the Court of Appeals for the Sixth Circuit is reversed.[14]

Like the plurality, Justice Breyer rejects the argument of the 6th Circuit Court by *distinguishing* the Michigan initiative from the initiatives in the two cases they rely upon, but he does so in a different way. *Hunter* and *Seattle,* he writes, "involved efforts to manipulate the political process in a way not here at issue." The political level at which policies were enacted was changed in those cases. "This case, in contrast, does not involve a reordering of the political process" because, in Michigan, *in fact* "unelected faculty members and administrators, not voters or their elected representatives, adopted the race-conscious admission programs affected by Michigan's constitutional amendment. The amendment took decision-making authority away from these unelected actors and placed it in the hands of the voters."[15] This movement from an administrative process to an electoral process did not diminish the minority's ability to participate meaningfully in the political process, because formerly there had been no electoral process directly determining the outcomes.

Justice Breyer's commitment to democracy is as complete as that of Justice Kennedy. After *Grutter v. Bollinger,*[16] he writes, the U.S. Constitution permits but does not require the use of race-conscious admissions programs. How then are we to decide when and where they are appropriate? "[T]he Constitution foresees the ballot box, not the courts, as the normal instrument for resolving differences and debates about the merit of these programs."[17] If the people, or their elected representatives, have the right to adopt race-conscious policies for reasons of inclusion, "they must also have the right to vote not to do so."[18]

Justices Scalia and Thomas, vigorously supporting the legitimacy of the Michigan amendment, did not seek to distinguish the Michigan circumstances from those in Akron and Seattle. They simply rejected those precedents, finding them upon scrutiny to be seriously mistaken. "Patently atextual, unadministrable, and contrary to our traditional equal-protection jurisprudence, *Hunter* and *Seattle* should be overruled."[19]

Whether distinguished or discarded, *Hunter* and *Seattle* are dispensed with. Those cases being the only remotely plausible grounds for judges to strike down a decisive vote of the Michigan citizenry, the constitutional amendment created by the MCRI has been solidly reestablished. Michigan is not alone. Statewide initiatives specifically aimed at this result have almost invariably won the support of preponderant majorities. Seven other states have banned preference by ethnicity in public education: Arizona, California, Florida, Nebraska, New Hampshire, Oklahoma, and Washington.

In the pages of the five thoughtful opinions in *Schuette* appears an exchange, between Justice Sotomayor and Chief Justice Roberts, that cuts deeply and deserves reflection. Sotomayor fully understands, as we all do, that this case is not about the wisdom or the rightness of preference for minorities. It is, as Justice Kennedy made clear, about the extent of voter authority and the constitutional status of the amendment adopted by Michigan voters in 2006. But Sotomayor believes earnestly that preference for ethnic minorities is called for, and she will not be silenced. She herself benefited from minority preference, as she reported in her recent memoir.[20] The underrepresentation of minorities in selective universities troubles her deeply, as it must trouble us. And so, after arguing in her dissenting opinion that *Hunter* and *Seattle* should govern this case, she adds eleven pages of material—charts, statistics, and historical reflections—defending the proposition that race preference in admissions is a good thing. But these data, Chief Justice Roberts observes, cannot bear upon the question of the constitutionality of the Michigan amendment. His very short opinion, concurring with the judgment of the plurality supporting the amendment, questions the wisdom of the race preference that Sotomayor defends.

In a 2012 case, Roberts famously wrote, "The way to stop discrimination on the basis of race is to stop discriminating on the basis of race."[21] In her dissent, Justice Sotomayor asserts that this view "is a sentiment out of touch with reality."[22] She almost mocks him. "The way to stop discrimination on the basis of race is to speak openly and candidly on the subject of race, and to apply the Constitution with eyes open to the unfortunate effects of centuries of racial discrimination. . . . Race matters because of the slights, the snickers, the silent judgments that reinforce that most crippling of thoughts: 'I do not belong here.'"[23] She had written of her "fevered insecurity" as a student at Princeton and the Yale Law School, conscious of the ethnic preference from which *she* had benefited. "I had been admitted to the Ivy League through a special door. . . . I lived the day-to-day reality of affirmative action."[24]

Roberts's response is gentle but incisive. It is not "out of touch with reality to conclude that *racial preferences may themselves have the debilitating effect of reinforcing precisely that doubt* and—if so—that *the preferences do more harm than good.*"[25] The disagreement between Roberts and Sotomayor about the costs and benefits of race preferences reflects a disagreement that pervades our national conversation on this topic. The 6th Circuit court could suppose that ending race preference in Michigan injured the minority there because it seemed to members of that court that a benefit formerly enjoyed by the minority had been taken away. But do admissions preferences really benefit a minority in the long run? Bearing in mind the many injurious consequences of preference noted previously in Chapter 30, as well as the cruelties so painful to Justice Sotomayor in her youth, and observing that no such "slights and snickers and silent judgments" are justified at the University of Michigan today where applicants of all races are treated equally, we may conclude that ending preference by race is a step needed to transcend racial discrimination.

I conclude by calling attention to the near absurdity of the argument we were obliged to combat. The amendment to the Michigan Constitution that we put forward, which explicitly forbids discrimination, had been held discriminatory! Can the demand that all people be treated equally violate the Equal Protection Clause? Justice Scalia too is struck by the manifest implausibility of the claim. He calls it "frighteningly bizarre. . . . Does the Equal Protection Clause of the Fourteenth Amendment *forbid* what its text plainly *requires*? . . . The question answers itself."[26]

With the solid reaffirmation of the MCRI by six justices of the U. S. Supreme Court my story ends. Justice Scalia provides an eloquent summary of the core:

> The Constitution proscribes government discrimination on the basis of race, and state-provided education is no exception. It is precisely this understanding—the correct understanding—of the federal Equal Protection Clause that the people of the State of Michigan have adopted for their own fundamental law. By adopting it, they did not simultaneously *offend* it. . . . [A] law directing state actors to provide equal protection . . . cannot violate the Constitution. Section 26 of the Michigan Constitution (formerly Proposal 2) rightly stands."[27]

Appendix A

Freedom of Information Act Requests

Here follows the full text of the two letters I sent (on 18 and 19 December 1995) to Freedom of Information Act Officer Lewis Morrissey of the University of Michigan, requesting all guidelines and reports pertaining to any uses of ethnic or racial categories in our admissions—to the Law School, the Medical School, or the College of Literature, Science, and the Arts.

Mr. Lewis A. Morrissey
Freedom of Information Act Officer
The University of Michigan
2064 Fleming Bldg.
Ann Arbor, MI 48109-1340
Dear Mr. Morrissey:

Cordial greetings. Under the provisions of the Michigan Freedom of Information Act [Sec. 4.1801] I request, hereby, copies of all correspondence, memoranda, and minutes still in effect, from or to the Director of Admissions for the College of Literature, Science and the Arts, and the Law School, and the Medical School, of the University of Michigan (or persons they supervise) in which are given as directives or as guidance, or are in any other way identified, the principles or criteria, numerical (pertaining to the use of test scores and/or grade point averages) and non-numerical, for the offering of admission, or the denial of admission, or the evaluation of candidates for possible later admission, of applicants of different ethnicities: white, black, Hispanic, and in other ways categorized.

I also request copies of all correspondence, memoranda, and minutes still in effect, from or to the above-mentioned persons, which identify for the purposes of guidance or any other use by admissions officers, the numerical goals and timetables discussed or adopted for the recent, current, or future admission of applicants by ethnic category, or the delineation of the numerical profiles (by ethnic category) to be viewed as targets or objectives sought for recent, current, or future entering classes.

Please note that I do not want the names of any applicants for admission, or any other information that would constitute an invasion of privacy for any applicant.

Please note that the volume of material I request is small. I do not seek information about the treatment of any named individual; I do not seek any information about instructions given to applicants, or the forms for application used by applicants. I do not seek any of the material distributed by the university in its general advertising, to applicants or to the public at large. I do not seek any of the many publications widely distributed by the university.

I seek only accurate and up-to-date records of admission policy guidelines, used by admissions officers or other administrators, governing or guiding the consideration or disposition of applications for admission to the three Colleges mentioned, or which bear in any way upon the admission of majority and minority applicants.

I would of course be pleased if these document copies could be provided within the time period set forth in the Michigan Freedom of Information Act; however, realizing that it may take several days for these documents to be located, I accept in advance the extension of this period by 10 business days, as provided in the Act.

Being anxious to cooperate with you, Mr. Morrissey, I would be happy to come to your office to consult with you, explaining with greater care, if that would be helpful, the nature of the documents and information I seek. If you think such a meeting would be useful, please give me a call at 313-665-0090.

Thank you for your time and attention.

Respectfully yours,

Carl Cohen

Because I sought also to learn what the University of Michigan had actually done in this sphere, I needed numerical data about applications and actual admissions by ethnicity. I therefore wrote a second letter the next day, with the same formal structure but with important additional requests.

Mr. Lewis A. Morrissey
Freedom of Information Act Officer
The University of Michigan
2064 Fleming Bldg.
Ann Arbor, MI 48109-1340
Dear Mr. Morrissey:

Cordial greetings. Under the provisions of the Michigan Freedom of Information Act [Sec. 4.1801] I request, hereby, the following information, stated separately for the College of Literature, Science and the Arts, the Law School, and the Medical School of the University of Michigan: for all applicants seeking admission in the fall of 1995 (or alternatively in the fall of 1994, if records pertaining to 1995 are not yet available) the records of Grade Point Averages, raw LSAT or MCAT scores, race and ethnicity, in-state and out-of-state status of applicants, and the record of offers of admission by each of those numerical and ethnic categories.

While I believe the request above is clear, I thought it might be helpful to you if I provided an illustration of what records I seek. Enclosed, therefore, you will find two samples of records provided by the University of California (with reference to the entering classes of 1994) in response to an almost identical request. One of these sample records reports admissions offered, and admissions applied for, at the UC Berkeley School of Law. You'll note that the categories of applicants by GPA are listed vertically on the left; the categories of applicants by their LSAT percentile scores are listed horizontally on top; totals appear in the two right-most columns; each of the four sheets reports the figures for one ethnic group: white, Asian, Hispanic, and black. The second sample provides a similar record for the UCLA School of Medicine. The same categories by GPA appear vertically on the left; the horizontal categories are the percentile performance on the Medical College Admission Test. Totals again appear in the two right-most columns; ethnic categories are only two, white/Asian and black/Hispanic, hence this sample contains only two sheets.

Of course the University of Michigan and its colleges may record its data regarding the performance and ethnicity of applicants, and those offered admission, using somewhat different numerical or ethnic categories; the records I seek may therefore be different from these, which I enclose only to help explain my object. The information I am requesting may be available only in a very different form. But the university does carefully collect data of the kind here requested, and in whatever form those records are kept, for the above-mentioned three colleges, I ask for the records of that data.

Please note that I do not want the names of any applicants, or any other information that would constitute an invasion of privacy for any applicant. Please note also that the volume of material I seek is small, comprising only the records of actual applications and admissions, by ethnic and performance categories, for the three Colleges named, for 1995.

I would of course be pleased if these records could be provided within the time period set forth in the Michigan Freedom of Information Act; however, realizing that it may take several days for this information to be gathered, I accept in advance the extension of this period by 10 business days, as provided in the Act.

Being anxious to cooperate with you, Mr. Morrissey, I would be happy to come to your office to consult with you, explaining with greater care, if that would be helpful, the nature of the information I seek. If you think such a meeting would be useful please give me a call at 313-665-0090.

Thank you for your time and attention.

Respectfully yours,

Carl Cohen

Appendix B

The Cohen Report, 20 March 1996

To convey to the President and Regents of the University of Michigan the highlights of the information pertaining to race preferences in admission that I had obtained as a result of my Freedom of Information Act requests of December 1995, I prepared a report entitled: "Racial Discrimination in Admissions at the University of Michigan." This report, completed and first sent on 20 March 1996, later came into the hands of journalists and legislators in Michigan, and the Center for Individual Rights in Washington. It led to the Federal litigation that began in October of 1997 and concluded with the decisions of the U.S. Supreme Court in the *Gratz* and *Grutter* cases, in June of 2003. Here follows an exact copy of that original report.

20 March 1996

Carl Cohen
16 Ridgeway
Ann Arbor, MI 48104

Racial Discrimination in Admissions at the University of Michigan
Preference by race is given systematically at the University of Michigan to applicants for admission—to the Law School, to the Medical School, and to the College of Literature, Science and the Arts. The evidence for this is overwhelming, the conclusion indisputable. The passages cited below, and figures given below, are all taken from official University documents obtained in response to Freedom of Information Act requests which carefully avoided all individual identifications. Some of the docu-

ments requested were not provided, but the figures appearing on those that were provided are damning.

I. Equal Treatment Professed

The policy publicly professed by the University of Michigan is one of strictly equal treatment of the races. Here follows the language of the disclaimer appearing in official University catalogues (and elsewhere) in the fall of 1995:

> The University of Michigan is committed to a policy of nondiscrimination and equal opportunity for all persons regardless of race, sex, color, religion, creed, national origin or ancestry . . . in employment, educational programs and activities, and admissions.

The formally approved practices of several colleges within the University—as will be seen in detail below—do not accord with this professed commitment.

Reasonable persons will agree that non-numerical factors—community service, character, special circumstance of earlier schooling, and the like—are appropriately considered in offering admission to applicants. Such factors will (rightly) account for many anomalous cases. But if weighed fairly, non-numerical factors will be considered for applicants of *every ethnic group*. In all groups there will be applicants with special needs, special talents, or special achievements; good character and dedication to one's community and the like are not found disproportionately among the members of any one race or nationality. Therefore, while such factors may be wisely weighed in individual cases, they cannot explain systematic bias by race.

II. Racially Preferential Admissions in the College of Literature, Science and the Arts (LS&A).

Preference in admission to LS&A for some racial groups is formally manifested in several ways.

1. Decisions Made on First Review of Applicants

The Office of Undergraduate Admissions prepares a many page document entitled "College of Literature, Science and the Arts/ Guidelines for All Terms of 1996."[1] The first page of this document gives admissions officers ("counselors") a table that directs their responses to applications on first review; some applicants are admitted at that time, some are rejected then, some decisions are postponed. Many decisions to admit or reject are specified as to be made automatically, by clerks. The table is headed "CONFIDENTIAL Internal Use Only."

All applicants are divided into ninety (90) intellectual categories, or "cells" on the official table. Each cell is delineated by a combination of grade-point average in earlier schooling (on the vertical axis) and ACT scores or SAT scores (on the horizontal axis). In each cell is written two or three lines of code, indicating the responses to be made to applicants on first review. At the top of the table appears this instruction, in bold:

"In general, use the top row in each cell for majority applicants and the middle and bottom rows for underrepresented minorities and other disadvantaged students."

There are many cells, many categories of performance, in which the directed response to majority applicants is rejection, but (with exactly the same scores) the directed response to minority applicants is acceptance. For example:

In ten cells in which GPA is 3.0 and above but SAT scores are below 1,000, majority applicants are rejected, minority applicants accepted.

In twenty-four cells in which earlier Grade Point Averages are below 2.7, majority applicants are rejected by clerks without further attention, while minority applicants, although not automatically admitted, are channeled for special processing.

In nine mid-range cells in which GPA is somewhat above 3 and SAT scores somewhat above 1090, minority applicants are accepted for admission, majority applicants are postponed for further review.

A careful review of the LS&A decision-grid provided leaves no possible doubt that the system of first-review response distinguishes sharply between minorities and non-minorities, giving substantial preference to the former. Whether the "Affirmative Action Objectives" of LS&A are quotas in fact is, as Justice Powell said in *Bakke*, a "semantic distinction [that] is beside the point. . . . it is a line drawn on the basis of race and ethnic status."

2. Application for Admission to the Integrated Premedical-Medical Program (INTEFLEX).

Pages 9 and 10 of the document identified above indicate the responses to be given for applicants to the highly prized INTEFLEX Program.

Sub-section (b) under this heading directs the responses to be given to "non-minorities," Sub-section (c) directs the responses to be given to "ALL Underrepresented Minority Students," as follows:

Highest category (code AINT) is granted to non-minorities having ACT score of 30+ or SAT scores of 1320+, and GPA of 3.8 (if out-of-state) and 3.6 (if in-state).

Highest category (code AINT) is granted to minorities having ACT score of 26+ or SAT scores of 1170+, and GPA of 3.4, in-state and out-of-state.

This is compelling evidence that preference by race is given in admission to the INTEFLEX Program at the University of Michigan.[2]

3. Guideline Exceptions.

The preferences above are formally ensconced in the undergraduate admissions system. Other preferences are given in informal ways impossible to document, since many decisions are discretionary and made in secret. However, the principle of informal preference for minority applicants is formally announced under Section G, "Guideline Exceptions."

The first paragraph of that Section reads in full:

1. Underrepresented Minority Groups:

All qualified American Indians, Black/African Americans, and Hispanic/Latino American applicants will be admitted as soon as a high probability of success can be predicted. Delayed Decision (DD) letters should not be sent to underrepresented minority students. Instead, use DGF, DSF, DGSF, etc., to require specific information.[3] Students who do not qualify for selected admissions, INCLUDING ON THE SPOT REVIEW,[4] might be admitted under CSP or Bridge Program guidelines after fall semester grades and/or tests are submitted. In general, admission to summer bridge should not occur during early sessions of On-the-spot Admissions.

It is impossible to determine how much preference is given by race under this exception. But it is certain that preference by race is given, since for those who are not in the favored groups, admission is certainly not assured "as soon as a high probability of success can be predicted."

Under another heading, "Special Considerations," (on page 13) students with "severe earlier life experiences" are briefly mentioned, after which is added the following:

"Only underrepresented minority students are considered under Affirmative Action Objectives."

Those "Affirmative Action Objectives" are not identified in this document. The fact that affirmative action objectives apply, in this College, to minority applicants only is strong evidence that race is not merely "one among many factors considered" as affirmative action spokespersons commonly insist, but is a fundamental threshold factor, dividing all applicants by their skin color or group.

On 18 December 1995 I requested, under the Michigan Freedom of Information Act, all documents

"which identify for the purpose of guidance or any other use by admissions officers, the numerical goals and timetables discussed or adopted for the recent, current, or future admission of applicants by ethnic category, or the delineation of the numerical profiles (by ethnic category) to be viewed as targets or objectives sought for recent, current, or future entering classes."

I was advised by the Chief Freedom of Information Officer, by letter of 28 February 1996, that "There are no documents responsive to this request."

Since emphatic emphasis is made, in the guidelines prepared by the Office of Undergraduate Admissions, to "Affirmative Action Objectives," and since it is unlikely that such objectives are communicated by the Director of Admissions to admissions counselors by voice only, there appears to be some reluctance on the part of that Office to respond to my request.

There are other informal preferences given by race. For example: One category of outstanding applicants discussed on page 6 is called "Instant Admits" to the Honors Program, requiring a very high GPA, and very high SAT scores. Immediately below the statement of the cut-off scores for Instant Admits, appears this additional note to admissions officers:

"If a minority student is very close to being an Instant Admit and you would like to make that designation, take the entire application to ----
who will get a decision from Honors within 24–48 hours."

Non-minority students do not receive that special accommodation.

4. Admission Percentages to LS&A, by Ethnic Group, Fall of 1994.[5]

In addition to the preferential *policies* identified above, it is possible to exhibit the marked preferential *results*. Again I would emphasize that non-numerical factors might wisely be considered in admissions decisions, but that they cannot plausibly account for systematic favoritism by race.

A document headed "Office of Undergraduate Admissions" and subheaded "Profile of the University of Michigan, Fall 94, For All Units" gives a table, or grid, with 108 categories or "cells" delineated by "former school GPA" on the vertical axis and "best test score" (SAT or ACT) on the horizontal axis. In each cell appears the number in that category who *applied*, and the number in that category who were *offered admission*.

Grids of identical form are prepared for "underrepresented minorities,"[6] and for all students. The fraction, admits/applications, gives the percentage in that cell who were offered admission. Those percentages, for minorities and for non-minorities, may be readily compared. These comparisons reveal strong systematic preference in favor of minorities in LS&A for 1994. In almost every cell in which there were any minority applicants at all, the percentage of minority admissions was higher than the percentage of non-minority admissions. In many cells and groups of cells the minority admissions rate very much higher. Here are the figures for some representative cells:

(a) If applicant's GPA was between 2.80 and 2.99 (B–),
    and SAT scores were 1200–1290:
        non-minority admission rate was 12%;
        minority admission rate was 100%.
    and SAT scores were 1100–1190:
        non-minority admission rate was 11%;
        minority admission rate was 100%.
    and SAT scores were 900–990:
        non-minority admission rate was 17%;
        minority admission rate was 92%.
(b) If applicant's GPA was between 3.40 and 3.60 (B+)
    and SAT scores 900–990:
        non-minority admission rate was 13%;
        minority admission rate was 98%.
(c) If applicant's GPA was between 3.60 and 3.79 (A–)

and SAT scores were 900–890:
   non-minority admission rate was 12%;
   minority admission rate was 100%.
And so on and on. There is no shadow of a doubt that, flatly on the basis of minority group membership, strong preference is given in admission to the College of LS&A.

III. Racially Preferential Admission to the Law School of the University of Michigan

The Law School Admissions Office prepares a document (latest version available is dated 7 December 1995) entitled: "Admission Grid of LSAT and GPA for All Applicants" that is very much like the grids prepared by the College of LS&A. Applications to the Law School are broken down into 120 cells; the vertical axis of the grid is the undergraduate GPA of applicants; the horizontal axis is the score of the applicants on the Law School Admission Test (LSAT). The number of applicants, and the number of offers of admission is given in each cell, so that, again, the percentage rate of admission within each category can be readily calculated. A grid identical in form is prepared for each of the several ethnic groups distinguished: "Native Americans," "African Americans," "Caucasian Americans," "Mexican Americans," "Other Hispanic Americans," "Asian/Pacific Island Americans," and "Puerto Rican Applicants." No grid is prepared (at least none was sent to me) for minorities as a whole. Comparing admission rates by ethnic group for almost any given cell reveals strong racial preferences.

Here are comparisons of four critical groups of cells, especially important because they contain the applicants whose performance, although not outstanding, has been good, and who are likely to believe that they have a decent chance for admission.

(a) For applicants with GPA 3.00–3.24 (B), and LSAT 161 and up (top range):
   Caucasian Americans: Applications 115. Admissions 17; Rate: 14.8%
   Mexican Americans: Applications 7; Admissions 7; Rate 100%
(b) For applicants with GPA 3.25–3.49 (B+) and LSAT 161 and up (top range):
   Caucasian Americans: Applications 217; Admissions 16; Rate 7.4%
   Native Americans: Applications 3; Admissions 3; Rate 100%
(c) For applicants with GPA 3.00–3.24 (B+) and LSAT 148–163 (6 cells in mid-range):

Caucasian Americans: Applications 319; Admissions 7; Rate 2.2%
African Americans: Applications 35; Admissions 26; Rate 74.3%
(d) For applicants with GPA 3.00–3.24 (B) and LSAT 156–166 (4 cells in mid-range):
Caucasian Americans: Applications 124; Admissions 6; Rate 4.8%
African Americans: Applications 20; Admissions 17; Rate 85%

The pattern of Law School preference by ethnic groups is very marked. Bear in mind that all Law School applicants must pay a $70 non-refundable fee with their application. But mid-range applicants (B or B+ students with decent LSAT scores) who remit that sum are for the most part wasting their time and their money *if they are white.* If they are Native American, or Mexican American, or African American their chances of admission are excellent. The University publicly assures applicants that there is no discrimination by race in admissions, and that applicants of all races are treated equally. Those who apply recognizing that their chances of acceptance are not excellent nevertheless believe (because they are *told*) that they will be treated like all others with equivalent credentials. They are misled. If that information was given to them with knowledge that it was not correct, they have been defrauded.

IV. Racially Preferential Admission to the Medical School of the University of Michigan

In the University of Michigan Medical School minority applicants are classified, following the practice of the Association of American Medical Colleges, into four groups: "Mexican-Americans, Mainland Puerto-Ricans, African Americans, and Native American Indians." It would appear likely that grids for each of these minority groups, and for the total pool, would be prepared by the Medical School, as they are in the Law School and in LS&A. However, a Freedom of Information Act request for those grids has not been granted. Nevertheless, documents prepared by the Medical School are sufficient to exhibit (although without as much detail as in Law and LS&A) marked preference in admission by race.

1. Racial Preference in Screening Applicants for Interviews

The first screening of applicants for admission to the Medical School is to determine who among them will be interviewed. A document headed "UM Medical School Admissions Office, SCREEN GROUPS for applicants," dated July, 1995, indicates the cut-off scores above which an interview (not necessarily admission, of course) will be automatically offered.

The different cut-off scores for Michigan Residents, and for Non-Michigan Residents are given, the groups coded R1, NR1, R2, NR2, R3, NR3. Then follows this notice:

"M" in front of the screen group designation indicates a minority applicant, e.g., MNR1, MR2."

It appears highly probable that, for groups designated with an "M" different standards are applied for screening. If not, there would be no point in the special designation. But what those differential standards are cannot be discerned from this document. A formal request for the document(s) that do(es) set forth these differential standards was not granted.

2. Admission Percentages to the Medical School by Ethnic Group, Fall of 1995.

The "Annual Report of Admissions, 1995" prepared by the Medical School reveals, on page 3, the number of applicants to the Medical School, and the number of offers of admission to the Medical School, in total and by various categories. On this table all four minority groups are clumped under the heading "Minorities." Here follows a sample of what this document reveals:

Total <u>applications</u> to the Medical School in 1995 numbered 5,873. Of these, 791 were applications by minorities, and 5,082 were applications by non-minorities.

Total <u>offers of admission</u> to the medical School numbered 245. Of these 46 were offers to minority applicants, 199 were offers to non-minority applicants.

The <u>rate of admission</u> for all minority applicants in 1995 was 5.8%.

The <u>rate of admission</u> for all non-minority applicants in 1995 was 3.9%, two-thirds of the minority rate.

Such preferences are established Medical School practice. During the three years 1992, 1993, and 1994 the average rate of admission for all minority applicants was 7.4%. The average rate of admission for non-minority students during that period was 4.2%.

3. Racially Preferential Admissions Not Disclosed

(a) Because the Medical School grids for applications/offers, by GPA and Medical College Admission Test (MCAT) scores, have not been revealed, it is not possible here to exhibit preference by race in especially important cells or categories, as can be done for the Law School. But it is probable that, in those cells containing applicants in the middle range the preference by race in Medical School admissions is very much more pronounced than in Medical School admissions as a whole. By clumping all minority admissions into one category in the annual report, the full account of admissions practices is hidden. If in fact the full account does not exhibit the more marked racial preference in the middle ranges that are exhibited in LS&A and in Law, the publication of those grids by the Medical School would make that clear.

(b) The table reporting applications and offers to minorities and to non-minorities, which appears in the Annual Report, is not a complete account of medical applications and offers. A footnote, qualifying the figures for the academic year 1995 and three preceding years, reads as follows:

> "Figures include only the standard admission pool (not including students entering from special programs such as the post baccalaureate program)."

Since the special programs referred to are specifically designed to enlarge the number of minorities admitted, it is reasonable to suppose that, with the inclusion of the admissions granted through those special programs, the contrast in ethnic admission rates would be yet greater.

V. Concluding Observations

Admission practices at the University of Michigan show very marked preferences by race and ethnic category. This is not consistent with our formal profession of strict equality of treatment by race, cited above in I.

This question arises: Do the University officers who make the public declaration of commitment to equal treatment know or believe that in fact our practice does not accord with that profession?

If they do, troubling issues of honesty arise.

If they do not, if they have been truly unaware of the racial preferences we give in admission, then changes certainly ought to be made very promptly now. Either we must change our practices to bring them into accord with the public declaration of our University, or we must change our public declaration to so that it reports honestly the racial preferences that we give.

Appendix C

The Michigan Civil Rights Initiative (MCRI)

The MCRI asked voters whether they approved of the addition of the following amendment to the Michigan Constitution:

Amendment to the Constitution of the State of Michigan
Adopted by state-wide vote on November 6, 2006.
Article 1, Section 26
Civil Rights.

The University of Michigan, Michigan State University, Wayne State University, and any other public college or university, community college, or school district shall not discriminate against, or grant preferential treatment to, any individual or group on the basis of race, sex, color, ethnicity, or national origin in the operation of public employment, public education, or public contracting.

The state shall not discriminate against, or grant preferential treatment to, any individual or group on the basis of race, sex, color, ethnicity, or national origin in the operation of public employment, public education, or public contracting.

For the purpose of this section "state" includes, but is not necessarily limited to, the state itself, any city, county, public college or university, community college, school district, or other political subdivision of governmental instrumentality of or within the State of Michigan.

This section does not affect any law or governmental action that does not discriminate on the basis of race, sex, color, ethnicity or national origin.

This section does not prohibit action that must be taken to establish or maintain eligibility for any federal program, if ineligibility would result in loss of federal funds to the State.

Nothing in this section shall be interpreted as prohibiting bona fide qualifications based on sex that are reasonably necessary to the normal operation of public employment, public education, or public contracting.

The remedies available for violations of this section shall be the same, regardless of the injured party's race, color, religion, ethnicity, or national origin, as are otherwise available for violations of Michigan's anti-discrimination law.

This section shall be self-executing. If any part or parts of this section are found to be in conflict with the United States Constitution or federal law, the section shall be implemented to the maximum extent that the United States Constitution and federal law permit. Any provision held invalid shall be severable from the remaining portions of this section.

This section applies only to action taken after the effective date of this section.

This section does not invalidate any court order or consent decree that is in force as of the effective date of this section.

This Amendment to the Michigan Constitution was approved by Michigan voters on 6 November 2006 by 58 percent to 42 percent.

Notes

CHAPTER 1. HOW IT ALL BEGAN

1 Introduced on July 27, 1995, as Senate Bill 1085, but not enacted, it was a bill to prohibit discrimination and preferential treatment on the basis of race, color, national origin, and sex with respect to federal employment, contracts, and programs and for other purposes.
2 416 U.S. 312 (1974).
3 Washington 507 P2d, 1191.
4 416 U.S. 312, at 319.
5 416 U.S. 332, at 342.
6 Ibid.
7 Ibid, at 350.
8 John Dewey, "The Need for a Recovery of Philosophy" (1917), in *John Dewey: The Middle Works, 1899–1924*, vol. 10, ed. Jo Ann Boydston (Carbondale: Southern Illinois University Press, 1980), 46.
9 "The Extreme Test of Free Speech," 15 April 1978.
10 "The Village of Skokie vs. Carl Cohen: An Exchange," 6 May 1978.
11 438 U.S. 265. I will refer frequently to this case henceforth as *Bakke*.
12 82 Wash. 2d 11; 507 P.2d 1169.
13 The Washington Supreme Court was very forthright about this matter, writing, "The minority admissions policy [at the University of Washington Law School] is certainly not benign with respect to nonminority students who are displaced by it." 82 Wash 2d, at 32.

CHAPTER 2. *BAKKE* AND THE RISE OF DIVERSITY

1 *Bakke v. Regents of the University of California*, 18 Cal. 3d 34.
2 "Equality, Diversity, and Good Faith," *Wayne Law Review* 26, no. 4 (July 1980).
3 Civil Rights Act of 1964, 78 Stat. 251, 2000d, Section 601.
4 Powell wrote, "The guarantee of equal protection cannot mean one thing when applied to one individual and something else when applied to a person of another color." *Bakke*, at 289, 290.
5 Ibid., 315 ff.
6 Ibid., 307 ff.
7 Ibid., 311 ff.

8 In an essay I published twenty years later, "The Uses of Race in Admissions under *Regents v. Bakke," Journal of Law in Society* 1, no. 1 (Winter 1999), I scrutinized different interpretations of the diversity argument but could find no version that did not in the end conflict with the clear prohibition of racial discrimination in the U.S. Constitution. Our university president, Lee Bollinger, had acknowledged on national television, "We do discriminate." His motives were honorable, but good motives do not make wrong acts right.

9 Heather MacDonald, "Less Academics, More Narcissism," *City Journal*, 14 July 2011.

10 "What Is Affirmative Action?" *Texas Law Review* 58, no. 4 (April 1980).

11 "Honorable Ends, Unsavory Means," *Civil Liberties Review* 2, no. 2 (Spring 1975).

12 "Racial Preference Is Dynamite," *The Chronicle of Higher Education* 14, no. 10 (May 2, 1977).

CHAPTER 3. FROM *THE NATION* TO *COMMENTARY*

1 *Annie Hall*, directed by Woody Allen, screenplay by Woody Allen and Marshall Brickman, produced by Charles H. Joffe, 1977.

2 *United Steelworkers of America v. Weber*, 443 U.S. 193 (1979). I refer to it henceforth as *Weber*.

3 42 U.S. Code 2000e, 2(d) (1970).

4 "Why Racial Preference Is Illegal and Immoral," *Commentary* 67, no. 6 (June 1979).

5 California Proposition 209, the California Civil Rights Initiative, was a ballot proposition approved by the voters in November of 1996. Modeled on the 1964 Civil Rights Act, it amended the California Constitution to prohibit state government institutions from considering race, sex, or ethnicity in public employment, public contracting, or public education. The Michigan Civil Rights Initiative, discussed in Chapters 29–31 and Chapter 33 of this book, was modeled after the California Civil Rights Initiative.

6 *Hopwood v. the University of Texas*, 78 F. 3rd 932 (1996).

7 *Weber*, at 204.

CHAPTER 4. FROM WASHINGTON TO BERLIN AND BEYOND

1 Hearings, Fair Housing Amendments Act of 1979 (S. 506), Committee on the Judiciary, Subcommittee on the Constitution, 96th Congress (Washington, DC: Government Printing Office, September 17, 1979), 458–466.

2 Carl Cohen, "Affirmative Action and the Rights of the Majority," *Dahlem Workshop Reports, Minorities. Report 27, Community and Identity* (Berlin: Springer Verlag, 1983).

CHAPTER 5. NAKED RACIAL PREFERENCE

1 Carl Cohen, *Naked Racial Preference* (New York: Madison Books, 1995).

2 *Wygant v. Jackson Board of Education*, 476 U.S. 267 (1986).

3 Ibid.

4 *Plessy v. Ferguson*, 163 U.S. 537 (1896).

5 Ibid.

6 *Official Transcript of Proceedings before the Supreme Court of the United States*, November 5, 1985, Case 84-1340, 35.

7 In the *Nürnberger Gesetze* of 1935 the Nazi principles for identifying Jews and Aryans were set forth. A Jew was a person with three or four Jewish grandparents; a person with one or two Jewish grandparents was a *Mischling*, a crossbreed. However, in some cases a person with exactly two Jewish grandparents was classified as Jewish; legal tests were devised to determine if such a person was a Jew or a *Mischling*. White non-Jewish Europeans were classified as Aryans. Detailed charts were prepared to explain the application of these laws.

8 *Wygant*, 476 U.S. at 274 (emphasis added).

9 Ibid., at 275.

10 Ibid., at 294.

11 Ibid., at 296.

CHAPTER 6. THE UNIVERSITY OF MICHIGAN COMES INTO FOCUS

1 "Acceptance Rates of Blacks in Leading American Universities and Colleges," *Journal of Blacks in Higher Education* (August 1995).

2 Carl Cohen and Irving Copi, *Introduction to Logic*, 14th ed. (Upper Saddle River, NJ: Prentice Hall, 2011). Used in universities around the world, this textbook is now in its fourteenth edition.

3 *New York Times*, 25 May 1993.

4 *Michigan Daily*, 21 October 1993.

CHAPTER 7. CONFRONTATION

1 The case was decided by the 5th Circuit Court of Appeals, 78 F. 3rd 932 (1996). The U.S. Supreme Court chose not to accept it for further review.

2 My testimony was published in *Congressional Digest* 75, nos. 6–7 (June–July 1996): 183–187.

CHAPTER 8. PULLING TEETH

1 Robben Fleming died at the age of 93 in January 2010.

CHAPTER 13. ON TO THE FEDERAL COURTS

1 Lee C. Bollinger, *The Tolerant Society: Freedom of Speech and Extremist Speech in America* (New York: Oxford University Press, 1988).

2 Carl Cohen, "Race, Lies, and *Hopwood*," *Commentary* 101, no. 6 (June 1996).

3 *Metro Broadcasting v. FCC*, 497 U.S. 547 (1990).

4 78 F. 3rd 932.

5 515 U.S. 819 (1995).

6 Larry Purdy, *Getting Under the Skin of "Diversity": Searching for the Color-Blind Ideal* (Minneapolis, MN: Robert Lawrence Press, 2008). Purdy's book shows, in the style of a penetrating litigator, that a much-discussed book defending race preferences, *The Shape of the River* by Derek Bok and William Bowen, was deceptive and in some ways intellectually disreputable. I will have more to say about Purdy's acumen and argumentative skills in Chapter 19.

7 Jennifer Gratz later played a key role in the campaign for the Michigan Civil Rights Initiative, as I will report in detail in Chapters 29–31. She is at present the chief executive officer of Foundation XIV, an organization devoted to the Fourteenth Amendment to the U.S. Constitution.

CHAPTER 14. THE CLIMATE OF OPINION AT MICHIGAN

1 Carl Cohen, "Race in University of Michigan Admissions," *University Record: Faculty Perspectives,* February 25, 1997.

2 Full report available at http://www.nas.org/roper/textsum.htm.

3 Full report available at http://www.udel.edu/DAS.

4 "Diversity and Affirmative Action: The State of Campus Opinion," *Academic Questions* 15, no. 4 (2002): 52–66.

CHAPTER 15. THE READING ROOM

1 Richard H. Sander, "A Systemic Analysis of Affirmative Action in American Law Schools," *Stanford Law Review* 57 (2004): 367.

2 Richard H. Sander and Stuart Taylor, *Mismatch: How Affirmative Action Hurts Students It's Supposed to Help, and Why Universities Won't Admit It* (New York: Basic-Books, 2012).

CHAPTER 16. MOVING TARGETS

1 See: Jerome Karabel, *The Chosen: The Hidden History of Admission and Exclusion at Harvard, Yale, and Princeton* (Boston: Houghton Mifflin, 2005). If there are only so many places, and one wants to enroll more Xs, it may be necessary to enroll fewer Ys.

CHAPTER 17. INTERVENORS

1 38 F. 3rd 147 (1994).

2 See, for example C. J. Sowa, M. M. Thomson, and C. T. Bennett, "Prediction and Improvement of Academic Performance for High-Risk Black College Students," *Journal of Multicultural Counseling and Development* 17 (1989): 14–22; J. L. Mumpower, R.

Nath, and T. R. Stewart, "Affirmative Action, Duality of Error, and the Consequences of Mispredicting the Academic Performance of African American College Applicants," *Journal of Policy Analysis and Management* 21, no. 1 (2002): 63–77.

3 Mario Palmieri, *The Philosophy of Fascism* (1936), selections appearing in Carl Cohen, *Communism, Fascism, and Democracy: The Theoretical Foundations*, 2nd ed. (New York: Random House, 1962).

4 Zarco sent copies of those reports to two sophisticated statisticians at the Center for Equal Opportunity (CEO) in Washington, D.C., Robert Lerner and Althea K. Nagai. While the university was publicly singing the praises of diversity, Lerner and Nagai published a study of the data Zarco had uncovered: "Diversity Distorted: How the University of Michigan Withheld Data to Hide Evidence of Racial Conflict and Polarization" (Washington, DC: Center for Equal Opportunity, 2003).

5 Richard H. Sander, "A Systematic Analysis of Affirmative Action in American Law Schools," *Stanford Law Review* 57 (November 2004): 213.

6 Ibid., 367.

7 Alger soon left the University of Michigan to become vice president and general counsel at Rutgers. In 2013 he became president of James Madison University, in Harrisonburg, Virginia.

8 Originally published in 1971 by the University of Georgia Press, and then by the Free Press of Macmillan Publishing Company, this book was republished by the University of Michigan Press in 2013.

CHAPTER 18. THE THIN LINE BETWEEN PERMISSIBLE AND IMPERMISSIBLE

1 Readers wishing to examine Judge Duggan's opinion can find it online or in any law library: *Gratz v. Bollinger*, 122 F. Supp. 2nd 81 (E.D. Mich. 2000).

2 That grid appears in Chapter 9 of this book on pages 54–55.

CHAPTER 19. 128 HONORARY DEGREES AND A COAT CHECK

1 The best report of the proceedings is to be found in Friedman's long and detailed opinion, readily accessed at 137 F. Supp. 2d 821 (E.D. Mich., 2001). I rely upon that opinion as well as my own recollections and a transcript of the testimony given.

2 This and all other quotations from the examination and cross-examination of John Hope Franklin are taken from a transcript of the oral testimony.

3 John Hope Franklin, *Race in History* (Baton Rouge: Louisiana State University Press, 1989).

CHAPTER 20. THE HEART OF THE TRIAL: 257 TO 1

1 The following account of the testimony of university witnesses denying the reality of a double standard, and their cross-examinations, relies chiefly on the official transcript of the proceedings of the trial.

2 Some of these grids were described earlier in this book. Two of the grids prepared by the Law School are combined in the one grid shown on pages 62–63 in Chapter 16 of this book.

3 The account of the testimony of Kinley Larntz, including quotations, relies upon the official transcript of the trial.

4 See Chapter 16.

5 The transcript does not show italics, which are added. They are appropriate, however, in conveying the intensity of the testimony as it was actually given.

CHAPTER 21. VINDICATION

1 *Barbara Grutter v. Lee Bolinger, et al. and the University of Michigan Law School,* 157 F. Supp. 2d 821 (E.D. Mich. 2001).

2 Ibid., p. 31 (page numbers reported are from the typescript of the decision as it was originally issued).

3 Ibid., p. 32.

4 Ibid., p. 33 (emphasis added).

5 Ibid., pp. 34–35.

6 Ibid., p. 35.

7 Ibid., p. 36.

8 Ibid.

9 *Wygant v. Jackson Board of Education,* 467 U.S. 267 (1986), at p. 273, quoting *Hirabayashi v. United States,* 320 U.S. 81 (1943), at p. 100.

10 *Grutter v. Bollinger,* F. Supp. 2nd 821 (E.D. Mich. 2001).

CHAPTER 22. PETITIONS DON'T DECIDE LAWSUITS

1 137 F. Supp. 2nd 874, 878.

2 *Grutter v. Bollinger,* 288 F. 3d 732 (6th Circuit). This appellate court opinion will be cited below simply as *Grutter* (6th Cir.). Readers interested in the detail may find it online at 2002 FED App. 0170P (6th Cir.)

3 *Grutter* (6th Cir.), 752.

4 Ibid., Judge Daniel Boggs dissenting, 773.

5 Ibid., 776.

6 Ibid., 800.

7 Ibid., Judge Ronald Gilman dissenting, 816.

8 Ibid., 817.

CHAPTER 23. WHY IT SMELLED FUNNY

1 *Grutter* (6th Cir.), Judge Daniel Boggs dissenting, 814.

2 Ibid., Judge Eugene Siler, dissenting, 815.

3 Ibid., Judge Karen Moore, concurring, 752.

4 Ibid., 753.

5 Ibid.

6 Ibid., Judge Eric Clay, concurring, 772.

7 Ibid., 772.

8 Ibid., Judge Alice Batchelder, dissenting, 815.

CHAPTER 24. BACK ON THE HOME FRONT

1 That *60 Minutes* episode, "A Negative on Affirmative Action," was first broadcast on Sunday, 29 October 2000. CBS must have liked it, because the station reran it several times thereafter, through the following two summers.

2 Several studies have that same result. See Chapter 17, n. 2.

3 Nicholas Lemann, "The Empathy Defense," *New Yorker*, 18 December 2000, 50.

4 The exact date on which that *Dateline* episode, "A Question of Fairness," was broadcast I cannot recall. It must have been during 2002 or 2003, however, because I recall referring, during the interview, to the fact that certain materials are "before the Supreme Court now."

5 Emphasis added. Thurgood Marshall, brief for NAACP, *Brown v. Board of Education.*

CHAPTER 25. SOME PERSONAL QUESTIONS

1 Carl Cohen, "A Very Bad Compromise," *Journal of Blacks in Higher Education* (Spring 1997): 106.

2 Richard H. Sander and Stuart Taylor Jr., *Mismatch: How Affirmative Action Hurts Students It's Intended to Help, and Why Universities Won't Admit It* (New York: BasicBooks, 2012). The results of statistical analysis presented in this book are stunning; what were thought to be supports for minority students are quite conclusively shown to have been the reverse, wreaking damaging impact upon those very students.

CHAPTER 26. PREPARING FOR THE BIG EVENT

1 Stephen Carter, "The Best Black, and Other Tales," *Reconstruction* 1 (Winter 1990).

2 Anthony Kennedy, *Metro Broadcasting v. FCC*, 497 U.S. 547. Kennedy wrote, "I cannot agree with the Court that the Constitution permits the Government to discriminate among its citizens on the basis of race in order to serve interests so trivial as 'broadcast diversity.'"

3 *Metro Broadcasting v. FCC*, 497 U.S. 547 (1990).

4 Alger is now president of James Madison University, in Harrisonburg, Virginia.

CHAPTER 27. THE BIG EVENT

1 All quotations in this account are from the official transcript of the hearing.

CHAPTER 28. THE END OF LITIGATION

1 *Grutter v. Bollinger*, 539 U.S. 306 (2003).
2 *Gratz v. Bollinger*, 539 U.S. 244 (2003).
3 Ibid., at 251.
4 *Grutter*, at 337.
5 Ibid., at 325.
6 Seymour Martin Lipset, Stanley Rothman, and Neil Nevitte, "Does Enrollment Diversity Improve University Education?" *International Journal of Public Opinion Research* 15, no. 1 (October 2002).
7 Russell K. Nieli, *Wounds That Will Not Heal: Affirmative Action and Our Continuing Racial Divide* (New York: Encounter Books, 2011). I published a long review of this book: "Both Wrong and Bad," *Academic Questions* 26, no. 1 (Spring 2013).
8 *Grutter*, at 322–325.
9 Ibid., 539 U.S. 306, at 343.
10 David L. Featherman, Martin Hall, and Marvin Krislov, eds., *The Next 25 Years: Affirmative Action in Higher Education in the United States and South Africa* (Ann Arbor: University of Michigan Press, 2010).
11 Sandra Day O'Connor and Stuart J. Schwab, "Twenty-Five Years: A Need for Study and Action," in ibid.
12 *Grutter*, 306, at 349.
13 Ibid., at 347.
14 Ibid.
15 Ibid., at 350.
16 Ibid., at 353.
17 Ibid., at 358.
18 *Plessy v. Ferguson*, 163 U.S. 537, at 559.
19 *Grutter*, at 381 and 383. Emphasis added.
20 Ibid., at 386. Emphasis added.
21 *Gratz*, at 251.
22 Ibid., at 271–272.
23 Ibid., at 275.
24 Ibid., at 305.
25 Ibid., at 275.

CHAPTER 29. FROM LEGAL BATTLES TO POLITICAL BATTLES

1 Carl Cohen, "Winks, Nods, Disguises—and Racial Preference," *Commentary* 116, no. 2 (September 2003).
2 Ibid., 38.

CHAPTER 30. DEFENDING THE MICHIGAN CIVIL RIGHTS INITIATIVE

1 Carl Cohen, "Political Controversy and the University," in *Public Policy in the 1980s: Implications for Liberal Education*, ed. Neal R. Berte (Savannah: Southern University Conference, 1980).

2 *Williams Reports*, April 1983.

3 R. P. Wolff, *The Ideal of the University* (Boston: Beacon Press, 1969).

4 H. D. Aiken, *The Predicament of the University* (Bloomington: Indiana University Press, 1971).

5 Executive Order 10925, 6 March 1961.

6 Ibid., Part Three, Subpart A, Section (301) (1). Emphasis added.

7 Executive Order 11246, 24 September 1965. Emphasis added.

8 Carl Cohen, "Open Letter to the President of My University," *Academic Questions* 19, no. 4 (Fall 2006). The same letter was published in the *Michigan Daily*, 4 October 2006.

9 Shelby Steele, *White Guilt: How Blacks and Whites Together Destroyed the Promise of the Civil Rights Era* (New York: HarperCollins, 2006).

10 Ibid., 39–40.

CHAPTER 32. RACE PREFERENCE AT THE UNIVERSITY OF TEXAS

1 *Fisher v. the University of Texas*, No. 11-345, U.S. Supreme Court, June 24, 2013. Cited hereafter simply as *Fisher*.

2 *Grutter*, at 326.

3 *Fisher*, slip opinion, Kennedy, at 12.

4 Ibid., 13. Emphasis added.

5 See Chapter 28 of this book.

6 *Fisher*, slip opinion, Thomas, at 17.

7 Ibid., at 5.

8 Ibid., at 7.

9 Ibid., at 8.

10 Ibid., at 10.

11 *McLaurin v. Oklahoma State Regents*, 339 U.S. 637 (1950).

12 *Fisher*, slip opinion, Thomas, 10–11.

13 *Fisher*, University of Texas brief, 53–54.

14 *Brown v. Board of Education*, brief for the State of Kansas, 1953, 56.

15 *Sweatt v. Painter*, 339 U.S. 629 (1950), brief for the State of Texas, 96. In this famous case a black applicant to the University of Texas, Heman Sweatt, was obliged to enroll in a separate law school established for him by the state, at Texas State University for Negroes. "Separate but equal" was the principle of that time—but the Supreme Court held that the separate law school in Texas was grossly *un*equal. Sweatt and I had a mutual friend; the outcome of that case was particularly heartening to me.

16 *Fisher*, slip opinion, Thomas, at 11.

17 416 U.S. 312 (1974), at 342. See Chapter 1 of this book.

18 *Fisher*, slip opinion, Thomas, at 2. Emphasis added.

19 Ibid., 12–13.

CHAPTER 33. RACE PREFERENCE IN MICHIGAN IS PERMANENTLY ENDED

1 393 U.S. 385 (henceforth referred to as *Hunter*).

2 Ibid., at 390–391.

3 Ibid., at 395.

4 458 U.S. 457 (henceforth referred to as *Seattle*).

5 701 F. 3d 466, at 475.

6 *Seattle*, at 472.

7 Ibid., at 470.

8 *Schuette, Attorney General of Michigan v. Coalition to Defend Affirmative Action, Integration, and Immigration Rights and Fight for Equality by Any Means Necessary (BAMN) et al.*, No. 12-682. Decided April 22, 2014 (henceforth referred to as *Schuette*).

9 Ibid., slip opinion, Kennedy, 12.

10 Ibid., at 13.

11 Ibid., 14.

12 Ibid., at 15.

13 Ibid., at 16–17.

14 Ibid., at 18.

15 Ibid., at 5.

16 539 U.S. 306 (2003).

17 *Schuette*, slip opinion, Breyer, at 5.

18 Ibid., at 6.

19 *Schuette*, slip opinion, Scalia, at 7–8.

20 Sonia Sotomayor, *My Beloved World* (New York: Knopf, 2013).

21 *Parents Involved in Community Schools v. Seattle School District No. 1*, 551 U.S. 701 (2007), at 748.

22 *Schuette*, slip opinion, Sotomayor, at 45.

23 Ibid.

24 Sotomayor, *My Beloved World*.

25 *Schuette*, slip opinion, Roberts, at 2. Emphasis added.

26 *Schuette*, slip opinion, Scalia, at 1. Emphasis in the original.

27 Ibid., at 1, 3. Emphasis in the original.

APPENDIX B. THE COHEN REPORT

1 Sent to me in response to my formal request under the Michigan Freedom of Information Act. A document just like it is apparently prepared each year, since the cover page indicates that "1996 changes are double underlined." There are few such changes.

2 The INTEFLEX program at the University of Michigan was phased out in 2007.

3 These are codes to identify the special delaying letters to be sent: DGF = delay for grades; DSF = delay for scores, etc.

4 The principles to be applied in granting admission after "on-the-spot review" are not specified in the formal guidelines document. Block capitals are used in the original.

5 Figures for the fall of 1994 are used because I was told (in March of 1996 upon repeated request) that the figures for 1995 admissions were not available.

6 The phrase "underrepresented minorities" as used by LS&A in this document, is comprised of three groups, identified in the document as: "American Indian, Black/African American, and Hispanic/Latino American."

Index

ACLU (American Civil Liberties Union)
    author's affiliation with, 1, 2, 5, 75, 83, 103,
        104, 119, 229
    and *Defunis*, 2
    "political correctness" of, 83
    and race preferences, 2, 119, 120, 194
ACT (American College Test), 52, 58, 111, 121,
    273, 274, 276
Adkins, Ray, 236
affirmative action
    in Civil Rights Act of 1964, 177–178,
        235–236
    in employment practices, 178, 180, 235–
        236
    Michigan Civil Rights Initiative and,
        215–218, 222–224, 231–232, 235–236,
        247–249, 250, 257–258, 260
    Michigan Law Review and, 32–34
    in President's Committee on Equal
        Employment Opportunities, 177–178,
        235
    and race preferences, 1–2, 98–99, 177–179,
        180–181, 235–236, 243–245
    and *Schuette*, 257–265
    in *60 Minutes'* "A Negative on
        Affirmative Action," 171–173, 175,
        286n1
    Supreme Court and, 2, 198, 213–214,
        257–265, 273
    University of Michigan and, 7, 53, 92–95,
        98–99, 111, 135, 161, 180–184, 230–231,
        243–244, 247–249, 274–275
    See also Gratz v. Bollinger; *Grutter v.
        Bollinger*
African American Alumni Council, 236
Aiken, Henry David, 230
Alger, Jon, 129, 192, 285n7, 287n4

"Ali," 32–34
Alito, Samuel, 251, 258, 260
Allen, William, 234
American Arbitration Association, 70
American Association of University
    Professors (AAUP), 70–72, 107
"A Negative on Affirmative Action" (CBS *60
    Minutes*), 171–173, 175, 286n1
Ann Arbor News, 189, 221, 231
Ashford, Susan, 100
Asian American Law Students Association,
    237
Askin, Frank, 2
Association of American Medical Colleges,
    59, 278

Baker, Deane, 68–69
Bakke, Allan. *See* Regents of the University
    of California v. Bakke
Bakke case. *See* Regents of the University of
    California v. Bakke
BAMN. *See* Coalition to Defend Affirmative
    Action by Any Means Necessary
    (BAMN)
*Barbara Grutter v. Lee Bollinger and the
    Regents of the University of Michigan.*
    See *Grutter v. Bollinger*
Barry, Elizabeth, 172–173
Batchelder, Alice, 164, 170
Black Action Movement (BAM), 124
Boggs, Daniel, 162–163, 164, 166–167, 168–170,
    185
Bollinger, Lee
    in Bradley *60 Minutes* interview, 172, 173
    career and background of, 78–79
    and Carl Cohen Reading Room
        controversy, 104, 105, 107–108

Feikens, John, 116
5th Circuit Court of Appeals, 16, 80, 82–83,
    84, 160, 250, 253, 283n1
Fisher, Abigail. *See* Fisher v. University of
    Texas
Fisher v. University of Texas, 250–256
Fleming, Robben, 45
Foundation XIV, 284n7
Fourteenth Amendment, U. S. Constitution.
    See Equal Protection Clause,
    Fourteenth Amendment
4th Circuit Court of Appeals, 120
Franklin, John Hope, 138–144, 145
Friedman, Bernard
    and BAMN intervention in *Grutter,* 133–134
    on consolidation of *Gratz* and *Grutter,*
        116, 117
    and diversity argument in *Grutter,* 137–
        138, 149, 150
    Grutter decision by, 151–156, 157, 164, 166,
        177, 185
    and 6th Circuit Court reversal of *Grutter*
        decision, 164, 165, 166, 167, 185
    and University of Michigan appeal of
        Grutter decision, 156, 157–159, 162–164

Gikas, Paul, 29
Gilman, Ronald, 164, 165
Ginsburg, Ruth Bader
    in *Gratz,* 212, 213–214
    in *Grutter,* 195, 198, 206
    and Michigan Civil Rights Initiative, 258
    and race preferences, 191
    in *Schuette,* 260
GPA
    and race preference at University of
        Texas Law School, 80–81
    in University of Michigan Law School
        admissions grid system, 60–62, 63
        (figure), 64, 148–149, 152, 153, 277–278
    and University of Michigan Medical
        School admissions, 279–280
    in University of Michigan undergraduate
        admissions grid system, 48–50, 52–54,
        55–56 (figure), 57, 273–274, 275, 276–
        277
    in University of Michigan undergraduate
        admissions Selection Index, 111,
        114–115 (figure)

grade-point average. *See* GPA
Graff, Matt, 160
Granholm, Jennifer, 226
Gratz, Jennifer
    as lead plaintiff in *Gratz,* 89–91, 109–110,
        111, 118, 172, 194, 199, 201, 205, 212
    and Michigan Civil Rights Initiative, 220,
        221, 223–224, 234, 247, 284n7
    See also Gratz v. Bollinger
Gratz v. Bollinger
    and *Bakke,* 135, 137
    CIR filing of, 91
    in District Court, 115–117, 122, 133–136,
        161–162, 186, 199–200
    diversity argument in, 135, 160–162,
        200–201, 205, 213, 214
    John Payton as University of Michigan
        lead attorney in, 134, 135, 161–162, 196,
        200–201
    and Lee Bollinger, 135, 160, 161
    plaintiffs in, 87–91
    and quota systems, 161, 200, 273
    in 6th Circuit Court, 161–162, 165, 185–
        186, 199–200
    Supreme Court and, 171, 185–186, 190,
        192–194, 199–202, 204–205, 212–214, 271
    See also Center for Individual Rights
        (CIR); Gratz, Jennifer
Greve, Michael, 83–85, 86, 118, 171
grid system, University of Michigan
    undergraduate admissions
    applicant categories in, 48–54, 55–56
        (figure), 57
    in Duggan District Court opinion, 135–
        136
    and Fourteenth Amendment Equal
        Protection Clause, 51, 115, 134–135, 199
    race preference policy in, 51–54, 85–86,
        87, 109–110, 134–136, 185, 276–277
    Selection Index as replacement for,
        111–112, 114–115 (figure), 115, 134–136,
        199–200
    in 6th Circuit Court appeal, 161–162
grid system, University of Michigan Law
    School admissions, 60–62, 63 (figure),
        64, 147–150, 152, 173, 277–278
Grutter, Barbara
    as lead plaintiff in *Grutter,* 90–91, 116, 118,
        142, 145, 154, 156, 161, 204, 233

Kowich, Debra, 129–130
Kozodoy, Neal, 13
Krislov, Marvin, 107–108, 160, 196, 202, 208, 209, 234

LaCroix, Jeston, 128–129, 130
Larntz, Kinley, 147–150, 152, 153, 162–163, 173
Law School Admissions Test (LSAT) scores, 60–62, 64, 80–81, 90, 138, 148, 152, 153, 277–278
LDF (NAACP), 119, 120, 122, 123, 133–134, 138–139, 160, 161, 162
Lehman, Jeffrey, 145–146, 172, 173, 202, 208
Lemann, Nicholas, 173–175, 177
Lempert, Richard, 145–146, 151, 177, 178–179
Lerner, Robert, 284–285n4
Levin, Carl, 193–194
Lipscomb, James, 176–177
LSAT. *See* Law School Admissions Test (LSAT) scores

Madrigal, Jose, 102
Mahoney, Maureen, 196–199, 202, 209
Marshall, Thurgood, 138–139, 179, 254–255
Martin, Boyce, 159, 160–161, 164, 166, 167, 169
Maslon Edelman Borman and Brand, 87–88
Massie, Miranda
    as BAMN lead attorney, 122, 133–134, 137, 138–141, 145, 160, 161, 163, 201–202
    and *Grutter* in District Court, 138–141, 145
    and *Grutter* in 6th Circuit Court, 160, 161, 163
MCAT. *See* Medical College Admissions Test (MCAT) scores
McDonald, Michael, 83–85, 87, 88, 89, 90–91, 118
McDonald, Terrence, 36
MCRI. *See* Michigan Civil Rights Initiative (MCRI)
McWilliams, Carey, 5–6
Medical College Admissions Test (MCAT) scores, 42, 269, 279–280
Metro Broadcasting v. FCC, 82, 190–191, 287n2
Mexican American Legal Defense and Education Fund (MALDEF), 120
Michigan cases. *See* Gratz v. Bollinger; Grutter v. Bollinger
Michigan Civil Rights Initiative (MCRI)

and affirmative action, 215–218, 222–224, 231–232, 235–236, 247–249, 250, 257–258, 260
as amendment to Michigan Constitution, 216–217, 224, 247–249, 257, 261, 263, 265, 281–282
and ballot campaign, 218, 219–227
and BAMN, 222, 223–224, 226, 233, 234, 257, 262
Board of State Canvassers and, 225–226, 227
California Civil Rights Initiative as model for, 215–216, 219–220, 282n5
and Civil Rights Act of 1964, 217, 238
and employment practices, 216–218, 221, 248–249, 282n5
and Fourteenth Amendment Equal Protection Clause, 257, 258–261, 265, 267
Jennifer Gratz as executive director of, 223, 224, 247, 284n7
opposition to, 220, 221–222, 223–224, 226–227, 229, 230–233, 234, 235, 242–246
and Proposition 2 campaign, 228–229, 230–232, 234, 235, 236–246
Race and Admissions course related to, 232–234
race preference prohibited by, 216–218, 234, 235–238, 245–246, 248–249, 257, 259, 261–265, 281–282
in *Schuette,* 257–265
University of Michigan opposition to, 230–233, 238–242
Michigan Daily, 46, 93, 97, 104, 231, 243
Michigan Law Review, 32–34
Michigan Mandate, 27, 66, 76, 98
Michigan State University (MSU), 73, 74, 89, 90, 216, 242, 248, 281
minority classifications. *See* underrepresented minorities at University of Michigan
Moore, Karen, 158, 164, 167, 168–170
Morrissey, Lewis A., 40–41, 42, 44, 45–46, 267–270

NAACP Legal Defense Fund (LDF). *See* LDF (NAACP)
Nagai, Althea, 284–285n4

race preference, *continued*
  in University of Michigan Law School
    admissions grid system, 60–62, 64,
    147–150, 152, 173
  in University of Michigan undergraduate
    admissions grid system, 51–54, 62–63,
    85–86, 87, 109–110, 134–136, 185, 276–
    277
  and University of Michigan Medical
    School admissions, 29–31, 54, 59–60,
    67, 271, 278–280
  and *Wygant,* 26
racial discrimination
  and *Brown v. Board of Education,* 255–256
  Chief Justice Roberts on, 264
  Civil Rights Act of 1964 and, 15–16, 154,
    191, 217, 235, 238
  Michigan Civil Rights Initiative and,
    214–217, 248–249, 281
  and President's Committee on Equal
    Employment Opportunities, 235
  prohibition of in U.S. Constitution, 134,
    197, 282n8
  Supreme Court and arguments justifying,
    190–191, 210–211, 253–254
  in University of California admissions, 16
  in University of Michigan admissions,
    1–2, 48, 66–67, 85–86, 89, 91, 92–93,
    116, 134–135, 136, 154, 185, 197, 211, 241,
    271–272, 282n8
  in University of Texas admissions, 251,
    254–256
racial self-identification forms, 99–100
Raudenbush, Stephen, 153
Regan, Donald, 151–152
Regents of the University of California v. Bakke
  Civil Rights Act of 1964 and, 9, 16, 191
  diversity argument in, 9–13, 80, 81–82,
    135, 137, 163–164, 166, 175, 205–206,
    208, 209, 252, 282n8
  Fourteenth Amendment Equal
    Protection Clause and, 9–10, 80, 81,
    82, 154
  and *Gratz,* 135, 137
  and *Grutter,* 137, 154, 162–163, 165, 166,
    205–206, 208, 252
  Powell opinion in, 9–11, 12–13, 25, 26,
    80, 81–82, 135, 137, 163–164, 166, 175,
    205–206, 208, 209, 252, 273, 281n4

  and quotas, 165, 273
  Stevens in, 9, 16, 191
  Supreme Court in, 6, 8–13, 16, 26, 78, 80,
    81–82, 135, 137, 154, 162, 163–164, 166,
    171, 175
Rehnquist, William
  diversity argument and, 166, 201, 211–212,
    214
  in *Gratz,* 205
  in *Grutter,* 166, 196, 198, 199, 214
  in *Metro Broadcasting v. FCC,* 82
  and race preferences, 190–191, 205
Residential College, University of Michigan,
  32, 99, 101–105, 219, 232
Rice, Warner, 110
Roach, Tom, 68–69
Roberts, John, 258, 260, 263, 264
Rosenberger v. University of Virginia, 84
Rosman, Michael, 202
Rothman, Stanley, 94, 208
Rule 11, Supreme Court, 186

Sandalow, Terry, 105–106, 192, 204
Sander, Richard, 106, 127–128, 184, 253
SAT, 48–49, 50, 51–54, 55–56 (figure), 57, 111,
  273–274, 275, 276–277
Scalia, Antonin
  and diversity argument, 82, 196–197, 210
  in *Gratz,* 200–201
  in *Grutter,* 196–197, 198–199, 210, 211
  in *Metro Broadcasting v. FCC,* 82
  and race preferences, 82, 190–191, 198–
    199, 200–201, 210
  in *Schuette,* 258, 260, 263, 265
Scholastic Aptitude Test. *See* SAT
Schuette, Bill. *See* Schuette v. Coalition to
  Defend Affirmative Action by Any
  Means Necessary
*Schuette v. Coalition to Defend Affirmative
  Action by Any Means Necessary,* 257–265
Seattle case. *See* Washington v. Seattle School
  District No. 1
Selection Index system, 111–112, 114–115
  (figure), 115, 134–136, 161, 199–200
Shape of the River, The (Bok/Bowen),
  283–284n6
Shaw, Theodore, 119, 120, 122, 123, 133–134,
  135, 160, 161, 162
Sherburne, Jane, 118